Rethinking Therapeutic Culture

Rethinking Therapeutic Culture

Edited by Timothy Aubry and Trysh Travis

The University of Chicago Press CHICAGO & LONDON

TIMOTHY AUBRY is associate professor of English at Baruch College, CUNY. He is the author of *Reading as Therapy: What Contemporary Fiction Does for Middle-Class Americans*. TRYSH TRAVIS is a cultural and literary historian who teaches in the Center for Women's Studies and Gender Research at the University of Florida. She is the author of *The Language of the Heart: A Cultural History of the Recovery Movement from Alcoholics Anonymous to Oprah Winfrey*.

The University of Chicago Press, Chicago 60637
The University of Chicago Press, Ltd., London
 Published 2015.
Printed in the United States of America

24 23 22 21 20 19 18 17 16 15   1 2 3 4 5

ISBN-13: 978-0-226-24993-3 (cloth)
ISBN-13: 978-0-226-25013-7 (paper)
ISBN-13: 978-0-226-25027-4 (e-book)
DOI: 10.7208/chicago/9780226250274.001.0001

Library of Congress Cataloging-in-Publication Data

Aubry, Timothy Richard, 1975– author.
Rethinking therapeutic culture / Timothy Aubry and Trysh Travis.
pages cm
Includes bibliographical references and index.
ISBN 978-0-226-24993-3 (cloth : alk. paper) — ISBN 978-0-226-25013-7 (pbk. : alk. paper) — ISBN 978-0-226-25027-4 (e-book) 1. Therapeutic communities. 2. Self-help groups.
I. Travis, Trysh, author. II. Title.
RC489.T67A93 2015
615.8'528—dc23
2014033249

⊗ This paper meets the requirements of ANSI/NISO Z39.48-1992 (Permanence of Paper).

CONTENTS

ACKNOWLEDGMENTS

I have been thinking about therapeutic culture for over a decade, and during that time many people have responded to my ideas, challenged my arguments, and offered extremely useful provocations, among them Diana Fuss, Michael Wood, Mark McGurl, Leah Price, Joe Parsons, John Brenkman, Jon Baskin, Mary McGlynn, Shelly Eversley, Robert Devens, Timothy Mennel, Rita Felski, Sandra Parvu, and Tala Dowlatshahi. In the past several years, I have been particularly inspired by the contributors to this volume and the careful, textured accounts they have offered of how therapeutic culture functions in particular places at particular times in history. But more than anyone else, my coeditor, Trysh Travis, has underscored for me the remarkable complexity of this collection's subject matter. The project has been a complete collaboration; reflecting that fact, our names appear in alphabetical order. But I would nevertheless hold that she deserves more credit than I do, at least for the book's moments of greatest clarity and insight. Her indefatigable commitment to the editorial process—to finding the clearest, sharpest, and most precise formulation for every given idea—not only resulted in more polished essays, it also inspired many of the volume's most surprising and original arguments. From her, in other words, I learned just how important the task of *rethinking* can be. It was, admittedly, an exhausting process; fortunately Trysh's ever-reliable, often pugnacious sense of humor also made it an extremely amusing one.

Timothy Aubry

A group project like this one involves so many people doing so many things over such a long period of time that to write an adequate acknowledgments page—always a daunting task—seems nearly impossible. But attention must be paid. Lea Johnston and Jan Snyder provided encouragement along the way with their persistent questions about the project's progress, while Mark Fenster and Rachel Rebouche pushed me to think more deeply about every concept covered in the volume. Jean-Christophe Agnew, Robert Devens, Ann Fabian, and Sian Hunter were key cheerleaders and critics, often at the same time. Tim Mennel's willingness to send me photographs of his lunch sustained the last revisions. All of the writers involved in the project have inspired me with their willingness to revise and rethink their work as the book took shape. This has certainly made for a richer volume. Perhaps more importantly, our conversations and e-mails about therapeutic culture have made, for me, a richer collegial life. And on that note, my greatest debt is to my tireless, creative, and always insightful coeditor, Tim Aubry, who has kept the integrity of this volume front and center since we first began to discuss it back in 2009. It's no exaggeration to say that working with Tim has revitalized my belief in the political, intellectual, and aesthetic possibilities of scholarly collaboration.

Trysh Travis

INTRODUCTION

Rethinking Therapeutic Culture

Timothy Aubry and Trysh Travis

Our age is therapeutic. If prior generations turned to their local pastors, their first selectmen, or their community elders for help and guidance, twenty-first-century Americans tend to believe that mental health experts hold the answers to their problems. The well-off willingly seek out therapists and gurus, pursuing the elusive state of happiness that their affluence has, curiously enough, failed to secure. Meanwhile the poor are referred to social workers who vet their mental and moral fitness for government benefits. Just about any individual who violates social norms—by committing violence, using ethnic slurs, or refusing to work or attend school—will invariably be encouraged to see a mental health counselor. And those who lead perfectly conventional lives but nevertheless find themselves frustrated, bored, sad, unfocused, or angry will likely end up, at some point or another, in the same place. Whether we are "in treatment" or simply know people who are, we all recognize the jargon. Whether with heartfelt zeal or an ironic shrug, we all acknowledge the importance of "attitude adjustment," "emotional fulfillment," and "personal growth." Why? Because we have made the individual psyche the primary object of our attention. We treat its improper functioning as the principal source of society's ills and see its balance and well-being as the ultimate goal of our strivings on this earth.

This therapeutic orientation is so prevalent that we rarely question or examine it. It is now a matter of common sense that people are defined primarily not by their social roles, their class status, or their political commitments but by their interior feelings. As a corollary, we believe that the exploration and expression of those feelings benefit both the individual and society. This investment in the private emotive self means that immediate familial relationships become the key to understanding not only personal identity but also each person's potential for success or failure. The ideal and healthy self, we often insist, is both individuated and happy. And of course the cultivation of such a self is not merely a personal good, but a social obligation, the central purpose of human existence.

These beliefs have played a central role in shaping our era. But while they may pass as "natural," they are in fact historically specific and therefore neither eternal nor inescapable. This book invites the curious reader (whose experience of therapeutic culture may stem from scholarly research or lived experience) to "denaturalize" them. This is not because we believe the assumptions of therapeutic culture should automatically be cast aside or rejected as categorically wrongheaded or pernicious. We certainly do want to investigate whether our therapeutic views and practices actually work for us in the ways that we are invited to believe they do, but it seems important first to understand the specific kinds of work they actually perform. We think such an understanding requires close scrutiny—attention both passionate and dispassionate. This book aims to pay that attention.

While many of the institutions and practices of therapeutic culture originated in Europe, and its contemporary reach is global, we argue here that therapeutic culture is an especially American phenomenon.[1] A central justification for the founding of the United States, after all, was the "pursuit of happiness"—a right enshrined in the Declaration of Independence. Benjamin Franklin famously helped to popularize that pursuit through his autobiographical writings, which detail his own lifelong efforts at self-improvement. His modern-day counterpart, Oprah Winfrey, urged her seven million daily viewers to "live your best life" during her talk show's twenty-five-year run. [2] The resonance of that message spawned a multimedia empire that promises to perpetuate Winfrey's sway over the national consciousness indefinitely. Given this abiding belief in a malleable inner self, it is no surprise that the number of practitioners who tend to the psychological needs of Americans has increased a hundred-fold in the past fifty years. The industry was earning sixty-nine billion dollars annually at the turn of the millennium and has grown steadily since then.[3] For those who cannot afford or do not want professional help, Alcoholics Anonymous (AA) and its offshoots are contemporary examples of the American tradition of "mutual aid"—like-minded individuals working together to support one another in the quest for personal betterment; estimated membership in AA at the turn of the century topped two million.[4] More than any other nation, it seems, the United States is passionately committed to the therapeutic promise of "self-actualization" and to whatever industries and policy regimes promise to facilitate it.

The therapeutic is a mode of healing; for those who find themselves healed, it can easily become a worldview. But given its power to work through a variety of forms, in a multitude of professional and casual settings, on a national and individual scale, we contend that it is best understood not merely as a healing technology, or even a zeitgeist, but rather as a culture, a complex web of shared assumptions, behaviors, and institutions that brings individuals together and shapes their values and ideals. Such a claim may seem counterintuitive. After all, cultures are generally thought to bind communities together, while the therapeutic appears to focus on the problems of the private individual—indeed, it plays a key role in constituting those problems as private. And yet therapeutic culture seems, bizarrely, to unite people—to foster community—through the individualistic discourse that it disseminates. Its patterns of cognition and affect unify us even as it invites us to believe that true meaning can be found only within our individual selves. The processes through which this happens are sometimes calculated, other times coincidental. Unsurprisingly, our experiences of therapeutic connectivity and isolation are sometimes conscious and critical and other times symptomatic and unreflective. If our age is therapeutic, our therapeutic culture is multivalent—maybe even perverse.

Our interest in this paradox—which we have observed in our lives as well as in our research—is what drives this volume. We argue that therapeutic culture's complexity, its capacity to serve seemingly incongruous ends, has been overlooked by scholars and critics of the therapeutic, even by those who have understood it as something more far-reaching than just a series of clinical interventions. The result has been a cultural history of the therapeutic that is conceptually thin, ideologically blinkered, and, unsurprisingly, not very useful. This volume is our attempt to change the direction of that history by beginning to rethink therapeutic culture. We want to better understand the vagaries of its evolution, the nuances of its aesthetics, and the diverse implications of its politics, broadly defined.

One issue that has hamstrung would-be critics of therapeutic culture in the past is its ubiquity in contemporary life. Therapeutic culture's omnipresence, along with its multiple and proliferating forms, has encouraged a critical engagement markedly similar to Supreme Court Justice Potter Stewart's famous take on pornography: "I know it when I see it."[5] A popular novel, a politician's speech, a set of legal arrangements, a particular form of exercise, a mobile app, a boss's pep talk: all can be celebrated (or impugned) as therapeutic. What's a critic to do with such diversity and abundance? Our goal in this volume is not to produce a catalogue of therapeutic culture's myriad manifestations, nor to serve up a set of high-profile examples from which we can derive a tidy theoretical unity for this unruly category—though either endeavor would be at home in a conventional academic collection. Instead, the essays that follow engage in varied ways with distinct examples of American therapeutic culture, analyzing them on their own terms while also casting an eye towards identifiable patterns, shared resonances, and homologies. Individually and as a collection, they aim to tease out some common threads of therapeutic discourse without pretending to reveal its warp and woof or to render a final judgment on the quality of the weave.

In this, our project differs from much extant scholarship on therapeutic culture, which tends to excoriate rather than to analyze. Perhaps as a reaction against the utopian claims of its partisans, many of whom present therapeutic nostrums as the very key to our salvation, critics from every discipline and from across the ideological spectrum have decried therapeutic culture for reducing the United States to a country of insular navel gazers unable to engage with anything beyond their own feelings. For those on the left, this preoccupation with the self disables the structural critique necessary for progressive change; as seen from the right, it cancels out the commitment to personal responsibility and civic duty that has historically underpinned American democracy. And on one thing everybody can agree: therapeutic culture dupes, demoralizes, and pacifies those it claims to help—it deepens their problems rather than resolving them.[6]

Both the power and the limitations of this peculiar intellectual history inform our goals for this volume. Just as we examine the complexity of therapeutic culture and the diversity of its forms in everyday life, we also grapple here with "therapeutic culture" as a critical canard, a convenient term designed to denigrate cultural formations that fail to rise to critics' political (or intellectual or aesthetic) standards. If the boosterish style of the therapeutic's proponents seems hyperbolic to us, so, too, do many of the apocalyptic arguments of its detractors. Indeed, the strong feelings on either side of the issue are what intrigue us: they are obviously central to the work that therapeutic culture performs every day, for critics who use it as an analytical category as well as for laypeople who use it to make sense of their lives. In this volume we hope to draw attention to such partisanship rather than to replicate it: if we do not pretend to create either an exhaustive compendium or a grand unified theory of the therapeutic, in the same spirit we aim neither to recuperate nor to vilify it. Our intent is simultaneously more modest and more grand: rethinking—giving voice to a group of thoughtful observers variously invested in therapeutic culture as a practice, an object of study, and a critical discourse. Their insights, we believe, begin to chip away at the received meanings of therapeutic culture and suggest new frameworks through which we may better understand our therapeutic age. The power and originality of the observations collected here should illuminate a trail that readers of all stripes can follow, whether they read diligently, from cover to cover, or haphazardly, attuned to the possibility of serendipitous connections. On the assumption that either reading mode will benefit from a comprehensive historical backdrop, we sketch here a brief overview of therapeutic culture as both a lived reality and a critical discourse.

THERAPEUTIC CULTURE: AN INSTITUTIONAL HISTORY

A central premise of therapeutic culture—that the self is something we can work to cultivate and improve and that its economic, ethical, intellectual, and emotional possibilities are not predetermined by heredity or inherited social position—has a long history in the United States. Jefferson and Franklin were particularly adroit early spokesmen, but the belief in the self as a malleable entity with a duty before God to pursue happiness predates them. It was a central plank in the liberal political philosophy underpinning the whole of the American experiment.[7]

This self was popularized across the nineteenth century in religious tracts, conduct manuals, the popular press, and both fictional and "true life" bestsellers. Self-examination and self-renovation became central themes in public meetings of reformed drunkards and in the "friendly visits" of church volunteers to fallen women. The same imperatives are evident in Henry David Thoreau's injunction (1848) to "live deliberately . . . and suck out all the marrow of life" and in Harriet Beecher Stowe's call to the readers of *Uncle Tom's Cabin* (1852) to "see to it that *they feel right*" about slavery.[8] By the time that the Mind Cure mystics of the Gilded Age began urging their followers to discover "the Divine within," Americans had already been scrutinizing their interiors for more than a century.

The United States has provided an especially fertile ground for the flourishing of therapeutic culture, but that culture's origins may have less to do with American exceptionalism than with the broad forces of modernization at work in Europe in the eighteenth and nineteenth centuries. The gradual decline of the church as a unitary source of knowledge and authority meant changes in traditional religious practices during this period—including the proliferation of Protestant sects, the modernizing streak within Catholicism, and the rise of evangelicalism and mysticism. These led to a flattening of church hierarchies and a newly personalized experience of spirituality. Simultaneously, what historian Joyce Appleby calls "the heroic model of science" evolved in the new European nation states, laying the foundation for the empiricism, rationalization, and mind-body dualism that would structure the assumptions of clinical psychiatry.[9] Alongside of them, romanticism's celebration of creativity, spontaneity, originality, and self-expression provided a repository of self-centered values that would eventually become central to a therapeutic sensibility.

Underwriting all of these developments was the growth of industrial capitalism, which brought with it an increasingly rigid division between public and private spaces, work life and home life, the labor of the body and that of the mind. The existence of routinized, bureaucratic, oppressive, and mercenary labor during the eighteenth and nineteenth centuries helped to create the idea of private life as the site of fulfillment and safety, the place to express and satisfy authentic needs. The interior, inner life—for which the home served as both metaphor and sanctuary—thus acquired a heightened value, even as perceived threats from the outside created a sense of its fragility. In a reinforcing loop, the perception of the domestic/interior as besieged increased its relative importance, both to individuals and to the culture writ large.[10]

The rising standard of living brought on by the spread of capitalism throughout Europe and North America played a key role here. If in earlier times economic scarcity had dictated relentless labor, deferral of gratification, and a belief in the virtue of asceticism, by the end of the nineteenth century a relative abundance of affordable material goods allowed even the average citizen of the metropolis to believe that personal fulfillment and happiness need not be postponed. The result was not just a new pursuit of everyday luxuries but also a reorienting of spiritual life in accordance with the norm of abundance. This tendency is most pronounced in the theosophical religions and associated Mind Cure movement that flourished in this period. Promulgated by a loose assortment of mental healers, preachers, and mystics, these popular, polyglot spiritualities downplayed the importance of hard work and self-sacrifice, arguing for the presence of a cosmic "divine supply" of love and health, wealth and power, and positing that they were readily available to all those who would attune themselves "with the Infinite."[11] Most traditional denominations, unsurprisingly, scorned the metaphysical orientation and focus on personal uplift. But their own shifts away from a stern and demanding God the Father and towards a personal and loving Jesus, directly accessible through individual prayer, reflect a similar reorientation. If older theologies had focused on the humility of the self in the face of the divine, these new discourses emphasized the self's potential for greatness when properly partnered with the divine. Religion, argued William James, the most prominent and persuasive observer of these developments, had become a channel through which to seek rich subjective experiences and with them "mental health."[12]

But if personal happiness suddenly seemed far more attainable than ever before, various conditions associated with modernity—the rise of crowded urban centers filled with strangers, the emergence of bewildering new high-speed communication and transportation technologies, and a sense of disorienting and rapid social and cultural change—also helped to produce in the 1800s an outbreak of what physicians referred to as "nervous disorders." In earlier times, the scant attention paid to mental health had been focused on the insane and sequestered. But the new disorders of modernity were mundane and manageable, the complaints of individuals who remained integrated within society, if not perfectly comfortable with it. A new class of caregivers arose to address them. In the United States, this meant that a colorful array of practitioners (some religious, some medical, some claiming to wield psychic or occult powers) began to offer prototherapeutic interventions aimed at relieving mental suffering. In Europe, Sigmund Freud developed and popularized the one-on-one office visit and the talking cure as palliatives, challenging as he did so the view promoted by asylum physicians working in the tradition of Phillipe Pinel and Jean-Martin Charcot of mental illness as necessarily rooted in neurological dysfunction. The result was a sense of the mind as an autonomous realm requiring its own kind of professional attention.[13]

Theosophy had been a pan-European innovation, but the unique and deep-seated American commitment to self (combined with a polyglot and opportunistic medical profession) meant the insights of mental healing were particularly resonant in the United States. As Eric Caplan notes, "when Freud first set foot on American soil [in 1909], psychotherapy was already integrally woven into the fabric of American culture and American medicine."[14] The Progressive era had already seen the development of a mental hygiene movement that aimed to alleviate the stresses and harms associated with life in urban slums; now the need to promote mental health began to appeal to a broader clientele.[15] It is not surprising that Freud's ideas moved rapidly beyond a narrow professional audience and into the lives of the country's growing middle class.[16] Two world wars contributed immeasurably to the proliferation of what were now known as "psychological" pathologies. Indeed, the growth of mental health services for soldier and veterans, especially during and after World War II, helped to destigmatize therapy, as huge numbers of purportedly normal individuals availed themselves of it. Shell-shocked combat veterans, neurotic housewives, and maladjusted youth alike sought help from—or were remanded to—the newly legitimate counseling professions.[17] While therapeutic culture did not originate in the United States, by the mid-twentieth century, it was avowedly American—and vice versa.

In postwar America, the stream of therapeutic ideas flowing into mainstream culture grew to a gusher, and a profession that had previously served a small segment of the population—urban eccentrics, wealthy elites, and the visibly disturbed—experienced extraordinary growth, coming to treat a significant percentage of the general population.[18] In 1949 the federal government created the National Institute of Mental Health, and in the decade that followed universities across the country developed degree programs in clinical psychology, creating a world of mental health apart from the medical field and thus paving the way for a multitude of new therapeutic strategies and practices—behaviorist, cognitive, humanist, gestalt, and family systems, to name just a very few.By the latter half of the twentieth century, psychology's concepts and practices had thoroughly permeated popular culture, to the extent that therapeutic principles began to shape the worldview of many people who never had any direct contact with mental health workers.Tabloid confessions, Hollywood melodrama, the advice columns of popular magazines, moralizing made-for-TV movies, self-improvement books for adults, and "social problem" novels for teens—all these and more addressed a population whose newfound prosperity and concomitant insecurity made fully realized psychological well-being seem elusive yet achievable. Belief in that distinctly modern possibility is what critics have derisively called "the therapeutic worldview."[19]

THE THERAPEUTIC CULTURE CRITIQUE: AN INTELLECTUAL HISTORY

No sooner did it emerge as a salient phenomenon in the late nineteenth century than the therapeutic worldview became an object of scathing critique. Orthodox clergy, unsurprisingly, were among its first critics. They condemned the drift of both theology and worship toward what one early Unitarian tract characterized as "A Display of Love Not of Wrath." The end of the nineteenth century saw these positions harden, as evangelicals, eager to retain their claim to biblical prophecies regarding miraculous physical healing, decried New Thought recommendations as liberal heresies. During the 1950s, when Norman Vincent Peale made Christian faith into a source of psychological health and worldly success with his phenomenally popular *The Power of Positive Thinking*, religious leaders ranging from Reinhold Niebuhr to Elmer George Homrighausen offered fierce rejoinders, claiming that Peale was watering

Christianity down, obscuring its more complex and tragic elements so as to lend it a mass appeal.[20] This strain of critique has persisted largely unchanged into the present, fueling fundamentalist splinter groups convinced that only a focus on sin and atonement addresses the self that really matters—the soul.[21]

If religious critics were early observers of therapeutic culture's emergence, their secular counterparts waited until the immediate postwar period to sound the alarm—and then quickly made up for lost time. Prominent liberals spearheaded the most direct and influential of these assaults. But several other camps, including libertarians, countercultural iconoclasts, feminists, neoconservatives, and radical Foucauldians, have contributed to the chorus of condemnation. One index of therapeutic culture's power may be its ability to unify so many otherwise antagonistic schools of thought.

Recasting arguments made by Frankfurt school theorists such as Theodor Adorno and Herbert Marcuse, R.D. Laing and Thomas Szasz of the antipsychiatry movement of the 1960s argued that psychological discourses and the mental health industry that grew out of them served as a means of social control. Their analysis was complemented by Michel Foucault's contemporaneous excavations of the disciplinary technologies of modernity, particularly of science, medicine, and imprisonment. Categories designed to identify mental illness were not, these skeptics held, neutral scientific descriptions of actual preexisting conditions but part of a coercive, ideologically motivated taxonomy designed to extend legitimacy and legal rights to those who adhered to social conventions while marginalizing those labeled deviant or subversive.[22] Many American feminists, including Betty Friedan and Kate Millett, while focused on a different set of problems and political goals, reached remarkably similar conclusions. Noting that attitudes among mental health professionals ranged from sexist to downright misogynist, they argued that therapeutic labels and treatment norms served to exclude women from full participation in society and recast the feelings of dissatisfaction produced by gender inequality as the symptoms of psychological disorders.[23]

Further attacks based on a stance of critical suspicion grew out of Foucault's later work. In *A History of Sexuality, Volume One* (published in the United States in 1977), he famously argued that the talking cure was not, as Freud had suggested, a means to free up repressed feelings and thoughts about taboo subjects but instead a covert tactic for constructing the very thing it pretended to liberate: a self-regulating subjectivity that served the needs of bourgeois society. Inspired by Foucault's insights into the ways therapeutic techniques subtly complement the workings of other structures of power, social theorists like Nikolas Rose and Wendy Brown have argued that people are now paradoxically governed through their "freedoms." Constantly told that they can and should be happy, individuals become their own jailers: policing their bodies and minds in search of what they believe to be self-fulfillment, they align themselves ever more perfectly with the agendas of the overweening state and the interests of the corporation.[24]

These arguments against the purportedly specious freedoms afforded by therapeutic culture have exerted considerable influence, especially among academics who work within the tradition of continental critical theory. But a different mode of criticism has played an equally if not more central role in establishing therapeutic culture as a critical commonplace in whose shadow we currently labor. The liberal public intellectual tradition of postwar America informs what we term the "canonical" critique of therapeutic culture, as articulated by (among others) Philip Rieff, Richard Sennett, Christopher Lasch, T.J. Jackson Lears, Robert Bellah et al., and Wendy Kaminer. These authors, for the most part, acknowledge the intellectual and clinical power of psychoanalysis and its offshoots and believe that therapeutic culture performs a liberating function, freeing people up from angst-inducing obligations and responsibilities of all sorts. But this is precisely the source of their alarm. Less concerned with the possibility of ideological coercion than with social fragmentation, and animated more by nostalgia than suspicion, the canonical critics mourn the debasement of *civitas*, the classical public sphere, and the traditions of artisanal republicanism.

It is telling that their complaint does not spring from the history of science or the therapeutic professions. It originates instead from the general intellectual predispositions of midcentury America, specifically the arguments against "mass society" mounted by spokesmen for the anticommunist left like Richard Hofstadter, David Riesman, C. Wright Mills, Dwight MacDonald, and Leslie Fiedler.[25] They, too, drew on the Frankfurt school's insights, although agonistically, seeking a critical paradigm with the explanatory power of popular front Marxism but free from its communist taint. Their solution was to analyze capitalism in cultural rather than structural ways, focusing on a zeitgeist or a set of lifeways rather than class structure or political economy. Their chief object of concern was mass society—a term that, in their writings, designates a structure of feeling as much as anything and a state characterized primarily by loss: of authenticity and community, of true religiosity and meaningful work. All these, they opined, had figured prominently in an imagined American past but had been degraded by current circumstances and reduced to little more than haunting residues.

Emerging from this intellectual tradition in the 1960s and '70s, the canonical critics of the therapeutic elaborated the argument against mass society into something simultaneously more precise and more far-reaching. At the center of their critique lay consumer capitalism, a dynamic force that cultivated personal dissatisfaction in order to drive the economy. Lofty notions of personal happiness, the possibilities of self-improvement, and the authentic self constrained by an oppressive social order—these were nothing but advertising slogans dressed up to look like philosophies. The panaceas touted by therapists and admen undercut the powerful logic of delayed gratification that had underpinned an older mercantile capitalism and its handmaiden, organized religion. As the self and its needs became the dominant preoccupation of "the affluent society," the world became "weightless" absent the structures that had given it meaning.[26] Self-restraint, decorum, and personal responsibility ceased to exercise their inhibiting but ultimately productive powers. "Permissiveness" reigned; chaos ensued.

We call this tradition of critique "canonical" in part because of its staying power, but also because of its capaciousness: it has been endorsed by everyone from Republicans to radicals.For the former, as energies are siphoned off in the frivolous pursuit of individual happiness, political participation, civic involvement, and public life decline accordingly. The public sphere dissolves into "a nation of victims," bereft of agency and political will.[27] For the latter, overinvestment in individualism breeds political quiescence. Significantly, this argument shares certain key assumptions with the Foucauldian tradition discussed earlier: participation in twelve-step groups keeps women from recognizing their oppression by patriarchy; organizational psychologists direct workers' attention away from their poor working conditions; a diagnosis of post-traumatic stress disorder negates principled resistance to war.[28]

In short, the therapeutic worldview is a smoke and mirrors game, inviting people to believe their problems lie in themselves, not in the world, and encouraging them to adjust their attitudes rather than to fight against injustice. Although they define its content differently, right- and left-leaning canonical critics alike agree that therapeutic culture empties out the vital and rigorous realm of "the political," replacing its stern but rewarding traditions with the ethical equivalent of junk food. The result is a world largely devoid of community or collectivity, populated by selves that are simultaneously overvalued and weak and thus vulnerable to control by the authoritarian bureaucracy of the welfare state as well as by the whims of capital.

As if such degradation were not enough, a crushing irony lies at the heart of this realignment of societal priorities: therapeutic culture fails to live up to its own promises. The freedom to pursue happiness does not in fact make people happier. Quite the opposite. Continental and canonical, right- and left-wing critics agree that therapeutic culture formalizes and exacerbates unhappiness. It encourages individuals to discover and label every possible symptom of mental disquiet, produces additional anxiety on top of the anxiety it purports to cure, and makes people neurotic about their own neuroses. It deceives, weakens, and intellectually stifles those whom it claims to help; it comforts its adherents only by falsifying their conditions; it offers delusions rather than honest assessments of or viable solutions to the problems it pretends to solve. And in doing so, it ensures a receptive market for its own continued interventions into people's lives.

The fall narrative offered by the therapeutic culture critics is seductive—it promises in fact to explain almost all contemporary problems. But a capacious term of art like "the therapeutic worldview" is ripe for reductive deployment. Its vagueness can be exploited in order to make it apply to all manner of phenomena, thus expanding the scope of an argument—and it can also be strategically narrowed, reduced down at crucial moments to a few negative attributes and connotations, which can then be claimed as the basic DNA of contemporary consciousness. If therapeutic culture simplifies the world by laying all its problems at the doorstep of the individual psyche, then many of its critics uncannily repeat the error, laying those problems at the doorstep of therapeutic culture.

Different authors, of course, locate the dawning of the therapeutic age in different historical moments: Lears situates it in the Gilded Age; Rieff in the decades following Freud's ascendance; Lasch, Bellah, and Kaminer in the aftermath of the 1960s, and so on. But whenever the therapeutic day breaks, it looks the same—and, interestingly, it is almost always a dystopian image of the critics' own historical moment. To be sure, the reactionary quality of some of these arguments does not automatically render them invalid. The canonical critics were probably right to treat the increased permissiveness of the Cold War era with skepticism. Cultivating the self and engaging with civic society both take time; prioritize the former, and the latter may suffer. Righteous demands for the redress of political grievances can melt away into complacency. And in particular, hedonism, sexual liberation, and primal spontaneity, so often touted as revolutionary, seem quite amenable to capture within the iron cage of capitalism and hence far less emancipatory than many of their original partisans believed.

But the antipathy of the canonical therapeutic culture critics to these liberationist energies too often turns from principled to shrill.[29] Perhaps their uneasiness is provoked by a social landscape and an intellectual climate no longer hospitable to their sweeping pronouncements; perhaps insecurity, as well as principled disagreement, fuels their vitriol. Along with calls for political liberation, the cultural foment known as "the '60s" gave us a plurality of ethnic, sexual, and affective subcultures, and the identity politics that have flowed from them insist upon the existence of multiple critical paradigms, none more legitimate than any other. Emerging first as radical political movements—black nationalism, radical feminism, gay rights—during the 1960s and '70s, these oppositional frameworks reject not only traditional forms of authority but also the ideal of cultural unity, of "American" or "civic" values. Such decentering impulses pose a threat to traditional public intellectuals, particularly those invested in grand explanatory narratives.

Institutionalized within the academy during the culture wars of the 1980s, the critical legacy of such identitarian movements has included a recognition that the perspectives of those who consume, enjoy, and use popular culture are no less valid than those of experts—a premise that attacks the very foundation on which the canonical therapeutic culture critics stand. Reviewed in this light, their central concerns—anxieties about social fragmentation, claims about the so-called fall of public man, and laments over the weakening of civic commitments—begin to appear suspiciously tactical, attempts to stigmatize the rival worldviews whose appearance threatens to render their own modes of analysis obsolete.

We are not the first to suggest that a nostalgic impulse may lie back of the therapeutic culture critique. Robert Bellah and his coauthors acknowledge the possibility in their preface to the 1996 reissue of their classic 1985 book *Habits of the Heart*—and just as quickly dismiss it: "If some readers of *Habits* saw us as nostalgic for an idealized past, we would now like to disabuse them" (xvii). No more full-throated rebuttal is forthcoming, however; instead, the authors acknowledge with scant chagrin a personal preference for the "biblical and republican traditions" (xvii) of an earlier era, as exemplified by the traditional American small town.

Such a human-scale community—where families reside for generations, where collective prosperity serves the interests of local business owners, where altruism and individualism work together organically and civic activities lend a sense of communal purpose to the lives of the town's citizens—is an enticing picture. But missing from Bellah et al.'s description is any serious concern for the patriarchal lines of authority and the racial and ethnic exclusions through which such communities achieved their appealing coherence or for the dogmatism, provinciality, and intolerance that they nurtured and directed toward anyone who did not fit the demographic and cultural profile of the community's dominant members. Such inattention to power is both symptomatic and significant. Central to the utopian pasts that the canonical therapeutic culture critics juxtapose to the debased present are coercive forms of moral authority and cultural homogeneity, which often operated by excluding, subjugating, or disregarding significant portions of the American population.[30] The discourse of individual gratification sponsored by therapeutic culture may have licensed narcissism and indulgence, but its liberatory energies have also challenged these older and intransigent forms of authority, empowering those who have been denied a meaningful role or sphere of agency within the organizing schema of traditional American communities.

We concede that this, therapeutic culture's chief virtue, may also be its greatest limitation. Like any mass-produced, popularly acclaimed, or one-size-fits-all product, therapeutic culture promises to meet everyone's needs but does so incompletely, fully satisfying no one. The inspirational language employed by self-help gurus such as Ralph Waldo Trine, Dale Carnegie, and Oprah Winfrey, for instance, appeals to a broad and democratic audience. As such, the meanings and values that it offers its adherents cannot help but be more attenuated than those that operate within a more exclusive community—whether of civic Republicans or radical anarchists. But perhaps this very attenuation, this falling away of traditional supports, is what allows new forms of agency, selfhood, and struggle to emerge within both individual and communal life on the ground. It is possibilities of this kind, unleashed by therapeutic culture and generally disregarded by so many of its critics, that we hope to entertain in this collection.

NEW DEVELOPMENTS

We hold that existing blind spots in the therapeutic culture critique require us to rethink it. But another key reason for a reconsideration is that therapy and therapeutic culture continue to change. Recent developments in science-based mental health as well as in more popular forms of therapeutic engagement cry out for analysis grounded in an understanding of the institutional and intellectual histories of the therapeutic. We sketch a few of these innovations now in order to suggest some areas that we believe are particularly ripe for future debate.

The most glaring development is, of course, the rise of psychotropic prescription drugs designed to alleviate mental conditions like depression, anxiety, mania, psychosis, attention deficit disorder, insomnia, and so on. The list of these elixirs grows continually; it includes Prozac, Pristiq, Cymbalta, Ixel, Tolvon, Remeron, Avanza, Zispin, Strattera, Zoloft, Effexor, Mazanor, Sanorex, Edronax, Vivalan, Stablon, Coaxil, Tatinol, Valdoxan, Melitor, Thymanax,

Elavil, Endep, Anafranil, Adrafinil, Wellbutrin, Adapin, Paxil, Ritalin, Lithium, Haldol, Serenace, Droleptan, Thorazine, Trileptal, Xanax, and Ativan. These drugs promise to stabilize moods, forestall suicidal impulses, aid concentration, minimize antisocial behavior, and promote overall psychic wellbeing. The peculiar aural quality of this list of trademarked names should be enough to suggest that with them we enter an alien universe. While their growing presence in our world raises myriad theoretical issues, we find ourselves compelled by one particularly significant question: Does the popularity of these pharmaceuticals indicate that we have moved beyond the central insight of Cartesian rationalism (which informed neurology, psychology, and psychoanalysis at their founding and have shaped most of the therapies that follow from them), that is, that the mind is separate from the body, a phenomenon in and of itself? If indeed we are now, a century later, reversing Freud's efforts to distinguish psychological and bodily complaints, how will this alter our conception of the subjective interior or, for that matter, of the subject itself?

A second and related development is the proliferation of new pathological categories—among them obsessive-compulsive disorder, codependence, sex addiction, body dysmorphia, borderline personality disorder, and Asperger's—that seem, in many cases, to be invented and deployed primarily to justify new psychiatric interventions. The popularity of such terms and labels testifies, on the one hand, to Americans' continued reliance upon licensed experts in their efforts to achieve self-understanding. But it also indicates, on the other hand, our ongoing investment in self-help and mutual-help movements, whose strategies tend to focus on what Mariana Valverde has provocatively labeled "diseases of the will," problems that are neither wholly moral, nor wholly medical, and thus evade mastery by professionals operating within any institutionalized spheres of knowledge.[31]

Such movements—particularly those inspired by the principles of AA—both embrace and call into question many concepts and tenets of the therapeutic paradigm. They seem to affirm the American faith in individual agency, holding addicts responsible for their behavior and, especially in the case of codependency groups, pathologizing unseemly dependence on others. And yet they also seem to trouble this faith, encouraging, as their critics so often note, an unhealthy dependence upon the group itself. Moreover, while these organizations often champion normative relationships between husbands and wives and parents and children, the cultivation of strong ties within the group also challenges the traditional privileging of the nuclear family as the incubator for proper psychological development. Indeed, recovery groups tend to highlight dysfunctions caused by the immediate families of their members and to volunteer themselves as healthier surrogates, thus encouraging individuals to seek fulfillment outside the home, in public spaces marked by the congregation of strangers.

If face-to-face self-help groups have smudged the bright line between the public and the private, the Internet's therapeutic cultures threaten to obliterate it. The Internet is a place people go, typically alone, in order, paradoxically, to be with other people—sometimes strangers, sometimes friends, and often, on social networking sites, with those who fall somewhere in between the two categories. A "status update" often contains intimate details, but it reaches hundreds; its position as just one disclosure among many depersonalizes its content. Indeed, it is the impersonality of the site that enables—or compels—disclosure in the first place. We often discover more about our friends and family members from these peculiar new hybrid discourses than we do from our direct interactions with them, but this personal knowledge is no longer a sign of privilege or a source of intimacy. Instead it is the common currency of a reading public.

The confessional rhetoric associated with therapeutic culture has also infiltrated the political sphere in recent decades. Details about the personal lives and domestic dramas of our leaders attract constant media attention. Their perceived psychological or emotional states drive public opinion as much as their ideological positions or their policies. Politicians routinely perform empathy in choreographed scenes, one eye misted over and another on their poll numbers. Bill Clinton may have been the master of such tactics, but Barack Obama, despite his perceived aloofness, obviously recognizes the therapeutic character of contemporary politics. His 2008 campaign produced a coalition of voters organized not around a unified political program, but around a simple state of affect, hope. It should surprise no one that when his campaign flagged during the primaries, he revived it with the help of Oprah Winfrey, therapeutic culture's foremost spokesperson. If Americans now pick their leaders the same way they decide which books to read—on the basis of their "relatability"—is this just one more sign of how therapeutic culture is ruining our society, supplanting rational analysis with personal feelings? Perhaps . . . but not necessarily. We recognize the dangers of our current cultural climate. What interests us here are its untapped possibilities and unexplored complexities.

RETHINKING THERAPEUTIC CULTURE: A ROADMAP

A phenomenon as amorphous, pervasive, and diffuse as therapeutic culture, one whose influence spans the boundary between the political and the personal, whose truths flow from the mouths of world leaders and celebrities, whose assumptions shape the quarrels we have in the privacy of our homes as well as our published fiction, editorials, and policy statements—such a phenomenon demands a diverse and refined set of critical tools. For this reason our approach to instantiating a rethinking has been deliberately idiosyncratic. The authors assembled here come from various disciplines, have different perspectives, and deploy diverse rhetorics and methodologies to make their points. Our editorial mandate to them was simple: take a term that was central to their understanding of therapeutic culture (or its critique) and run with it. For some authors, this meant historicizing or problematizing a discrete term or moment in traditional scholarly style. In at least a few (appropriately therapeutic) cases, the subject matter forced authors out of their academic comfort zones to follow certain wayward realities into unfamiliar conceptual territory. As a result, the forms as well as the content of these essays register the complexity and scope of our subject matter. Unsuspecting readers may be surprised by shifts in style and focus as they move from one piece to the next; we hope they will also be pleased by unexpected moments of resonance among our authors' seemingly disparate reflections.

The structure of the volume encourages the active search for such resonance. Our very rough chronological ordering of the essays invites an understanding of therapeutic culture's emergence over time as a defining feature of postwar American life. The traditional reader will see that story develop as she moves from beginning to middle to end; our volume first considers therapeutic culture's relationship to its prehistory, then tracks its dramatic growth in the immediate post–World War II era and the anxieties, hopes, and ambivalences that growth inspired. It then explores countercultural reactions to the so-called culture of consensus and the impact they had on therapeutic practices. It concludes with a series of examinations of therapeutic culture in contemporary society. This structure follows the changes therapeutic culture has undergone over time as the institutions that underpin it have developed and as it has become an explicit object of intellectual critique.

The less linear, more opportunistic reader may treat this collection as a simple compendium of stand-alone pieces or trace key thematic motifs that develop across it: gender's preeminence as an organizing category within the therapeutic ("Motherhood," "Confessions," "Pain"); the peculiar malleability of therapeutic terminology ("Gospel," "Spirit," "Narcissism"); the persistence of political commitment within this supposedly depoliticizing discourse ("Race," "Pills," "Radical"), and so on. The microabstracts included in the Contents are intended to help both types of readers navigate the broad territory we cover and to provide points of entry into the provocative (if sometimes implicit) conversation these essays instantiate.

To invite readers into that conversation, we conclude this Introduction with several propositions designed to foster debate. Their purpose is not to impose upon readers a particular attitude toward therapeutic culture, nor is it to offer prescriptions on how we as individuals or as a nation should proceed. Like the essays in this volume, these mini-manifestoes invite consideration of an assortment of assumptions, rituals, and habits (which may have seemed too natural, too commonplace, or just too banal to merit much reflection) as constituent parts of a historically specific and rather peculiar culture—and to think about the meaning of their participation in that culture. We assume that the conclusions readers reach will be as varied and complex as the perspectives offered by individual contributors.

"Therapeutic Culture" Lives

Although the institutions, practices, and habits of mind of therapeutic culture developed over generations, the concept of therapeutic culture burst into visibility as a result of the tireless (indeed sometimes feverish) efforts of a small group of postwar American public intellectuals—who now barely even figure in the footnotes of contemporary scholarship. Precisely because the theoretical paradigm instantiated by the canonical critics has suffered such critical neglect in recent years, it has never actually been discredited or even seriously challenged. One reason for its staying power, perhaps, is that its intuitive appeal is difficult to dismiss: who doesn't want a more robust public sphere or more sustaining communal ties? This vernacularization of the critique mounted by Rieff, Lasch, Bellah, and so on means that even while their names go unmentioned, their views persist. Foucault-inflected queer theory and, more recently, the "affective turn" in criticism offer an alternative, less sweepingly antagonistic approach to the therapeutic than that of the canonical critics, but these later schools have yet to engage with therapeutic culture as a critical construct.[32] Any rethinking of therapeutic culture must take on the canonical critics, if only as a prelude to creating a new position.

Therapeutic Culture Is No Monolith

In contemporary Western society (particularly but not exclusively American), myriad institutions, practices, and beliefs combine to form a therapeutic culture, which tends to propagate a fairly predictable set of ideas about the relationship between the self and society, the nature of happiness, and the purpose of life. But this apparent coherence masks a web of contradictions and conflicting allegiances. While critics on all sides of the spectrum, from Susan Sontag to David Brooks, from Michel Foucault to Germaine Greer, have sought to align therapeutic culture with a particular political regime or ideological bent, careful study reveals that such efforts are doomed to fail. In many cases, the language of therapy does prioritize the private sphere over the public; in others, it enforces accommodation to the status quo, as many observers have suggested. But in still other cases therapeutic discourse articulates dissatisfaction with social and political givens and challenges traditional forms of authority.

The Mental Matters

Until recently, scholars seeking to determine the key forces that shape history have not tended to assign much significance to the phenomena that play a central role within therapeutic culture. Whether carelessly or willfully, they have failed to recognize that mental and psychological states—including feelings, moods, memories, and dispositions—constitute a substantive part of social reality. To take therapeutic culture seriously is to recognize that these states are not merely symptomatic or epiphenomenal; they are not merely the passive products of economic or political developments; and they are not confined within the mind of the individual. They are public as often as they are private, collective as often as they are individual. Constantly communicated and shared, they can be deployed strategically to produce particular effects. The mental continually interacts with other registers, including the bodily, the economic, and the political. In some cases, mental states are the effects of other forces; in other cases they are the agents of change. To argue that therapeutic culture masks reality is to treat mental states as somehow unreal, or less real than economic or political registers, and thus to affirm an outmoded notion of what counts as history. It is also to trivialize the experiences, tactics, and forms of influence of those who, whether by choice or mandate, have traditionally operated outside the official public sphere.

The Therapeutic Is Social

The navel gazing that therapeutic culture purportedly promotes can serve to fragment society. And the landscape of the United States has arguably become more atomized in recent decades. But if therapeutic categories have contributed to this development, they have also promoted various forms of solidarity among strangers, most prominently in recovery and other mutual-help movements. The psychologization of experience can allow individuals divided by cultural context to feel a sense of empathy and communal purpose. Basic therapeutic concepts, like depression, anxiety, and happiness, are categories intended to specify internal mental states, without reference to the particular cultural contexts in which they emerge, suggesting that these states feel roughly the same to the individuals experiencing them, whatever their nationality, ethnicity, gender, or class. Although this deracinating language may at times elide important economic and social differences, it can also produce unlikely alliances. The strength and duration of such bonds have not yet been tested over long periods of time. But we know that the language of the self, when read carefully, often turns out to be the language of the social.

Diagnosis Is Identity

Therapeutic identity categories, such as Asperger's, codependence, and attention deficit disorder, have the potential to rival older identity categories derived from class, race, and gender. This may inaugurate unpredictable forms of identity politics, with new alliances and conflicts that cut across the old divisions. Class has rarely functioned as effectively as gender and race to mobilize pride and oppositional politics in the United States, since to use class in this way would require disadvantaged people to embrace a state of relative deprivation. Will therapeutic identity categories face an analogous problem, or will they successfully "flip the script" as other identity-based social movements have done, converting stigma into a source of power?[33] Debates over whether individuals should seek "cures" for their "dysfunctions" or embrace them are currently raging on discussion boards for "Aspies" and among those on the autism spectrum. Will therapeutic identity categories serve a minoritizing or a universalizing function? Will they play a role similar to other so-called disabilities, and do they even belong within this category?

The Liberal Subject Might Be Worth Keeping

Ever since Freud argued that we are shaped by unconscious drives, of which we remain largely unaware, philosophers and theorists have been challenging the notion of the self as a unified, coherent, and autonomous entity. Its boundaries, some noted, were porous; its apparent depth was entirely a fiction or performance; and its future was very much uncertain. But this was almost never a cause for alarm: the unified self, according to Roland Barthes, Michel Foucault, and other continental theorists, was the illusory product of a historically specific ideology, a key facet of the bourgeois individualism necessary to free market capitalism. Dismantling the liberal subject, in short, would help usher in a new society. In recent years, however, the most serious challenges to the traditional self have come from a quarter that is not known for encouraging political revolution, namely, the pharmaceutical industry, which incessantly markets psychotropic drugs as the solution to various mental "problems." Now that prescribed neurochemical supplements—institutionally sanctioned (or required) alterations of identity—have become commonplace, perhaps it is time to ask whether undermining the stability and coherence of the self is quite as subversive as theorists have hoped. When the profit-driven pharmaceutical industry hawks its own version of the deconstructed self, in other words, the liberal subject suddenly begins to look less like the barrier to all political progress and more like an endangered species worth preserving. Indeed, perhaps we should not be so quick to relinquish a host of other similarly discredited categories—including essence, character, and even soul—now that technological interventions far removed from the speculations of the intellectual elite threaten to do away with them.

And finally, there is no escaping therapeutic culture. While it will certainly continue to change, it will not disappear in the near future. Further denunciations will only corroborate perceptions of its critics as out of touch with the reality of everyday life. Acknowledging that therapeutic culture is here to stay takes us to the central concern of this book, namely how to rethink therapeutic culture in a critical fashion.

For many left intellectuals, the ultimate measure of a given cultural phenomenon's value is whether or not it serves progressive political ends. Some of the essays that follow explore the way certain therapeutic practices can be made to serve social causes. Others explore the history of therapeutic empowerment. Their point of departure is the recognition, popularized by the New Left and its identitarian offshoots, that psychological, sexual, and emotional language can be made to perform important political work. These groups' efforts to make consciousness itself the site for revolutionary engagement constituted a central weapon in the struggles for liberation that emerged in the 1960s and '70s.

The achievements of second-wave feminism represent one such exemplary alliance between therapeutic culture and political activism. Within that social movement, awareness that "the personal is political" led to vastly increased reproductive freedoms for women, greater equality within marriage, antidiscrimination laws, and a far more integrated workplace and public culture. Critical attention to the everyday psychological burdens of suburban housewives, as well as to the therapy industry itself, provided one impetus for this far-reaching movement. Psychotherapists, argued Betty Friedan in *The Feminine Mystique*, exacerbated female unhappiness. When women struggled with the depression they felt as a result of their second-class status, therapy mostly reaffirmed their subordinate positions and endorsed the stifling domestic arrangements that had helped to produce their dissatisfaction in the first place. Yet even as Friedan critiqued professional therapists and their pop culture proxies, she relied upon a humanistic psychological framework to understand why middle-class American women felt dissatisfied. At the center of *The Feminine Mystique* is the right to self-actualization, to what Friedan called the "basic human need to grow," as understood by psychologists ranging from Abraham Maslow to Karen Horney.[34] The only way to combat the potentially reactionary effects of therapeutic culture, Friedan argued, was to turn it to your own uses. Fifty years later, we have yet to realize the full potential of this insight.

Thus some of the essays in this volume illuminate the progressive political potential inherent in therapeutic culture. Others, however, call into question the unthinking default to "the political" as the yardstick with which we measure value. Therapeutic culture is interesting in part because it benefits (or possibly hurts) individuals in ways that may defy strict categorization along the ideological spectrum. In some cases those who engage with it find something incontestably valuable that serves no political or ideological function whatsoever. This is an observation so entirely obvious as to be almost banal, and one that would immediately be accepted by most people who engage even at arm's length with therapeutic culture. But it is nevertheless one that progressives (particularly in the academy) have had difficulty acknowledging.

To be clear, we do not oppose efforts to identify the covert political functions—liberatory or coercive—performed by ostensibly apolitical phenomena, nor are we suggesting that such efforts cannot yield important and compelling insights. But we believe that the scholarship on therapeutic culture demonstrates that when either conservative or progressive political ideals exercise too great an influence over an analytical framework, cultural critics are reduced to civic judges tasked endlessly with issuing either affirmative or negative verdicts: Does this text serve or subvert the cause? Is this group promoting political progress or is it not? When we measure the cultural formation against the political template—pharmacology creates dependence, counseling blunts resistance—our job is done, and we have little else to say.

The task of understanding how and when our personal lives intersect with the political and how and when they do not—the task, in short, of identifying the outer limits of the political and thinking beyond those limits—is not an easy one. We hope, at the very least, that this book will initiate a conversation about how such an unfashionable and necessary intellectual enterprise might become possible.

CHAPTER 1

Damage

Joseph M. Gabriel

I live next to a three-year-old boy who generally seems like a happy child. My wife and I are friendly with his parents, and at times our children play together; my own son is five, and the two boys enjoy each other's company. As they play ball and laugh and run about, all seems well. Yet at night when his parents put this child to bed, I hear him cry and scream through his window. He is learning to sleep on his own, so his parents put him in his room and say goodnight and shut the door and let him cry it out. He sobs and wails for what seems like a very long time. My wife has occasionally tried to bring the issue up with his parents, but they are distinctly uninterested in our opinions on the topic. I can't really blame them. It is probably not pleasant to be sitting in their living room while their son is screaming. Yet they do it, because they love him and believe they are acting in his best interests. My wife and I sometimes sit on our porch in the evening and listen to him until we can't take it anymore. We go inside and close our door. Later in the night he sometimes visits me in my dreams, and I wake in the dark, scared and lonely, thinking about this boy.

This anecdote captures something important about how we think about suffering. *Damage* is a word that appears regularly when we speak of pain, distress, and other types of trouble—damage to our bodies, our minds, our lives and relationships, damage to our souls. When used in this way, the word *damage* points to something in ourselves or others that is broken, something that needs to be fixed in order for us to return to how we ought to be. When I hear my neighbor crying through his window, I imagine that something is being done *to* him. Given that I have no reason to suspect physical abuse, I assume the harm being inflicted is primarily psychological in nature. Yet this does not mean I consider it unreal. Quite the contrary. I worry that this boy will suffer long after he learns to go to sleep without crying. I worry that he will have problems that might have been avoided, that his wounds will follow him as he becomes a man. And so, as I listen to his cries, I not only feel bad for him. I also feel bad about myself for not doing more to help.

It was not always like this. In the early years of this country's history, suffering—both physical and psychological—was widespread and generally considered a normal part of daily life. Although people certainly tried to improve their own lives and the lives of those around them, and at times railed against the hardness of the world, they also understood pain and suffering as an inescapable part of the world in which they lived. As a result, there was no sense that emotional or mental distress might harm the individual in a lasting way; nor did it occur to people that such distress might reflect harms that had been inflicted in the past. People simply did not think of those who suffered as damaged in the way that we do today. In the years before the Civil War, however, psychological suffering was reconceptualized as anomalous and potentially threatening to the normal functioning of the self. Increasingly, it seemed to be something that happened *to* people and thus to be something that could disrupt and harm the most intimate parts of the self. Since then, the belief that acute psychological suffering can harm people in lasting ways has been a central assumption in the popularization of therapeutic culture. So too has the idea that such harm can be ameliorated through therapeutic intervention.

I do not have a problem with this. Unlike many critics, I do not dismiss the importance of therapeutic culture in making the world a better place. Still, this framework has a tendency to foreclose other possible responses to the troubles of the world. If we look to the past, we see that people did not always respond to the problem of suffering as we do today, and while I would never suggest that we should return to those times, I do believe that we can learn something important from those who came before us. At the end of the essay, I offer one such possibility—that of keeping company—and suggest that sometimes simply being with those who are going through difficult times may be all that we can, and should, do.

A WORLD OF TROUBLE: PAIN AND SUFFERING IN EARLY AMERICA

The diary of Elizabeth Drinker (1735–1807) provides a remarkable glimpse into the extent of pain and suffering in the late eighteenth century. A devout Quaker, Drinker lived in Philadelphia; her husband Henry was a successful businessman and leader in the Quaker community. Drinker spent her days running the household, maintaining social obligations, and seeing to the needs of her family. Financially successful, the Drinkers had an active social life and by all measures should be considered among the city's elite class. Yet despite such privileges, as Elaine Forman Crane notes, Elizabeth Drinker's diary "offers convincing evidence that physical distress invaded daily life to a degree currently unimaginable." Rheumatism, fevers, severe coughs, painful discharges of urine, and other ailments were common. Spoiled and undercooked food led to frequent intestinal problems; gum disease was widespread, resulting in frequent pain in the teeth, gums, and face. Broken bones and other injuries failed to heal properly. Disease was rampant, in part owing to poor sanitation, and infections were common and sometimes deadly. "Why should we expect to be exempt from pain and trouble," Drinker noted one night. "How many of our friends have lately suffer'd sickness and death, lost near and dear relati[ons.]"[1]

Drinker's comments reflect the restrained attitude toward suffering characteristic of late eighteenth-century American culture. The constant and unrelenting fact of physical pain led to a stoic attitude that today might seem callous. In part, this reflected the simple reality that medical science was relatively primitive, that disease and physical ailments were far more common than they are today, and that pain relief was simply not possible in the way that we now take for granted. Physicians and other healers had few effective analgesics at their disposal, and in any event they tended to consider pain as a warning sign of other problems rather than a problem worth addressing in its own right. Indeed, physicians often understood pain to be a natural part of the healing process and something that should be allowed to express itself, or perhaps even encouraged, in order to help the patient recover. People in the late eighteenth century simply had to accept the reality of ongoing and often severe physical pain, both in their own lives and in the lives of the people they knew and loved.

Moreover expressions of grief, worry, and other painful emotions, while common in Drinker's diary, are surprisingly muted in tone. Drinker did not really distinguish these types of feelings from the torment she often felt in her body. Whereas today we tend to see physical pain and psychological distress as distinct, although perhaps related, types of problems, during the eighteenth century the two were frequently understood in overlapping terms. Drinker often referred to the difficulties she and her family faced simply as "trouble," without distinguishing physical from psychological suffering. Both were part of a difficult and painful world, and as she made her way through life, watching loved ones suffer and die, feeling her body torment her, Drinker tried to face her troubles as best she could. Little wonder that her emotional response to the suffering of others was, from today's perspective, modest. One night, when her daughter Sally lay in agonizing pain during labor, Drinker pondered her own restrained emotional response. "Is it that as we grow in years our feelings become blunted & Callous," she asked herself, "or does pain and experience cause resignation?"[2]

For Drinker, suffering was an ordinary part of the world that God had created. In the late eighteenth century, discussions of pain, emotional distress, and other types of trouble were largely confined to funerals and other rituals where religious leaders explained their meaning to their flocks. Doctrinal views varied, of course, but in general religious leaders suggested that the troubles of life were God's punishment for original sin and as such a natural part of a fallen world. These troubles might encourage ungodly behavior, such as drunkenness or cruelty, and as a result they needed to be mastered and controlled as a part of the battle against sin. From this perspective, a godly life depended upon accepting the pain and suffering of the world as an expression of God's will, composing and regulating oneself properly in the face of it, and orienting oneself to the promise of an afterlife in which suffering would be no more. Drinker fully embraced this worldview. "This is a world of trouble," she noted toward the end of her life, "may we so live as to find peace in the next."[3]

I do not want to equate everyone's experience in the late eighteenth century with that of Elizabeth Drinker. If anything, given the privileged life she led as a free, white woman of modest wealth, Drinker probably experienced less suffering than most. Nor do I want to collapse all responses to the troubles of the world into a narrative of godly submission. Not everyone was as resigned to the difficulties of life as was Drinker—people fled their jobs and homes, they struggled against those who oppressed them, and they worked to improve their lives in countless ways; such actions grew at least in part out of an effort to reduce the experience of physical and psychological distress. Moreover, as Amanda Porterfield has recently argued, by the 1790s religious skepticism had become commonplace in American society. Political and economic instability, social upheaval, and other destabilizing changes led to widespread doubt about the role of religion in people's lives. Preachers and other religious enthusiasts responded by demanding that submission to God's authority serve as both the foundation for a new national identity and as a guide to personal conduct, but their pleas did not always meet with agreement or compliance. Attitudes toward pain and suffering were a part of this contested process. While Drinker was largely resigned to a life of trouble, and she understood pain and other forms of suffering in the context of her faith, other diaries from the time reveal that people questioned the meaning both of suffering and of the doctrines that were supposed to explain it. For many, the difficult and painful nature of the world cast doubt on the presence and mercy of God.[4]

For the most part, such doubts were kept private. As personal matters, and topics for discussion in ritualized spaces, expressions of pain and suffering were not really a part of public or political discourse. This is not to say that physical pain, emotional distress, and other types of trouble had no effect on public affairs. Clearly, they were one of the many forces that motivated human action, then as today—the efforts of slaves, the poor, and others to improve their lives, sometimes in ways that directly impacted public affairs, make this abundantly clear. Yet despite such efforts, the experience of suffering was not, in general, a topic of public concern. For most observers, individual suffering did not point to a broader problem about how society was organized, nor was it something that could be addressed through political or social action. In general, people were not motivated by the suffering of others to change the world in which they lived. They noted the troubles of their families and neighbors and often tried to help, but they did not dwell upon such difficulties or consider them to be indicative of some type of broader problem. Suffering, whether physical or psychological, did not require much discussion. Efforts to heal were often futile, the world was hard, and for most people there was no real expectation that things might be different. As Drinker knew, in many cases there was nothing to do in the face of trouble other than to sit quietly and wait for it to pass.

SYMPATHY AND THE PROJECT OF REFORM

Running through Elizabeth Drinker's diary are small expressions of sympathy for the suffering of her family, friends, and neighbors. In an entry from 1796, for example, Drinker mentions her neighbor Molly Hensel, a young woman who had married a "drunken old man" and begun to regularly drink herself. "I look'd upon her with pity and compassion," she notes, "one of the many beings from whom much was not required."[5] Drinker's expressions of "pity and compassion" were modest in nature and primarily directed toward friends, neighbors, and most of all her family. Yet they also point to the intensification and proliferation of sympathy as an emotional response to the suffering of others in the coming years. Beginning in the early nineteenth century, what had once been a muted emotion became more strongly felt. Sympathy for those who suffered—even those whom one had never met—was increasingly experienced as a powerful emotion and was, at times, described as its own type of pain. It was also increasingly seen as a virtue, and to be unmoved in the face of suffering was, if not quite a sin, increasingly morally suspect. By the 1830s, the visceral experience of sympathy had become one of the ways that many people judged themselves to be ethical actors in the world.[6]

A complex web of causes underpinned the growth of sympathy. By the late eighteenth century, to name one important factor, physicians and other healers had begun to see physical pain as a meaningless result of illness that should be minimized, if not eliminated. Increasingly, physicians believed that people suffering acute pain deserved their sympathy and that increasing the comfort of their patients was an important part of medical care. Changes in religious sentiment were also tremendously important. As Margaret Abruzzo notes, theological changes in late eighteenth-century Protestantism "helped push benevolence to the center of Anglo-American Christianity."[7] Threatened by the erosion of biblical authority, protestant ministers began to reject the assumption that pain and suffering were a normal part of God's world and to suggest that those who followed the path of righteousness would prosper not just in the next life but also in this one. In this new vision, undue suffering thus indicated not God's will but rather a breach of the natural order he had so wisely ordained. Of course, despite these and many other changes, significant pain and suffering still colored daily life. The world was hard, after all, and people struggled on much as they long had. Yet increasingly, both physical pain and psychological distress were seen as unnatural, as outside the domain of how things ought to be. Increasingly, they were understood as things that happened *to* people. "Thou has robbed me of peace, of the blessing of rest," wrote one anonymous poet in an ode to pain in 1814, "and has flung o'er my shoulders grief's saddening vest."[8]

In the early decades of the nineteenth century, a great wave of religious fervor linked the idea that acute pain and suffering lay outside the proper order of the world to a moral critique of changing social relations and the spread of the market. By the 1830s, this surge of religious enthusiasm had made the suffering of others the rhetorical basis for a series of broad humanitarian movements that transformed the social and political fabric of the country, including abolition, temperance, and antiprostitution reform. Reformers loudly denounced the cruelty of the world and described in endless detail the agony of tortured slaves, abused women, and other victimized innocents. As feelings of sympathy proliferated and became more intense, and as suffering was redefined as a perversion of the natural order, reformers increasingly understood their own moral status to be intertwined with the condition of the world in which they lived. To ignore the sins of others, it seemed, was to be a part of its evil; one's own salvation seemed linked to the effort to transform the suffering world.

This was not just about physical pain. For many reformers in the antebellum period, the worst type of harm inflicted on the innocent was not to the body but to the spirit. Reformers described the terrible shame of the young girl forced into prostitution, the overpowering grief of the drunkard as he watched his family reduced to poverty, the humiliation of the man unable to support his family. Abolitionist literature depicted slavery not just as physically brutal but also as threatening the very souls of the enslaved. Frederick Douglass, for example, described the profound damage of slavery in psychological terms. "I was broken in my body, soul, and spirit," he wrote in his autobiography. "The dark night of slavery closed in upon me; and behold a man transformed into a brute."[9] For Douglass, as for other reformers of the time, psychological harm was an unnatural part of the world. It was inflicted on a person from the outside, distorting the inner life of its victim from what it ideally should be. Acute psychological suffering was both the cause and consequence of a broken, damaged self.

Following the Civil War, the assumption that excessive psychological suffering should be prevented or ameliorated underlay the efforts of reformers who sought to create a rational and bureaucratic modern regulatory state. Tragic narratives about dangerous consumer goods, unsafe work conditions, sexual violence, and other horrors filled the newspapers and magazines of the time, prompting the passage of numerous laws intended to protect the innocent. These narratives, like the stories that reformers told in the years before the war, often focused on the emotional and psychological anguish of those who were harmed. Meanwhile, psychiatrists, social workers, and other experts sought to promote—or enforce, depending on your perspective—both psychological health and social and behavioral norms in hospitals, schools, prisons, and other institutions. Finally, a variety of new diseases were identified that had behavioral and psychological components, such as neurasthenia and hysteria. These types of ailments might be caused by a physical injury, it was believed, or result from sudden shock or some other type of "emotional disturbance."[10] Whatever the cause, however, those who suffered from such problems had clearly been harmed in some way. They had been damaged.

By the first decade of the twentieth century, the early outlines of modern therapeutic culture had thus begun to emerge. An activist state worked to protect its citizens from undue suffering, sometimes using force to pursue its goals; mental health experts sought both to promote psychological health and to enforce what they believed to be appropriate norms of behavior; a growing number of mental and emotional states were understood and described as forms of disease. These and other related changes were the work of a range of reformers who sought to reduce the burden of suffering on those they considered victims of a cruel world. Many of them brought a secular attitude to their work, but like their predecessors in the antebellum period these reformers believed that the duty to help was a moral imperative. For them, as for us, the effort to reduce suffering was part of what it meant to be an ethical actor in the world.

COMPASSION AND HARM

We have come a long way since psychological distress was reconceptualized as something that impinges upon the self. The therapeutic culture that grew out of that reconceptualization has proliferated rapidly and is now, as Eva Illouz notes, "an essential part of the cultural and moral universe of contemporary middle-class Americans."[11] Therapeutic culture frames emotional and psychological suffering as an impairment of the self that results from some sort of previous harm. At the same time, it offers the possibility of healing through the sharing of stories, the establishment of practical goals, and other means that—supposedly—place distance between past wounds and the current organization of the self. If damage is a type of harm that is inflicted on the self from the outside, then healing results from the reordering of emotional and psychological states in a way that no longer prioritizes that harm as a central part of who the person is.

The assumption that significant psychological distress reflects—and/or causes—damage to the self pushes us toward action; when we are confronted with the suffering of others we are moved to help. As a result, our society has developed a massive therapeutic infrastructure dedicated to preventing and ameliorating psychological harm. In complex and overlapping ways, various psychotherapeutic techniques have been combined with the practice of medicine, endless numbers of self-help groups, the institutions of the media, and the police powers of the state—all to prevent and reduce psychological distress. Yet there is an important irony here. Our efforts to prevent and relieve suffering often cause their own types of harm; sadly, we often damage those we seek to help. Breaking up a family for the good of an abused child, for example, might be necessary, and morally justified, and in the best interests of the child—but, if we are honest with ourselves, we must admit that there are ways in which it is also hurtful, even if we decide that the harm we inflict is justified by other considerations. There are an endless number of such examples. Indeed, it sometimes seems as if we are trapped in a vicious cycle, one in which our efforts to help cause additional problems, which in turn prompt new interventions and further, often unexpected, harms.

I do not know what to do about this problem. I am less of a critic of therapeutic culture than many of my colleagues in this volume, and I would never advocate dismantling what Thomas Szasz has called the "therapeutic state"—even if, at times, it seems obvious that it needs to be curtailed and humanized.[12] Still, it occurs to me that we can learn something important from Elizabeth Drinker and others who lived in a world before the experience of suffering was linked to the expansion of institutional power. Drinker did her best to help those around her, offering them medicinal herbs from her garden and comforting them when they fell ill. Yet she also accepted the limitations of her own ability to relieve their suffering. She questioned her modest emotional response in the face of her daughter's agony, wondering if she had grown callous, but she knew that her ability to intervene in the situation was limited. In the end, she recognized that all she could really do when confronted by her daughter's anguish was to sit and keep her company. This she did, passing the time as best she could, waiting for the pain—her daughter's, and her own—to pass. And so it did.

I want to be careful here. I am not saying that we should passively accept the world as it is. Nor am I saying that we should deaden ourselves to the suffering of others or refrain from trying to help those in need. Far from it. Drinker lived at a time when the emotional response to suffering was significantly more muted than it is today. We are the beneficiaries of the increased emotional capacity that followed her death, and like the reformers of the antebellum period I believe that we are ethically obligated to help those around us who suffer. Yet, like Szasz and other critics of the therapeutic state, I also sometimes question the ethics of intervention. Our efforts to fix things do not always make the world a better place, and even when they do—or, at least, when we think they do—they are also quite clearly an expression of our own desires and power. No wonder those whom we seek to help do not always appreciate our efforts. No wonder our efforts so frequently lead to additional forms of harm.

Elizabeth Drinker did not face this problem. Although she did her best to reduce the pain and suffering of those around her, she also understood that trouble was a part of life and she had no real expectation that she could ever make it go away. I think that we can learn something from her in this regard, even as we embrace our own ability to feel strongly in ways that she could not. Perhaps, when confronted by the suffering of others, we can set aside the assumption that those in distress have been, or are being, damaged. Perhaps we can accept the fact that suffering is a part of who we are and what life has in store for us, even as we feel strongly, desperately, the sadness that comes with life in a troubled world. To do so is not to abandon the possibility of helping others. It is, in its own way, a part of how we can make the world a better place. For as we sit and keep company with those who suffer, as we witness their trials and hold space with them, we are in some way helping them through their difficult times. We are helping, even if there is nothing that we are trying to fix. When, exactly, this is an appropriate response to the suffering of others and when a more assertive intervention is called for I cannot say with any precision or certainty. All I know is that keeping company with those who suffer is sometimes the best that we can, and should, do.

This returns me to the story of my neighbors' son. I do not know whether or not the suffering he goes through at night will affect him as he grows older and becomes a man. Presumably it will shape him in some way. I like to think that he will, somehow, be better for it, if not in the ways that his parents predict. My own father was a violent man, and while coming to terms with my own history of family violence has been difficult for me, in a strange way I would not disown it. And so, as I listen to the sobs of my neighbor's child, I try to believe that this boy will flourish despite, or perhaps because of, what he is going through. I try to believe that the small moments of compassion I can offer him—sharing my child's toys, smiling at him when his father calls for him to come home—will somehow contribute to this flourishing. I try to believe that my efforts to keep him company will contribute in a positive way to the unfolding of his life and that my decision to set aside the question of whether or not I should do more is the right one. And I try to believe that the world is a place not just of pain and suffering but also one of beauty and compassion, even if those seemingly opposite things are in fact so frequently intertwined.

CHAPTER 2

Gospel

Kathryn Lofton

Today it seems that there is a gospel for everything. The March 2012 issue of *Edible Manhattan* features Rob Kaufelt, owner of Murray's Cheese, explaining that his business is not just about making money. "It's about spreading the gospel of cheese," Kaufelt explains. "Bring the best cheese to the largest possible number of people."[1] Whether it is the gospel of cheese (or jeans or happiness or slow cookers), a gospel has become a way to convey promises of something superlative: the best cheese, the best fit, the best way to live your best life. A gospel is always exigent—*you* need to hear about cheese *right now*—and always ambitious—"Bring the best cheese to the largest possible number of people." It is not a gospel message if it is not delivered ("*Bring* the best cheese.") or if it reaches only a few people ("to the *largest* number of people"). To qualify as gospel a message must be the brightest light for your inadequate circumstance, packaged for vast dissemination.

Since the beginnings of Christianity and through the Internet age, some have found gospels to be revelatory, while others have decried them as embarrassing. To some, Kaufelt's "gospel of cheese" may exemplify the easy heresies of advertising copy; for others, his words might testify to the spiritual power attached to contemporary consumption. (Some readers may even see this essay's repetition of Kaufelt's promotional language as an excessive response to a minor locution or, worse yet, a cynical rendering of a meaningful epicurean intervention.) Any and all of these responses participate in a long history of replies to the announcement of good news and its mass distribution. A gospel never appears without sparking all four reactions: some proclaim it heresy, while others deem it powerful; some dismiss it as nonsense, while others pronounce it essential. However a gospel may manifest—however it may be canonized or advertised, printed or sold—we know something is a gospel because it demands a reply. It does this explicitly by asking you to change your life. But it also does this implicitly through the very suggestion that your life needs changing. This dual solicitation—to change and to recognize you need changing—is the gospel function.

In this sense, gospel talk is not unlike therapeutic talk. Therapeutic culture, too, enjoys a bruising relationship with critics who doubt its transformational possibilities, even as individuals undergoing therapy find in it sustenance and survival. Quite often, "therapy" and "gospel" meet within particular documents and practices, as today's gospels quite regularly incorporate therapeutic promises. "*The Gospel of Joy* is your guidebook to creating the life you want—and are meant to have—in simple daily steps," advertises one 2010 volume. "If you follow the daily activities in this book, it will offer you the keys to reconnect with what's important in your life."[2] However newfangled such a gospel may be—however secularized, however removed from scriptural solemnity—in its proposal of a new life to the reader it is doing what a gospel has *always* done, which is to offer good news for someone supposedly struggling in the bad. Whether the twenty-first-century proposition of a gospel of joy or a first-century Gospel of Mark, a gospel has always been an attempt to convey an idea named as good for you—in as exigent means as possible—to individuals posited to need its ascriptions and prescriptions.

Having linked the first century with the twenty-first in a flattening gesture, I would like to now make more supple the entwined relationship between gospel propositions and therapeutic ones. Scholars of therapeutic culture tend to place its origins in the late nineteenth century and describe its indefatigable march through the twentieth, plotting its ascent alongside a simultaneous imagined secularization. As therapies increased, gospels decreased.

Such a narrative is too neat, obscuring the many connections between the story of therapeutic culture and the longer one of gospel messages. It cannot account, for example, for the strange penchant among critics of therapeutic culture for using religious descriptors to insult the power of therapy and accuse psychologists of demagoguery.[3] "We live in an age consumed by worship of the psyche," describes Eva Moskowitz at the beginning of her 2001 book, *In Therapy We Trust*. "Today Americans turn to psychological cures as reflexively as they once turned to God."[4] The flippant deployment of "reflexively" suggests that for suffering folk it's all the same opiate: religion, psychology, whatever. Naming therapy's effect a "gospel" is shorthand for a larger critique of cultic adherence—the problem is less the fact of the psychology (or the religion) than the dull-eyed adherence to anything prescribed. Therapeutic culture troubles such critics because it seems to foster the same unthinking obedience they perceive within religion. Critics of psychology perceive in its therapeutic relation something dependent, hierarchical, and manipulative; something, in other words, akin to what Enlightenment critics saw in revealed religion.

However caricaturing such critiques of religion—and psychology—may well be, their structural similarity makes them a productive starting point for deeper analysis. Psychology and theology do not offer the same gospels, but it may be useful to think about the gospel function within therapeutic discourse—especially as the therapeutic idiom begins to pervade even the most conservative religious cultures. Religion has long existed within, and been diagnosed by, therapeutic culture just as therapeutic culture has existed within, and been diagnosed by, religions. Once we understand the interconnection of these two categories, we can hope to better interpret their ongoing effects and appropriately critique their transformative limits.

GOSPEL ORIGINS

Through the fifth century, Christian writers used the word *gospel* in two different ways. For the authors of the New Testament, it referred to the glad tidings announced to the world by Jesus Christ about the kingdom of God. In this sense, gospel was not used in the plural (gospels). Rather, the singular *gospel* swept up multiple forms of description, including biographical accounts, ecclesiastical prescriptions, detailed parables, and moral imperatives that together made up the message of Jesus and his apostles. The texts of the New Testament did not consistently articulate the same message—Mark's narrative differs from that of Luke—but gospel provided (if sometimes misleadingly) a term that emphasized the hopeful unity of the New Testament, that is, this is *the* gospel message.

As the church fathers began to determine the canon of the New Testament, gospel also came to be understood as a designation for a specific genre within the broader array of documents testifying to church founding and formation.[5] Here, *gospel* referred to the books that specifically reported about Jesus's life and death. This usage of *gospel* did not appear in the New Testament except in the titles that were attached to the words attributed to Matthew, Mark, Luke, and John. The earliest use of *gospel* in this literary sense was in the writings of Justin Martyr and relied upon the opening statement in Mark 1:1 ("The beginning of the good news of Jesus Christ, the Son of God") in which the author equates the story of Jesus's life with a new beginning for its audience.[6]

A gospel was then a thing that would have been recognizable in part by its use of a singular life story (originally, that of Jesus) to explain something immediately and importantly relevant to a posited audience. Until the nineteenth century, such a gospel was invariably understood to be Christian, although just what kind of Christian, doing what kind of things, was always a matter of intense debate and disagreement. The history of gospel talk was never one-sided. Critics on every side named what they thought was right gospel (and what was not), even as they held in their hands the same actual gospel texts (Matthew, Mark, Luke, and John) that they were debating.

In the nineteenth century, the number of texts denominated as gospel expanded considerably. New strategies of scholarly inquiry, combined with archaeological discoveries that enlarged the archive of the ancient world, increased popular knowledge about the varieties of early Christianity. Although the printed New Testament included only four gospels, scholars identified noncanonical gospels from the late Antique period, such as the Gospel of Marcion and the Gospel of Peter. Biblical critics also examined the canonized gospels to discern inconsistencies among them, suggesting that the original gospel quartet emerged in different historical moments by authors of differing theological opinion.[7] Perhaps not coincidentally, dissident Christians, self-declared prophets, and leaders of new religious movements throughout the nineteenth century authored a raft of original scriptural writings, suggesting that the category of gospel could no longer be reserved solely for the New Testament by either church historians or religious innovators.[8] Alongside such new sacred writings, the word *gospel* also circulated in contexts distinctly unrelated to the canonical Christian tradition, as in Richard Grant White's *The New Gospel of Peace According to St. Benjamin*, a satire of the Civil War written in four installments between 1863 and 1866. But this new lexical malleability did not change the gospel function: gospel still was understood to be an ascription and a prescription, delivered (and consumed) with utmost urgency. *Gospel* was a word unmoored, even as its meaning remained largely the same.

MULTIPLYING GOSPELS

This enlarging archive of gospels appeared alongside the emerging comparative study of religions. In this more formal venture of a long-standing lay practice, scholars of and adherents to non-Christian religions used categories

Western audiences could relate to in order to translate and interpret religions. For example, in *The Gospel of Buddha* (1894), Paul Carus created a compendium of Buddhist teachings that offered "the gospel of Buddha"—despite the fact that Buddhism itself did not include either a singular canon or concept of good news.[9] Carus admitted that the diversity and number of Buddhist sects made it hard to distil a coherent gospel. Nevertheless, he argued it was possible to observe a consistent truth: "The present book follows none of the sectarian doctrines, but takes an ideal position upon which all true Buddhists may stand as upon common ground."[10] Formatted to resemble the chapter and verse arrangement of the Christian gospels, *The Gospel of Buddha* presented an "ideal" Buddhist perspective that might "set the reader a-thinking on the present religious problems of today." *The Gospel of Buddha* was therefore meant both to offer another version of the Christian gospel message and to provide a gospel template within which non-Christian religions could fit. Carus hoped that talking about Buddhism through the form of the Christian gospel might revive the content of the Christian message to Christians encountering alternative religious worlds.

The Gospel of Buddha lionized the life of Gautama Buddha in an effort to connect readers to an alternative vision of spiritual life in a way that kept them safely within familiar Christian formats. By contrast, Andrew Carnegie's "The Gospel of Wealth" (1889) used the gospel form to emphasize the exigency of his capitalist message for a new economic day. Carnegie labeled his millennial polemic a gospel because the word retained a certain spiritual urgency in an increasingly complicated social world and fractured religious landscape. In this usage, gospel became any testimony by a great man about a better future. If ancient biography used the life of a man as allegory, modern gospels like Carnegie's relied upon the assumed fame of the author to justify the affective aspirations of the text. Carnegie did not tell his life as a gospel story; rather, he distilled his life into a gospel message.

This presentation of self as message resonated in an era of new media, and the ambitions and foibles of Gilded Age tycoons created a nascent American celebrity culture for the masses to consume. Scholars of biography have interpreted the genre's quick ascendance during the period as a literary symptom of modernization, which included the interconnected experiences of rampant immigration, urbanization, industrialization, and, supposedly, secularization. Biographies like Carnegie's constructed a purposive self within this confused social maelstrom.[11] It is no coincidence that therapeutic culture—another "self"-centered concept—emerged in the same moment.

Scholars of psychology and religion alike look to William James to explain the story of the self that emerged triumphant in the twentieth century. As the science of psychology unfolded in the late Gilded Age, many psychologists acted as scholars of religion, naming the best religions for healthy minds. Among them was James, who, in *The Varieties of Religious Experience* (1901–1902) examined personal testimonies and famed spiritual biographies to determine the relationship between the individual and religious experience. After reviewing this trove of narrative, James argued that religion could be, in its healthiest form, a strategy by which individuals attained the highest form of happiness. This early instance of the psychology of religion sought to explain religious belief by diagnosing the individual self. James also suggested that the core of all religions, from Buddhism to Quakerism, offered the same mental rewards to adherents. This psychologized understanding of belief was not disconnected from the propositions of right religion; if anything, scientism gave its expositors newfound authority, allowing them to name the best religious news for the modern world.[12]

James thus repurposed religion for the modern individuals populating the sprawling cities and retreating countryside of his America. By focusing on personal narration, he highlighted—even prescribed—a turn away from ritual and toward belief, away from institutions of religion to religious individualism. In doing so, he offered not only a model for subsequent studies of religion but also a proposition for how religion might survive the broader criticisms that some of his fellow students of the mind were beginning to mount against it. Sigmund Freud's writings, for example, explained faith through diagnosis of the unconscious; his psychoanalytic methods provided psychical genealogies of religion and offered ritual forms that would supplant it. James's profiles of religious belief suggested that a new kind of mystical individualism could improve upon, even replace, institutional religious life, without explaining away what he saw as the positive power of spiritual experience. If Freud offered a critique of the gospel form, James resuscitated the possibility of the gospel message, insofar as he thought its good news could lead to individual self-sacrifice, self-improvement, and inner quiet.

PERSISTENT GOSPEL IN A THERAPEUTIC AGE

Some proponents of psychotherapy, if not Freud himself, believed it possible actually to end religion through therapeutic revelation—to replace the idea of God through a rational interpretation of the self. This takeover of the religious landscape by enlightened individuals did not transpire. Religions did, however, alter over the course of the twentieth century, owing in no small part to the circulation of therapeutic idiom and experience. Historians describe this shift in religiosity as a move away from more orthodox Christian emphases on sin toward therapeutic emphases on healing.

Evangelicals in the nineteenth century played a powerful role in the reshaping of Christianity to meet the various critiques of modernity, including those that appeared in nascent psychological writings. Ministers like Horace Bushnell (1802–1876) and Henry Ward Beecher (1813–1887) rejected aspects of Calvinist doctrine—especially that of original sin—while also embracing the contingency of scripture described by biblical criticism. The canonical gospels still mattered for these Christians; indeed, they seemed to matter all the more. But as ritual seemed less imperative and doctrine less pervasive, the gospels' stories of heroic self-sacrifice became the strongest argument for participating in religious life. Popular novelized renditions of Jesus's life, such as Charles Sheldon's *In His Steps* (1896) and Bruce Barton's *The Man Nobody Knows* (1925), indicate the power of a Jesus set free from ecclesiastical limits. Rendering Jesus as an accessible hero to whom everyone could relate—a striving self that other striving selves might take as a model—became the primary task of evangelism. This shift in emphasis meant that the difference between Protestant evangelicalism and liberalism in the twentieth century was less a difference of gospel form than of gospel message: liberals emphasized the importance of social progress and the good found in each individual, while evangelicals directed their energies toward the identification of social ills and the need to change the self by rooting out individual sin. Each held high the gospel accounts of Jesus that proved their reading of this singular figure to be the right one.

Far from diminishing evangelical efforts then, the late nineteenth-century shift towards the therapeutic in Protestant theology only seemed to energize them. A new message of evangelism poured forth into the world concomitant with new notions of psychological understanding. The number of American foreign missionaries, which stood at 934 in 1890, reached nearly 5,000 a decade later and over nine thousand in 1915. During this same epoch, the American Psychological Association was founded (1892), and Freud would publish *The Interpretation of Dreams* (1899), *Three Essays on the Theory of Sexuality* (1905), and *Totem and Taboo* (1913). The history of therapeutic practice cannot be disentangled from the history of Christianity as a converting force. This is not because psychologists and missionaries overlapped in a literal sense (although they at times did and would) but because they offered simultaneous replies to descriptions of modern ennui. This is how the history of therapeutic culture becomes inextricably tied to the histories of Christianity that supplied, and continued to supply, propositions directly to you, for your reformation.

THERAPY IN THE GOSPEL

It is strange then that for many American evangelicals, therapeutic culture has become a dogged enemy—even as they have coopted its messages and modes for the advancement of their ministries. In the mid-twentieth century, as public culture increasingly absorbed the secular discourse of psychotherapy, conservative religious groups developed agencies that offered modes of therapeutic practice informed by the content of the Christian gospel, such as the Christian Association for Psychological Studies (founded in 1956) and the School of Psychology at Fuller Theological Seminary (established in 1965). These developments inaugurated the separate but parallel lives of conservative churches and secular social sciences: liberal seminaries' models of pastoral counseling mirrored psychology programs at research universities. By the 1970s, evangelical churches developed entire institutional spaces within their communities to offer specifically Christian care of the self, emphasizing small-group ministries to treat addictions and promote self-esteem.[13] As liberal Protestants started to seem (to some observers) more secular than liberal in their theology (read: more spiritual than religious), evangelicals reacted with organizational fervor, working to create a counseling subculture that reiterated biblical moral standards and the necessity of God's presence in any transformation of the self. Evangelical agencies such as Focus on the Family and practices like biblical counseling emerged out of this scramble, focusing on sublimating individual inquiry to scriptural certainty.[14]

Cognizant of the multiple uses of gospel as a term of transformation, evangelicals became adept at monitoring the borders between their gospels and others offered in the modern marketplace. But such attention to difference manifests not only through carping rallies to old-time Christianity but also through strategic appropriation of secular subjects. For instance, Presbyterian publisher Westminster John Knox (WJK) Press uses secular material to articulate gospel propositions. Since 2000, WJK has published thirteen volumes of their "The Gospel According to" series, from *The Gospel According to Peanuts* (2000) to *The Gospel According to Twilight* (2011). In these books, authors recoup the potentially pagan content of the *Harry Potter*, *Lord of the Rings*, and *Twilight* books; reframe the heresies of Disney, Hollywood, and *The Simpsons*; and illuminate the spectral theologies in the lyrics of the Beatles, Bruce

Springsteen, and U2 by showing connections between popular culture and the gospel message.

To do so, WJK uses what Krista L. Phair calls a "transformative discursive allegory" to connect secular texts to sacred meanings. Phair observes that among Christians, "the gospel is often accessed through synecdoche," meaning that believers discern the whole gospel message from singular passages in the New Testament. "Thus, in *The Gospel According to* books, any biblical element that can be identified will in turn imply the full biblical message to an initiated reader," allowing "the secular to be read and experienced as an allegory for the sacred or ideological."[15] Bruce Springsteen songs do not replace the New Testament. Rather, by locating the gospel message in pieces of Springsteen's canon, WJK reiterates the primacy of the Christian gospels, identifying it through its pervasive contemporary echo. "The Gospel According to" series resuscitates the canonical Christian gospel by suggesting that nothing, no matter how decadently rock star, can remain profane if read with or as "gospel."

As a Christian publisher, WJK participates in the ongoing effort to assert right gospel readings in the face of alternative—and perverse—gospel hermeneutics. Since the Reformation, Protestants have taken this as their mission. Among many contemporary evangelicals, no perversion is observed more snidely than therapeutic culture itself, with purveyors of belief in the Bible warning against the false wares of therapeutic gospels. "Evangelicals' descriptions of twentieth-century American society parallel the observation of those scholars—Philip Rieff, T. J. Jackson Lears, and Christopher Lasch, for example, who argue that a pervasive 'therapeutic culture,' associated with the rise of psychiatry and clinical psychology, has profoundly shaped the modern world," writes David Harrington Watt.[16]

But while accusing liberals of letting therapy dilute their gospels, evangelicals have also sought to make therapy their own. In this, as David Watt has argued, evangelical Protestantism has shown itself to be "less a bulwark against than a variant of the therapeutic culture."[17] Evangelicals may have criticized a modern culture that included the pernicious influence of Freud, but they also shared the malaise of their secular peers, so much so that it is often difficult to distinguish a practical difference between the counsel of secular and of evangelical self-help materials.

THE THERAPEUTIC GOSPEL

This is what brings us to the present day: not a diminution of the gospel message in a therapeutic world but a relentless recycling of the same categories by different combatants locked in definitional struggles. In 2008, biblical counselor David Powlison authored a two-part essay on "The Therapeutic Gospel" for the online webzine *Boundless*. As one of the many magazines published by Focus on the Family, *Boundless* advertises itself as Christian counsel for the single set: "From college to career to relationships, we at *Boundless* want to cast a vibrant vision for the single years, helping you navigate this season while preparing for the challenges and responsibilities of the one to come."[18]

In his essay, Powlison, a faculty member at the Christian Counseling and Educational Foundation, offers a typical *Boundless* contribution, one that includes a strong description of who Jesus is and how he ought to be understood by those struggling to live in his community. "When Jesus takes us as His disciple, when our Father takes us as his children, we no longer need to be consumed by the craving to be loved, to make money, to be comfortable, to be beautiful, to find sexual ecstasy, to be successful, to control our world," Powlison explains, drawing the reader to his view by encapsulating her supposed cravings. The presumed reader is surrounded by worldly temptations, and Powlison seeks to temper her desires, first by actively acknowledging them and then by redefining the source from which they spring. In this discursive landscape, the terms of your diagnosis cannot help but be theological and psychological, as nearly every piece of advice seeks to transform your mind and your behavior by placing them in a new hermeneutic frame. The craving, desirous mind is the battlefield, the weapons are biblical, and the cause is a vibrant Christian modernity.

Powlison's text makes clear that therapeutic culture has not vanquished gospel cures; gospel cures have not been indifferent to therapeutic idioms. Today both exist in a persistent dynamic, with few religious products evading therapeutic talk and few therapies devoid of spiritual imperatives. Powlison merely illuminates the ardent edge of this negotiation in the heart of evangelical culture. Since its founding in 1977, Focus on the Family has supplied an avalanche of sermons that minister to (and perhaps help to create) the sheer confusion of contemporary life. "Through our radio broadcasts, websites, simulcasts, conferences, interactive forums, magazines, books, counseling and much more, Focus on the Family equips parents, children and spouses to thrive in an ever-changing, ever-more-complicated world," their mission statement explains, emphasizing the positive impact their media deluge will have on your "ever-more-complicated world."[19] To counteract that ever more complexity, Focus on the Family supplies ever more clarifications—cast not as a revelation but as a righting of wrong disposition, a tweaking of imperfect self.

Powlison's "Therapeutic Gospel" aims to adjust your outlook. "God doesn't gratify our instinctive longings," he explains. "[God] forgives them, and then changes what we most want. This is one facet of the gospel taught in the Bible." The reader may nod at this distinction between gratification and forgiveness, but Powlison only sets up the dichotomy so he can intervene in it. He quickly turns to a description of our culture, a culture in which we do not understand ourselves as in pursuit of God's forgiveness but of our own satiation, since "it's common to interpret human desires automatically as givens." Believing our desires are unalterable—and, therefore, valid—leads us to believe that desires deserve to be fulfilled, that they are inherently righteous. In doing so, we make theology serve our desire and not God's will.

> When this way of looking at things is ported into Christianity, then the gospel of Jesus becomes the better way to meet your needs. Perhaps your sin is that you look to your girlfriend/boyfriend or spouse to meet your need for love, when Jesus is the one who lives to meet that need. In this way of looking at things, God's chief purpose is often portrayed as merely giving us what we deeply desire, gratifying our deepest instinctive longings. This way of describing how God interacts with our desires is a "therapeutic gospel." It offers to heal the woundedness we feel because our needs weren't met. It offers to fill those empty places inside with Jesus.[20]

Powlison suggests that we believe in our hungers more than we believe in God. And so we imagine God as the satiation of our hungers rather than as a challenge to them.

The therapeutic gospel "gets it wrong," Powlison writes. "It gets God wrong. It gets people wrong. It gets suffering wrong. It gets the gospel wrong." His assault focuses on the "new gospel's" false appraisals of and subsequent wrong answers for real problems. The therapeutic gospel focuses on the self, rather than on a salvation knitted to a subjugation of self: "It's structured to give people what they *want*, not to *change* what they want. It merely makes people *feel* better." Powlison spends the rest of the essay refocusing readers on the "ordinary gospel" that exists over and above the new therapeutic gospel that seems to taunt and tempt them at every turn.[21] In doing so, he may seem to be a typical religious critic, nervously combating the incursion of a usurping new message with a rebuttal that argues for the importance of a gospel he believes to be more immediately relevant. The gospel function is hard to resist; it is pretty hard in the modern period to avoid making promises that through this news (about this gospel, or about this cheese) your life will be changed.

But Powlison dismisses the therapeutic gospel only insofar as he seeks to offer his own, that "ordinary" gospel that gets you away from just feelings for themselves and back to thinking through Jesus. He does so through a focus on the transfiguration of desire, on the belief that your mind can—and should—be changed. In this, his twenty-first-century critique of the therapeutic gospel invites an examination into the long, mutually constitutive history of gospels and therapies in the modern period.

What is constant in this account, and consistent in the conjoined histories of therapeutic and religious cultures, is that nobody—neither the liberal Protestants nor evangelical Christians, neither psychoanalysts nor their critics—have ever questioned that the mind is the terrain of our combat. Critics seeking to refute any gospel will have to offer a counternarrative to this certitude: that the psyche above all else—above all context and content—determines our quest to make an enlightened life.

CHAPTER 3

Spirit

Courtney Bender

Spirituality long ago slipped the bonds of religious specificity. As many critics of therapeutic culture have told us, it is present in alternative medicine, in advertising, in business and sports—it is just about everywhere we look. By now, spirituality has expanded well beyond even the homegrown cultures of Spiritualism and New Thought, Alcoholics Anonymous, and humanistic psychology. Even the critics who inveigh most strongly against the effects of down-market spiritual romanticism and the commercialized New Age now talk about spirituality. It is a term of art in political philosophy and legal theory, a troubled analytical category in the social sciences, and an awkward presence in art criticism.[1] Even the atheists are spiritual now. Given spirituality's ubiquity, how can we "rethink" it, and from what vantage?

It is helpful to begin by identifying what we mean by spirituality. Americans frequently invoke a negative understanding of spirituality that developed in post-war therapeutic culture critique. This critique frames spirituality as a kind of personal magic, characterized by narcissism, banal "commercialism," and consumerism. Spirituality frequently appears to be a debased religious impulse. Its expression and growth is a sign that Americans are still in the grip of anachronistic and imaginary thinking, for which critical thinking provides a ready antidote. Americans, even those who actively take part in various spiritual activities, talk about spirituality this way all the time. We might turn up our noses at spirituality, but we would never give up our 6 A.M. yoga class.

This understanding of spirituality, along with its allure and its critique, represents a relatively new discourse and set of practices (or what John Modern calls a "grammar of piety") that emerge within modernity and help make sense of its uncanny effects.[2] Thus, even while the modern world has become disenchanted thanks to the extensive professionalization and rationalization of the market, psychology, the state, the law, and even religion, individuals nonetheless encounter the world and its effects as uncanny, evocative of new possibilities, moods, and affects. Everything in modern life appears to be connected by hidden networks that shape our daily life in ways that no individual can measure, control, or understand. Spirituality emerges as one modern language with which we experience and speak of the secular promise (or peril) of these unseen connections and takes shape in a set of practices with which we manage those connections' effects.[3]

Considered this way, modern spirituality also announces a transformation wherein the multiple spirits of old are also rationalized into a single spiritual system. Mirroring transformations going on in other parts of American society, the motley and irrational variety of spirits, ghosts, voices, and visions gave way to a single rationalized spiritual universe. As a consequence, the occult handlers, mystical virtuosi, and priests who had mediated the unruly forces of gods and divinities were replaced by a new class of professional spiritual interpreter. These professionals, who figured prominently in the turn of the twentieth century New Thought movement and its various offshoots, offered democratically available, rational procedures that would lead to spiritual health for all.

Understanding spirituality as a response to modern secular conditions has implications for how we interpret and rethink the canonical critique of therapeutic culture. Viewing spirituality as a product of secularization, for example, poses a challenge to therapeutic culture critics' arguments that spirituality is best dealt with through ideology critique. As a consequence, rethinking spirituality in this light brings into relief the assumptions about modern life that are implicitly shared by proponents and critics of therapeutic culture. Both, it turns out, regard modernity as a single, unified system, and both offer strategies for confronting and thriving within that system. By paying attention to the optimistic resonances between the two positions, we can gain a broader understanding of the reflexively pious attitude that underwrites both.

SPIRIT OF CAPITALISM

Religious asceticism—whether finally, who knows?—has escaped from the cage. But victorious capitalism, since it rests on mechanical foundations, needs its support no longer.[4]

We should begin by getting a stronger view of the development of spirituality as I have sketched in the preceding paragraphs. There are lots of places to look, but perhaps none better than Max Weber's essay "The Protestant Ethic and the Spirit of Capitalism" (1905) in which Weber argues that the inescapable "iron cage" of a rationalized capitalism develops (ironically, and unexpectedly) from the intervention of an ascetic Protestant theology. Once this economic system is set in place, Weber notes, Protestant theology and practice are no longer necessary to its continuation. They become quite incidental to the material forces that are set in place.

Most contemporary readers, including critics of therapeutic culture, have been preoccupied with Weber's analysis of the "ethic" of Protestantism rather than the "spirit" of capitalism that forms the second part of his title. Occasionally the two terms are conflated, and their distinctions elided. As we will see, however, spirit is an important part of Weber's story—and Weber's text offers up a particularly good place to begin rethinking the spirit of therapeutic culture and its critique. This is particularly so, given that critics of therapeutic culture are among the most prominent popularizers of the term "Protestant ethic" and often rely upon an analysis that overlooks some of Weber's key understandings about the role of religion in contemporary culture. The consequence, as I hope will be clear, enables critics of therapeutic culture to characterize their own practices of critique and self-cultivation as ennobled and enlightened answers to what amounts to the same system. A closer look at Weber's texts, however, and his interesting discussions of the transformation of the spirit of capitalism, thus offer not only a rethinking of therapeutic culture's spirits but also the commonplace spirit of its critique.

Weber begins his essay by observing that the spirit of capitalism is elusive and rare in the historical record. Prior to the modern era, there are very few examples of individuals (and no examples of societies) possessed by this spirit. The infrequency of its appearance makes it, in Weber's metaphorical sense, a random and unaccounted for sighting that has only local, individual effect. Weber can provide only a few examples that predate the rise of industrial capitalism: unnamed swashbucklers, a "Dutch sea captain," and a "Neapolitan cab-driver." These individuals are characterized by their single-minded, often ruthless pursuit of money. They are not the great men of history. Overwhelmed by their passion for accumulating money, they have little interest in using it for any other end. Weber wants us to think about this spirit of capital in the old-fashioned sense. It is frightening; it possesses those who have it, inverting the natural order of life.[5] Those possessed with this spirit do not view their money as a means to an end; the spirit overrides not only commitments to normal regular ethical commands about wealth but also the pursuit of any other desire or pleasure. Those possessed have experienced "a reversal of the natural relationship" of life to money.[6] The effects of this spirit possession are clear. It absorbs all other pleasures and interests.

Weber argues that the spirit of capitalism is as unusual as it is unnatural. The life to which it leads is unappealing, and it is therefore not contagious. This is part of Weber's puzzle: how did this aberrant and frightening spirit of capitalism become the spirit of the age? What transformed it, and how was it, thereby, transformed? For, as readers of Weber's text know, by the time of Weber's writing in the early twentieth century this spirit of capitalism had become the norm: we had all become caught up in a system where rationalized wealth accumulation defined the conditions in which modern men toil. Weber asks, how does an unnatural, abnormal, dangerous spirit become the norm? Clearly, something else must intervene.

The intervention was the Protestant ethic. Unlike the spirit of capitalism, this ethic, in Weber's account, was neither irrational nor possessive. Indeed, Weber describes the application of Calvinist and Lutheran theologies as measured, logical, and based on an explicitly critical attitude toward wealth accumulation. The ethic is usually described as having two necessary theological components. Luther contributed the argument that all professions, cab driving, seafaring, and coffee trading no less than the offices of the priesthood, were holy callings and should be pursued as such. This sacralization of work was coupled with Calvin's theology of predestination, which placed salvation in God's hands alone. Good works or faith alone could not save a person or damn him. Yet, while works (or one's calling) did not offer salvation, no matter how devoutly they were pursued, good works might offer a sign of God's grace. Calvin urged his followers to examine their hearts and their actions for signs of grace, even if they were never fully knowable, and a believer needed to be wary of overconfidence (which was also a sin). In short, this existential theology compelled Protestants to continue to prove themselves worthy of God's grace while never being assured of it.

There could be nothing more different than a pious Protestant and a swashbuckling sea captain. Protestants frowned on the "irrational use of wealth" and all those who put Mammon before God. But as Weber points out, their theology led them to activities that suggested otherwise. While not possessed as the sea captain and the cabdriver were, their actions closely aligned them with those who had been occasionally possessed in the past—and quickly surpassed the latter in their effects. The Protestant ethic's "entry on the scene was not generally peaceful," Weber drolly notes. As a result of their obsession with deferred gratification and self-monitoring, Protestants disciplined laborers and instituted strict accounting measures in the counting house, the shop floor, and (not incidentally) the pew.[7] These activities expanded a web of rational capital development and caught up all economic actors, regardless of their religious predilections or lack thereof. Once these conditions had solidified, the spirit of capitalism was effectively unleashed on everyone. The Protestant ethic was no longer needed to keep it going, and Protestant leaders' increasingly concerned jeremiads against the effects of capitalism were equally ineffective at changing its course.

In sum, the aberrant and occasional spirit of capitalism had become the spirit of the system. It came to possess all men by virtue of their participation within capitalism. All men now worked in an economic system and found themselves in an unnatural relationship to money. They were possessed, in a newly modern way. Men and women found themselves "bound to the technical and economic conditions . . . which today determine the lives of all individuals who are born into this mechanism, with irresistible force."[8] The irresistible force of capitalism might be individually troubling or ennobling, but it was inescapably present. As Weber intoned, individuals could be critical of this system, they could offer theoretical critiques of it, they could find it distasteful or ethically wrong, or they could hope for escape. But these were more or less choices of interpretation, not choices of how to live, given that "the penalty for non-compliance is extinction."[9]

Weber's essay is a tale of modern spirit possession, one in which Protestantism is said to play an important yet historically limited role. Weber thus focuses our attention on the uncanny that accompanies modern capitalism. Modern people may no longer be afraid of ghosts, but we yield to the ghost in the machine. This seems to be Weber's metaphorical point. His invocation of spirit gestures to the modern social system's possession of us. It makes us do things against our will, and even against our better judgment. As such, we confront the spirit of modern capitalism as a real and present force. It is both outside of us and, insofar as we find ourselves aligning our desires with its aims, inside us as well. And as Weber glumly observes, modernity has brought with it no exorcists. Our new choice is not whether to believe or deny the spirit but rather to find the proper secular, religious, or "spiritual" response to it and to seek the best ways to thrive within its overwhelming embrace. Seen in this light, Weber prompts us to consider both spiritual self-help and critical readings thereof as responses and actions that develop within the new social conditions that he describes.

RESISTANCE IS FUTILE: THERAPEUTIC CULTURE'S SPIRITUAL SYSTEM

> Just as around our bodies is the physical universe, in dependence upon which we live so that we create no power of our own, but assimilate it—eat it, drink it, absorb it—so around our spirits and in them is the Spiritual Universe. It is really there and it is as law-abiding as the physical cosmos with which the scientist deals.
>
> HENRY EMERSON FOSDICK, "Concerning Prayer"

The first generation of spiritual therapeutic texts, many written contemporaneously with Weber's "Protestant Ethic," offer answers to the problem that Weber identifies. Promulgators of New Thought and Mind Cure such as Ralph Waldo Trine and William Walter Atkinson as well as liberal Protestant ministers contributed in turn to a new discourse of the spirit that emphasized and illuminated its unifying and systemic qualities. If there was no exorcism possible, they reasoned, perhaps people could be encouraged to understand and master this spirit. Indeed, if spirit was a rational system then it would be available for scientific investigation, learning, and mastery. And as spiritual writers argued, with mastery would come happiness, health, and an experience of real freedom.

According to spiritual writers, the first step to living well in the system was to recognize this spiritual force for what it is: an energetic force that is visible in its effects in the world and on the body. As "everything is everything," all matter and spirit are part of the same reality, so each person's body is a creation of this spiritual force and thus responds to spirit and mind as much as it does to matter. Spiritual writers agree with skeptics that this sounds all rather hokey, so they encourage their readers to pay attention and to use their own skepticism to observe the force of the universe at work in the world. There are many signs: luck, fortune, coincidence, and déjà vu. Learning to read the signs of the law-abiding spiritual universe is necessary to become in tune with this force and thus to succeed within it. Spiritual therapeutic writers from liberal Protestant theologian Henry Emerson Fosdick to New Thought great Ralph Waldo Trine similarly encourage their readers to discern the effects of the spiritual force within their bodies and their minds.[10] The universe, and everything within it, was equally imbricated in its webs of connection and energy.

The contemporary heir to these turn-of-the-century figures, Oprah Winfrey, frequently employs a similar rhetoric.

Lest all this talk of the energy within begin to sound too much like spirit possession, spiritual writers make it clear that the force they describe is akin to gravity or other scientifically understood yet not observable physical forces. Like these other natural forces, spirit is not capricious; it cannot possess people—rather, it is a powerful and distributed force in the world. And, much as coming to understand the rules of nature or the rules of science leads to a higher quality of life, so following the rules of the spiritual universe also leads to a much more joyful existence.

Such a joyful existence is, furthermore, a thoroughly modern one, according to the spiritual writers. This modern pose rejects religions in all their multiplicity, detecting instead the unifying and perennial spiritual force that underlies all religions. The scientific underpinnings of a modern spirituality furthermore exposes the limits of traditional religion which, these writers argue, places emphasis on an individual's capacity to believe or have faith. As spiritual writers put it, there is no point in believing or not believing in the infinite. Faith does not make the spirit more or less real. In a modern age filled with democratic promise, the expansion of scientific method and authority, and the norms of rational practice, spiritual therapeutics emerged as a new kind of discourse about the possibility of freedom within the limits posed by the "felt" force of the universal spirit.

Put this way, the spirit is ever present, and its rules apply to all people. The spiritual writers agree with Weber: resistance is futile. But spiritual writers announce to their readers that accepting the truths of the spiritual laws of the universe and learning to work with them leads to a new kind of freedom.

POSITIVE THINKING AND CRITICAL THINKING

> Disenchantment . . . means that principally there are no mysterious incalculable forces that come into play, but rather that one can, in principle, master all things by calculation. This means that the world is disenchanted. One need no longer have recourse to magical means in order to master or implore the spirits.
>
> MAX WEBER, "Science as a Vocation"

The postwar therapeutic culture's critics take issue with spiritual writers' stories of freedom through acceptance. The mind-cured individual's "happiness is brokered on giving up their freedom," Donald Meyer argues, clearly finding this choice to be a troubling one. The positive thinker, he says, can have "no personal economic desires and appetites. He (she) could not be in tension with the system . . . The wish for plenty was not the wish to have one's wishes fulfilled; it was the wish not to have to wish wishes of one's own at all." Barbara Ehrenreich, similarly, raises the specter of totalitarianism, following Adorno's line, linking positive thinking and spirituality to totalitarianism. "It's easy to see positive thinking as a uniquely American form of naiveté," she writes, "but it is neither uniquely American nor endearingly naïve . . . in vastly different settings, positive thinking has been a tool of political repression." She continues, "[w]e tend to think that tyrants rule through fear . . . but some of the world's most mercilessly authoritarian regimes have also demanded constant optimism and cheer."[11]

Critics find in spirituality false consciousness and misrecognition of the facts of modern life. As Meyer's comment makes clear, the system certainly exists, but it is a disenchanted one. Modern social life thus offers people the chance (for the first time!) not to misattribute the world's workings to spirits, gods, and other unseen things. Becoming spiritual, in this sense, seems out of step with modernity's promise, and perniciously so. Critics are quick to point out spirituality's myriad contradictions, its hokey-scientific imaginaries, its scribes' multiple cases of plagiarism and duplicity, not to mention its troubling political logics.

But in embracing the reality of modernity as a system (albeit a disenchanted one), critics of therapeutic culture seem to have missed the opportunity to read Weber's discussion of the transformation of spirits into spirit as a critique of their own critical gymnastics. Critics of therapeutic culture have often deployed Weber's essay in their interpretation of therapeutic culture but frequently misread Weber's central point that the Protestant ethic is, by the early twentieth century, utterly incidental to the systems that it has played a role in creating. Instead, therapeutic culture critics view New Thought therapeutics as the Protestant ethic in drag and a continuing source of power supporting the economic systems in which we live.[12] This conflation of cause and effect, so clearly articulated in Weber's argument, allows critics of therapeutic culture to offer their own form of ideology critique and their own special practices of self-cultivation as a way to live better within the system. Their language of overcoming through critical thinking shares clear parallels with the positive thinking that they criticize. It is fair, then, to read the critique of therapeutic culture as its own form of self-help therapy. In conflating the varied transformations and temporalities in Weber's complex argument, they often surprisingly seem to invert Weber's argument. In so doing they identify positive thinking's origins as debased theology, a holdout of religion, and argue that it is possible to overcome this ideology by critically examining its faulty logic, which can be found in various self-help texts.

Thus, contra Weber, critics of therapeutic culture spirituality connect spirituality to Protestantism and to enchanted, premodern religious life. They gloss over or ignore Weber's central claim altogether—namely, that the Protestant ethic is not legible in the spirit of capitalism as it is experienced today. Their reading turns away from a closer inspection of the secular spirituality that self-help literature invokes. And as a consequence, these critics overlook an uncanny fact: their own prescriptions for healthy living in modern life are remarkably similar to those made by the proponents of therapeutic culture. Indeed, we might consider how critics' identification of spirituality with religion rather than with secularity allows them to draw a portrait of spirituality that is substantially less threatening and that draws our attention away from the assumptions the critics share with the spiritual thinkers about how to live in modernity. It is, after all, quite easy for a disenchanted secular thinker to dispatch religious irrationalism and likewise quite reasonable to expect that a better day lies ahead for people cured of their simplistic views. It is another thing altogether to consider that both positive thinking and its critique emanate in response to what they both perceive as an inescapable set of social conditions.

Read the therapeutic culture critics carefully and they begin to sound remarkably similar to the self-help gurus they aim to attack: the techniques of critical thinking are clear and open to all, even if they are not widely used or diligently pursued. But those who follow them will be rewarded. The first step, of course, is to identify and detect the spread of therapeutic culture, happy and positive thinking, and to comprehend its sneaky premises and false promises. Everyone who learns to think critically can come to true self-awareness—which entails, among other things, the ability to see that therapeutic culture's language of freedom is false and in fact aligned with its opposite. But in rejecting the spiritual practices of self-help, one must also become a vigilant thinker and critic. Cultivating critical faculties, we learn, takes practice and time. But in the end, a life guided by the spirit of critique promises to return those who practice it to a better and more authentic, natural form of life.

"This is . . . not a path for utopians," Wendy Kaminer warns. "It promises us no earthly paradise, no ultimate resolution of conflict, no assurance of absolute rectitude, no rest." This restless, strenuous life of constant activity and no reward offers not happiness but rather "realism": the ability (or at least the promise of the ability) to see things as they really are. "Vigilant realism" is not easy, Barbara Ehrenreich likewise cautions: the task of throwing off positive thinking's "thought control" which "obscures judgment" and "shields us from vital information" nonetheless yields rewards. Yet, "*at all times* we need to be alert to the world outside ourselves, even when that includes absorbing bad news and entertaining the views of 'negative' people."[13] Critical thinkers, no less than the positive thinkers, promise a life of freedom if we submit to a life of constant discipline.

Therapeutic culture's critics are in this respect also positive thinkers, willing to imagine ways of envisioning and working toward self-fulfillment and social betterment through particular disciplines and techniques. They also offer freedom to those who would only submit to the self-evident promises of secular modernity.

Therapeutic culture's critics offer a no less (and no more) hopeful narrative of possible personal liberation than the positive thinkers. Both ideologies can be understood as responses to the "system" in which modern people live. What is striking is the frequency with which therapeutic culture's critics claim that by merely exposing and rejecting spiritual thinking, they can undercut its force and power in the world. This argument makes sense, however, only if spirituality is viewed in this systemic way. If we observe that this dominant view of spirituality itself emerges in modernity as a response to the effects and affects of an all-powerful system, then we see how critical and positive thinking align. Both parties have an equal role in articulating and promulgating diagnoses and responses to the modern worlds over which none of us has control, and from which none of us is ever free. Choosing critical thinking is as likely to change the world as bending spoons will create cosmic consciousness.

SPIRIT AND SPIRITS: THE ONE AND THE MANY

> The universe has always appeared to the natural mind as a kind of enigma, of which the key must be sought in the shape of some illuminating or power-bringing word or name. That word names the universe's principle and to possess it is after a fashion to possess the universe itself. 'God,' 'Matter,' 'Reason,' 'the Absolute,' 'Energy' are so many solving names. You can rest when you have them. You are at the end of your metaphysical quest.
>
> WILLIAM JAMES, "Pluralism, Pragmatism and Instrumental Truth"[14]

Weber, critical thinkers, and positive thinkers all agree that modernity is a system, or a system of systems. What differences there are lie primarily in how we come to convince ourselves that we can lead a life worth living within this system and how we might eke out some narrative of freedom or progress within it. These are all, in some respect, processes of secular enchantment. Spiritual writers provide an optimistic and hopeful view of the system, offering techniques in their books for how to best tap into its powers. Critics of spirituality, on the other hand, refuse to accept the enchantments of modernity as real (if they even notice them at all) and thus designate spiritual writers as not quite modern enough. Better, they say, to devote oneself to a life of critical reflection and toil: rooting out the last vestiges of religion will allow the promises of modernity to emerge. This is unquestionably a form of positive thinking, one that has increasingly even taken the term "spiritual" into its own orbit. Weber's commentary hovers nearby: neither the critics nor the spiritual writers seem aware of modernity's need for some kind of radical exorcism. Which was, of course, precisely Weber's concern.

Of course, at this moment we can also ask whether the worlds in which we live reflect or relate in any consequential way to Weber's theoretical arguments about modernity's overwhelming totality and its inescapability. Modern theorists and cultural critics (including positive thinkers and their critics) caution us against the dangers of asking this question, and of the folly of entertaining anything like freedom or independence of these totalities. Neither can imagine anything other than a world composed of systems.

But it is important to remember that the evidence for such a view comes from prescriptive texts and a particular method of reading them. In Weber's interpretive vision, Protestants listen to sermons and act predictably as a consequence. In Kaminer's and Meyer's interpretations, spiritual aspirants read self-help texts and duly follow the rituals and disciplines without thinking. While we know that people do not act in these ways, the vision of actors following through without thinking not only develops into a powerful vision of the blind follower but also takes attention away from how modern systems might actually work.

So, we might ask, how do people in the world actually use these texts? The self-identified spiritual practitioners in Cambridge, Massachusetts, whom I met in the early 2000s while researching a book on spiritual experience[15] were avid consumers of spirituality and self-help books, websites, DVDs, and so on. They read, reread, and discussed all the best-selling titles. Many sought out even more obscure volumes on their own. But they were without exception also all careful readers. They had particular tastes and judgments about what book might be worth their time. They were, moreover, quite adept at deploying the most scathing critiques of texts they found wanting, deftly utilizing every bow in the quiver of skilled critical thinkers.[16]

Significantly, whatever they read or experienced jostled around in other interactions and discussions that they had with other people and other spirits.[17] Their spiritual worlds and their practical commitments were both characterized by complexity that mirrored the various complexities they confronted in their daily life. While their striving for unity was real (and almost everyone I met during my years of fieldwork in Cambridge, Massachusetts, told me that they believed in the spiritual universe and its singularity), they did not fit the portrait often painted of them.

Indeed as I conducted fieldwork in Cambridge, Massachusetts, it became increasingly clear to me that the therapeutic and spiritual literature (and the literature of its critics) failed to characterize the world of spirits that my interlocutors encountered. Nothing prepared me for entry into a world where spirits were talkative, animative, and interactive. My respondents talked about spiritual forces, of course. But they also actively experienced the world populated by spirits, astral guides, and psychic personalities who spoke to them, and to whom they spoke back. Their nonsystemic encounters with the world of spirits demonstrated that spirits still had the ability to be irregular, disruptive, and pessimistic. They were rarely as uniform or law abiding as Fosdick and Trine claimed. A dead New York firefighter appeared at an otherwise placid discussion group, enraged at his own death, cursing Muslims. A woman found that her true love from a previous life had moved to town and her comfortable marriage fell apart. These were not the disenchanted spiritual forces we have become inured to expect. They do not fit easily into the normal stories that we tell about ourselves or about the modern people who are supposed to be attuning themselves to Spirit rather than spirits.

As I became increasingly aware of the long shadow that various interpretations of Weber cast on my analysis I began to take refuge in William James's writings about pluralism. James also lived in Cambridge, where he frequently engaged with the mind curers, mentalists, and spiritualists who were active at the turn of the twentieth century. Many scholars have offered explanations for James's interests in these spirits and their interlocutors, but the argument I find most compelling is that James found them to be an active and present challenge to the pronouncements of modernity's disenchantment that social scientists of his day increasingly proclaimed.[18]

James was not for enchantment. He was not an advocate for a return to a world of spirits and religion. But as a pluralist, he was interested (as many of us remain) in understanding the social and psychological effects of the prophets of a monistic, totalizing modernity. In conjuring up (or reporting on) the spirit world, James sought to explore and establish a vision of modern life and a way of being in it that was neither fully enchanted nor disenchanted, neither possessed nor possessing. In this milieu, spirits provided an unsteady and available way to point to something "multiple." Spirits were a local antidote, at the very least, to the overwhelming claims made by champions of modern materialism and science. "When you've got your true idea," James complains, "[y]ou're in possession: you *know;* you have fulfilled your thinking destiny." The restless James found nothing free in these terms and nothing valuable in either being possessed or in being in possession of a word. "'God,' 'Matter,' 'Reason,' 'the Absolute,' 'Energy.' . . . You can rest when you have them."[19]

James identified power in the strangeness and the unchartability of spirits—above all, they unsettled that modern claim that anyone could be "in possession" of their own solving words. Those words, rather, came to possess those who claimed them. Spirits, in other words, offered something beyond the intellectually limited quests (whether spiritual or secular) that emanated from modernity's "solving words." Strange and troubling, chatty, irresponsible, and definitely odd, these modern, nonpossessing, nonpossessive spirits spoke to, and of, a modern world that remained open to the possibility of contingency, externality, and otherness—and thus to the arrival of modernity's exorcist.

CHAPTER 4

Race

Gabriel Mendes

"Come in, sir. Tell me what's wrong with you."

"I am somewhat anxious."

"Tell me how in which way?"

"Well, doctor, when I go for a walk in the streets I have the feeling that people look at me with some distrust."

"What else?"

"When I enter a shop to buy something the salesgirl looks rather diffident and annoyed as though she does not want to sell anything to me."

"The doctor says: 'Well, in this profession, we have a phrase for your ailment. It is called 'subjective ideas of reference.' And the doctor adds: 'Well, you just come every Thursday from four to five and close your eyes and tell me all your thoughts and I can assure you that within two or three months, you'll be cured. It will cost you twenty thousand dollars. You understand?"

"Yes, doctor, I understand." And the white man leaves.

"Who's next?" the doctor says. It is the black man's turn.

"Good morning, doctor."

"Good morning. What's wrong with you?"

"Well, when I go for a walk in the streets people look at me with distrust, and when I enter a shop to buy something the salesgirl looks annoyed and diffident, and I have the distinct feeling that she does not want to sell anything to me."

"Well, I understand. In our profession, we have a phrase for this; it is 'subjective ideas of reference.'"

The black man is upset when he hears this and he says: "Pardon me, doctor but you must be raving mad."[1]

RICHARD WRIGHT, Interview with Georges Charbonnier, 1960

Wright's parable from fifty years ago conveys the impossibility of extricating race from the encounter between therapist and patient and illustrates how race inheres in the very tissue of models of mental health. As historian and psychiatrist Jonathan Metzl has recently argued, "To a remarkable extent, anxieties about racial difference shape diagnostic criteria, health-care policies, medical and popular attitudes about mentally ill persons, the structures of treatment facilities, and, ultimately, the conversations that take place there within."[2] In what follows, I consider the long history of the role race has played in American psychotherapy, through reference to a largely forgotten institution dedicated to psychiatric treatment founded on antiracist principles. Harlem, New York's, Lafargue Mental Hygiene Clinic linked black psychic well-being to social transformation at a time when to do so was deemed radical by mainstream psychiatry and by philanthropic and government funding agencies. The clinic was a landmark in the history of African Americans' encounters with the field of mental health care as well as an effort at redirecting the fundamental orientation of psychotherapy towards the social bases of mental illness and health. The years in which the Lafargue Clinic operated (1946–1958) preceded the heyday of the "canonical" critique of therapeutic culture, which emerged most saliently in the wake of the liberatory dreams and movements of the 1960s. Yet we can position the Lafargue Clinic within a set of debates over the role and purpose of psychotherapy in modern US society.

Housed in the basement of Harlem's St. Philip's Episcopal Church on West 134th Street, Lafargue opened its doors on March 8, 1946, and operated every Tuesday and Friday evening until November 1958. The result of a collaboration among the psychiatrist and social critic Dr. Fredric Wertham, writer Richard Wright, and clergyman Rev. Shelton Hale Bishop, this clinic embodied novel ways of thinking about mental health, race, and the experience of urban modernity that continue to yield insights about how to address the psychic dimensions of a raced existence in a racist world.

The importance of Lafargue being housed in a church must not be overlooked. The Harlem community regarded the church as a safe space where they would not be toyed with or treated as objects of scientific experiments, to be poked and prodded. The church's embrace of the clinic thus signaled to Harlem residents that they would be offered legitimate care and treatment with a truly human touch. In the St. Philip's Church newsletter, published one week after the night of the clinic's opening, Father Bishop captured the significance of the clinic's founding: "There is not one adequate community resource in New York City for the proper psychiatric treatment of colored people. This is well known by all social agencies that serve this community . . . [Lafargue] is for the people in the Harlem community, for both children and adults who have mental or nervous disorders of any kind, and who desire treatment. It is one more attempt on the part of this Parish to meet community needs in a very specific way . . . We would like to begin especially with the behavior problems of children and with veterans."[3]

Termed "an experiment in the social basis of psychotherapy" by Dr. Wertham, Lafargue explicitly incorporated the social experience of racial and class oppression into its diagnostic and therapeutic work.[4] The clinic was thus both a political and scientific gambit, challenging a racist mental health care system, as well as putatively color-blind psychiatrists who failed to consider black experiences of oppression in their treatment. At the core of the clinic's work was a social philosophy and scientific orientation that linked black psychological suffering to an oppressive social and economic order and saw therapy as transformative rather than palliative. Lafargue represents a prism through which to understand a genealogy of African American encounters with varieties of therapeutic culture as well as a suggestive attempt to understand the psychosocial significance of race and racism from within American psychotherapy.

*

The work of the Lafargue Clinic was part of a wider reckoning with the significance of race throughout mid-twentieth-century American political, social, cultural, and scientific institutions. In the years surrounding World War II, as many different groups and communities launched offensives against explicit racism and anti-Semitism in the United States, experts in various fields sought to understand race and "race relations" in scientific terms. Psychology in particular provided a language for understanding racism and its effects upon individual minority group members.[5] Many social and behavioral scientists contended that prejudice resulted from frustrated intrapsychic impulses and desires that led to aggressive thoughts and behavior expressed as hostility and discrimination. These same scientists argued that the behavior of minority group members victimized by discrimination could be explained in terms of individuals' ability or inability to manage their responses to frustration and aggression. Many social and behavioral scientists diagnosed racial prejudice as pathological and regarded therapy as the key to improving race relations.[6]

This "psychological reworking of race" represented just one part of a larger shift in the human sciences at midcentury toward a psychodynamic paradigm. Nowhere was this shift expressed more saliently than in the field of psychiatry. During World War II, psychiatrists were able to document and treat the effects of environmental stresses upon soldiers' personalities and behavior.[7] Extending their observations from the context of war to the rest of society, many psychiatrists contended that socioenvironmental conditions were important determinants of the American people's psychological health.

Although these ideas would seem to represent a promising complement to the efforts of behaviorists and other social scientists to understand the effects of racism, the new psychiatry largely overlooked black patients. Racism as a possible etiological source of mental disorder was mostly absent from the discourse of this psychiatric movement. It was left to a small group of black psychiatrists and psychologists and their more progressive white (mostly Jewish) colleagues to highlight the relationship between racism and mental illness.

If the popular 1940 book *Bellevue* by Lorraine Maynard is any guide, clinicians hardly regarded the Negro patient in any ward of Bellevue as a person possessing a mental makeup akin to that of any of the various "white peoples" who frequented the hospital. According to Maynard, who wrote her tabloid-style, behind-the-scenes exposé with the help of a Bellevue staff doctor named Laurence Miscall,

> [Often] it is possible, with a little practice, to estimate a person's general condition by his typically racial response . . . Most colored folk seem able to accept life as it comes and take trouble in stride. They are apt to make a fine recovery after operation because of this calm, positive flair for living in the moment. They do not get so tense and flurried as other people, and it just doesn't occur to them to expect the worst . . . the average negro [sic] is often too inured to discomfort for his own good. *Being less physically, mentally or aesthetically sensitive than a white*, what he will stand without a murmur is sometimes amazing to the staff.

Published in the same year as Richard Wright's *Native Son*, this book consistently trafficked in a variety of well-worn stereotypes about how "Polacks," "Hebrews," "Slovaks," "Spaniards," "negros" [sic] and other "races" interacted with hospital staff and used such stereotypes as a substitute for a truly therapeutic reckoning with the problem of diagnosis and treatment for both physical and mental traumas and diseases.[8]

In the 1940s, the state and private foundations created new agencies and institutions to promote the mental health of the general population in the United States, but little was done to consider the specific needs of African Americans. In fact, most mental health care professionals had little to say about and little interest in the psychic health of African Americans. Even in historical studies of this moment of expansion in the provision of mental health services to the American public, black Americans' needs rarely come under consideration.[9]

In the face of this systematic disregard, Fredric Wertham was adamant that the greatest need for mental health care existed among the most oppressed members of US society, people whose psychological needs were routinely dismissed or reduced to questions of material deprivation. "Negroes are not allowed the luxury of neuroses," he contended, adding that "[t]he official view is that they are just unhappy, or they need housing, or they feel downtrodden."[10] Further, Wertham argued that the state's liberalizing extension of various social services failed to address the fact of unequal access to care resulting from the ingrained belief among policy makers and health care providers, not to mention many academics, that black people were simple folk whose only need was to get a "fair shake" in the economy. Many whites and not a few black leaders framed the problem of race, or "the Negro problem" as it was termed, as simply a matter of fairness: Negroes' lots would improve if they got a fair shot at employment and other bread-and-butter issues.[11] Thus, prior to the establishment of Lafargue, most institutions and policy makers did not even consider that black people needed access to mental health care.

Soon after the two met in 1941, Wertham began to regale Richard Wright with stories of the terrible treatment of the mentally ill in New York City, black people in particular. As a psychiatrist in the New York City Department of Hospitals system, Wertham, a Bavarian-born nonobservant Jew who emigrated to the United States in 1922 to work with eminent psychiatrist Adolf Meyer at Johns Hopkins University's Phipps Clinic, had come into contact with black men, women, and children hospitalized for various mental disorders whose etiology he traced back to the oppressive social order of the Depression- and war-era United States. He had "a dark story to tell of how hospitals are run," particularly how black New Yorkers were treated at Bellevue and other hospitals and how they were excluded from services at centers such as the New York Psychiatric Institute attached to Columbia University. In the late 1930s, Wertham had interested the LaGuardia administration in his plan to open a mental hygiene clinic in Harlem. But the city never followed through.[12]

For Wertham the nature of the psychiatric treatment black New Yorkers received was just as significant as the question of access. He feared that even if black people did gain access to psychiatric facilities, they would receive treatment founded on a misguided approach, an approach that treated mental disorders as individual pathologies rather than as the product of an oppressive society.[13] Blacks comprised a reported "50% of the [annual] intake" at the Bellevue Psychiatric Ward, according to one early 1940s report, which of course means that they had access to a form of psychiatric care.[14] Even so, there is no indication that black New Yorkers considered Bellevue a place where they would be respected as human beings or receive the type of treatment that acknowledged the sociopsychological stress of living under oppressive conditions.

Wertham's efforts to address the specific mental health care needs of New York City's growing black population were animated by a combined scientific and political conviction that contemporary psychotherapy failed to adequately address the social bases of human thought and behavior.[15] There was at this time in the World War II era and early postwar America, according to Wertham, "a great contradiction between the tendency to apply psychiatric and psychoanalytic ideas to the social sciences and the failure of psychiatry so far to study adequately even those social problems which are most closely related to the care and treatment of mental patients."[16] He wanted his fellow psychiatrists to recognize that a patient must be understood first and foremost as belonging to a class, having a distinct social relation to the means of production, and experiencing specific concerns and problems based on this relation. The psychiatrist must be concerned with whether the patient is a boss, worker, or part of that group of have-nots that some have called the underclass—whom Marx called the *lumpenproletariat*. By paying close, clinical attention to the social basis of mental life, psychiatry would advance itself as a science. Wertham argued that "there is no contradiction between scientific and social psychiatry. Psychiatry cannot be social if it is not truly scientific, and it is certainly not scientific if it is not social. The road to progress is the integration of Kraepelin, Freud, and Marx—which means to do justice to the dynamic dialectic interaction of conscious, unconscious, and social factors."[17]

Wertham presented the emergence of social psychiatry as an historical progression from outmoded approaches to understanding and treating mental disorders and emotional problems. He argued further that psychiatric and psychoanalytic schools were rooted in the class interests of their practitioners and their patients and spoke exclusively to their sense of reality. For Wertham, a truly democratic people needed a truly democratic psychiatry. In one handwritten note Wertham offered these brief but telling guidelines for practicing psychotherapy within social psychiatry:

> To be active and brief;
> To consider the group interests of the individual;
> To emphasize the work aspects of life;
> To develop a pattern of solidarity in transfer;

To work toward the real liberation of sex impulses from outmoded taboos;
To include modifications of the environment as an intrinsic part of the treatment.

Scribbled beneath this list was a question Wertham posed to himself and by extension all psychiatrists: "Am I my brother's keeper?"[18] And he explained to his staff at Lafargue that "it is one of the tasks of social psychotherapy to strengthen the patient to such a degree that he is able to see and face the actual social situation, and to instill in him the will to survive in a hostile world."[19]

*

By the time the Lafargue Clinic had opened in the late winter of 1946, a number of schools of environmental, interpersonal, and cultural psychiatric thought had come to fruition. One important group coalesced around the work of the psychiatrist Harry Stack Sullivan, cultural anthropologist Louis Sapir, and Harold Lasswell at the William Alanson White Foundation.[20] Another was the "culture and personality" group whose primary home was Yale University and was best represented in the work of Dr. Karen Horney and the group of psychoanalysts who came to be known as "Neo-Freudians" or "Post-Freudians."[21] Throughout the life of the Lafargue Clinic, however, Wertham remained critical of the major trends in psychoanalytic psychiatry that explicitly incorporated what he termed suprapersonal factors into the total picture of human personality and mental health. He resisted the two predominating paradigms that contributed most to the environmental turn in psychiatry, namely, culture and personality and (ironically) social psychiatry.

It would appear that Horney's brand of psychoanalytic environmentalism would have considerable insight to offer Wertham in his work. Horney and the so-called Neo-Freudians challenged the biologism of both traditional somatic psychiatry and the orthodox Freudians' insistence on the primacy of the sex and death drives in man's personality. And more fundamentally, Horney challenged scientists and the public to confront the cultural forces that make people think and act the way they do, apart from the supposed instinctual drives fixed in their bodies and minds. But Wertham argued that the Neo-Freudians did not offer a substantive advance in psychotherapy because they still failed "to take into full account the dynamic interaction between personal and impersonal (social factors)." In Wertham's view it was not good science to equate cultural factors with social factors, namely because the former remained in the arena of the subjective. This meant that psychiatry, cultural or otherwise, would still treat the individual in terms of how he negotiated psychologically the culture of which he was a member. Wertham argued that a focus on culture elided the relationship of individuals and classes of people to the means of production and their place in the larger social structure, particularly how race and class intersect to structure individual and group experience.

Wertham's problem with the culture and personality psychoanalysts and the putative social psychiatrists was never theoretical or methodological alone. His main criticism was quite basic. All the progressive theories and treatments in the world would mean little if the majority of people never had access to psychotherapy. In order to treat anxieties, a doctor would need to grasp the origin and character of those anxieties. Wertham's brand of social psychiatry gave answers to this basic question of the origins and manifestations of mental disorders that addressed the concrete, reality-based nature of human personality and the psychological problems people confronted. There he saw racial discrimination and class exploitation and made the step that his putative colleagues had not, could not, or would not: he opened a clinic "in and for" the community of Harlem for the practical treatment of socially induced anxieties and mental maladies.

Practicality was central to the Lafargue Clinic's efforts to create a new type of psychotherapy. Since the clinic was only open two nights a week for about three hours each night, each therapy session was only thirty minutes, or an hour in special cases. Given this limited amount of time for each patient, the clinic staff would have to be creative in its use of professional resources. A September 1952 memo on the clinic's organization read, "The Clinic is entirely oriented to psychotherapy, to all the different forms of psychotherapy. Every staff member with the exception of clerical workers should get instruction in psychotherapy on all levels."[22]

Upon entering the Lafargue Clinic a patient would answer an intake questionnaire. Wertham directed the clinic staff to pay close attention to the broader context of the patient's experiences as sources of discontent, anxiety, delusions, and other mental distress. The clinic viewed the patient's presentation of his own case history as beginning the therapy process.[23] Dr. Luise Zucker, a psychologist at the clinic, offered these suggestions for first examinations: "Establish a good working relationship with [patient]. This can be achieved by showing him both your sympathy and your respect for him as a human being. Listen carefully to what he says and *how* he says it. Take notes while [patient] is talking, not in retrospect. His own formulations rather than yours can be very enlightening." Zucker further emphasized a focus on the patient's personal information as it related to his attitude toward his job and his various social relations. Moreover, Zucker warned fellow staff members not to "delude yourself into thinking that you will 'psychoanalyze' your [patient] in seeing him once a week or less often. You may do a good job by using a modified therapeutic approach, based on psychoanalytic principles. Both methods can be helpful, but don't get them mixed up."[24]

It must have been a remarkable experience for residents of Harlem to enter those basement rooms of the St. Philip's parish house. A contemporary report described the scene:

> The little waiting room was crowded. A good looking ex-GI smoked a cigarette nervously. A mother sat holding her 10-year old daughter's hand. Two men sat together quietly.
>
> A young lady in a white smock came in. "Mr. Carson next, please," she announced. He followed her into a large room and they both sat at a small circular table. She poised her pen and asked him numerous questions. When she was through, she led him to one of four cubicles formed by unpainted screens. Here, a psychiatrist was waiting to hear his troubles and start treatment . . .
>
> From the cubicles came the drone of steady talk as Dr. Wertham's three co-workers consulted with patients . . . Some patients remain for 15 minutes, others are not through for an hour.
>
> "I got out of the navy three months ago. I can't settle down to my job at the airport. I always worry about my family and about losing my job . . ."
>
> "I don't know how it happened, but when I came to I was lying on the floor. My tongue was bleeding. This is the second time . . ."
>
> "They're out to get me I tell you! I feel sure he put poison in my soup, I'm afraid to eat anything . . ."
>
> "Married? Of course, I want to get married. But if he even shakes hands with me I'm frightened . . ."
>
> "This is Harold, Doctor. He has always been a good boy up until a month ago. Then he started playing hookey . . . Yesterday the man at the newsstand caught him stealing . . ."
>
> And so on, far into the night, thousands of words uttered by hopeful lips in search of peace of mind.[25]

At the end of each night, Dr. Wertham and Dr. Hilde L. Mosse, the physician in charge, would assemble the staff to discuss each case seen that evening, to review the diagnoses and plan future treatment.[26]

The clinic staff often questioned and challenged the diagnoses and treatment plans of other agencies in New York. In a 1956 statistical report on the clinic's diagnoses over the years, there was a note reading, "*Re: Psychoses:* When we diagnose psychosis we mean it. We do not mean what all the other clinics and papers talk about, namely what they call 'latent' schizophrenia. We diagnose unquestionable psychoses . . . usually not recognized before they came to Lafargue . . . It is still amazing how many patients with major mental diseases are undiagnosed and untreated in spite of the increase in mental hygiene facilities in the past 10 years."[27] These diagnoses were indicative of both the clinic's rigorous social psychiatric therapeutic orientation and its attention to specific patients' presentation of mental disorders—despite its short hours and limited resources.

In 1954, the same year that the Supreme Court overturned "separate but equal" in *Brown v. Board* and the same year Dr. Wertham published *Seduction of the Innocent*, his controversial study of crime comic books' effects on youth, the State of New York passed a law that seemed to bode well for the future of Lafargue. The Community Mental Health Services Act represented the postwar shift in mental health care policy toward public health measures based upon localized efforts to prevent serious mental illness. Some of the clinic staff had always hoped they might be able to operate on a full-time, all-day basis, and the new law rekindled that hope. Each local board established by the act would now be responsible for the dispensation of the considerable funds newly allocated to licensed providers of mental health care.[28] Lafargue fit perfectly the model of locally based outpatient mental health services imagined under the 1954 act. But clearly the die had been cast long before the new legislation; no amount of persuasion or pleading could undo the calumny Wertham had directed against the psychiatric establishment in his publications, academic lectures, and activity. For he had become a staunch critic of what he termed orthodox psychiatry and its failure to act as a progressive force. Psychiatrists had become, in his view, guardians of the status quo.[29] And so Lafargue, Wertham's "experiment in the social basis of psychotherapy," never received any of the new money for community mental health care.[30] With the combination of Father Bishop's retirement from St. Philip's in 1957 and "an unforeseen accumulation of deaths and severe illnesses" among staff members in the subsequent year, the Lafargue Clinic announced in December 1958 that it would have to cease operating.

*

Contemporary newspaper and magazine articles about Lafargue focused on its novelty and hardscrabble operating conditions. Journalists portrayed the work of the clinic in terms that would appeal to a broad American audience in the early postwar years. Such articles offered narratives of redemption aimed at making their audience sympathetic both to the travails of individuals and families struggling with mental disorders and to the work of the clinic. Reporters often referenced the conditions of discrimination against Negroes that precipitated its founding. But they avoided discussion of the clinic's radical orientation linking racism and class subjugation to the increased anxiety and full-blown mental disorders among black New Yorkers.[31]

Richard Wright, by contrast, presented Lafargue as an underground anomaly, radically subverting the foundations of psychiatry. In his essay "Psychiatry Comes to Harlem," published in 1946, Wright explained that, "Though the Lafargue Clinic does exist, there is a widely prevalent feeling among many of the people that it does *not* exist." Wright and his fellow Lafargue booster Ralph Ellison would both use the trope of absence or nonexistence in their essays on Lafargue and its place in the world of 1940s Harlem. In his essay, Wright likened the establishment of Lafargue to the appearance of that which has been psychologically repressed in the individual. Like individually repressed needs, socially repressed needs such as basic medical care—in this case psychiatry—are made visible and treated often through methods that subvert the sanctioned social order. Thus the underground, in the absence of daylight, becomes the seedbed for radical social upsurges. Both Wright and Ellison argued that this was the importance of Lafargue as a new institution in black Harlem—a fugitive institution located tellingly in a basement, the actual underground, of the most prominent institution in black cultural and political life, a church.[32]

*

Lafargue was a modestly radical, local effort to confront directly the individual and social effects of intersecting racial and class oppressions in the mid-twentieth-century United States. By taking concrete, institutional measures to address the anxiety of the black individuals and communities living in New York, Lafargue chipped away at the edifice of Jim Crow in the North. While it anticipated the community mental health movement of the 1960s, the clinic did not shake up the entire system of mental health care in America, or even New York City for that matter. Yet the very of existence of Lafargue forced city officials, and at least some psychiatrists, to take seriously black people's need for humane and accessible psychiatric services.

It helps to place the antiracist work of Lafargue in conversation with the push for cultural competence, the most salient effort in contemporary mental health care to confront racial difference and the legacies of white supremacy in the therapeutic encounter. From the office receptionist to the chief psychiatrist/administrator, the attainment of cultural competence has become imperative among clinical staff at all levels. Promoters of cultural competence argue that an important step in reducing disparities is for health care providers not only to become aware of cultural differences among their clients and patients but to adopt strategies for incorporating that difference into their diagnostic and treatment protocols. Professional organizations, including the American Psychiatric Association, along with individual hospitals and clinics, have devised specific guidelines that signal to their members what to be aware of when treating members of different "ethnic" and "cultural" groups, that is, what to know about African Americans, Asians, Latinos, and Native Americans.[33] In their best versions, cultural competency guidelines promote awareness among the caregivers of their own possession of a culture, as well as the distinct culture of the caregiving environment, say, the clinic, hospital, or office. What cultural competency advocates hope will emerge from this stew of cross-cultural awareness is a reduction in miscommunication, misunderstanding, misdiagnosis, and mistreatment—and, ultimately, a reduction in health disparities among racialized populations.

In psychotherapy as in other spheres of American society, the language of cultural difference has emerged as a proxy—a stand-in for racial difference. Culture, as word and concept, emerged over the last century as a placeholder for that which used to be applied to and/or evoke race—race as defined by those embodied, intrinsic, fixed, and heritable traits/qualities within a population group and each one of its members. Reading culture becomes reading race, and that process of reading is governed by a fundamental, long-embedded ensemble of associations and expectations of what it means to be X type of person. And in Jonathan Metzl's words that opened this essay, this whole dynamic is fraught with racial anxiety.

Within the clinical encounter, the shift from race to culture has historically been a well-intentioned, often antiracist, attempt to address problems of alterity/difference. Yet the consequences of this well-intentioned shift from race to culture are profound evasions of the persistent significance, not only of racial identification and identity, but of racism as a determining force in constituting psychic health. And what's at stake in these evasions is nothing less than the very meaning of health and pathology, questions that will shape—that are no doubt shaping—the contours and substance of modern therapeutic cultures. In highlighting the efforts of cultural competency to confront the significance of racial and ethnic difference in the clinical setting, I wish to suggest that the emphasis on the patient's "culture" and the clinician's capacity to read and accommodate that patient's difference tends to elide the larger structures of inequity that perpetuate not race, but racism. And beyond that I wish to suggest that the focus on cultural competency evades the very fundamental issue of how racial difference structures how pathology is recognized, diagnosed, and treated.

By contrast, the Lafargue Clinic's emphasis on its Harlem patients' intersecting statuses as black, largely poor, and disempowered rather than on their "culture" in treating mental disorders or problems of everyday living eschewed the framework of culture as psychic determinant and offered a model of psychotherapy that was radical in the etymological sense of roots—of seeking answers and interventions in the fundamental social origins of anxiety and other mental health problems.

The Lafargue Clinic embodied a practical response to the need for low-cost psychotherapy and counseling for black Americans trying to survive in a hostile society. The clinic emerged not from a reformist political project or a desire "to study the Negro's personality" but instead from a more radical belief that psychotherapy could play an essential part in black New Yorkers' struggles against systemic inequality. "The Lafargue Clinic is not trying to help adjust people to a vicious environment," Dr. Wertham told one reporter a few months after the clinic's opening. "We give them the best psychiatric care to help build strong citizens, fighters against this debilitating ghetto! We want our patients to function in a changing world, and work with others to do it!"[34] It is the lesson of this modest radicalism, linking psychotherapy to social change on the racial and economic front, that the Lafargue Clinic has bequeathed to therapeutic culture's contemporary students and participants.

CHAPTER 5

Motherhood

Rebecca Jo Plant

Few American feminists in the 1960s and 1970s looked kindly on psychiatry and psychoanalysis. In *Sexual Politics*, Kate Millet described Freud as "beyond question the strongest individual counterrevolutionary force in the ideology of sexual politics."[1] She and many other feminist critics accused psychoanalysts and their popularizers of trafficking in spurious theories that legitimated women's subordination. Yet despite such hard-hitting critiques, feminists' stance toward psychological expertise cannot be characterized as one of straightforward repudiation. As both Ellen Herman and Eva Moskowitz have shown, the movement was also indebted to psychological thinking and enmeshed in the ambient therapeutic culture. The practice of consciousness raising, for instance, may have diverged widely from therapy in its ultimate goal—political change—but both were predicated on a belief in the value of self-exploration. To a significant extent, feminists seized the conceptual tools of therapeutic culture to critique the restrictive definitions of femininity that it so often and insidiously promoted.[2]

Building on these insights, this essay argues that psychological experts in the twentieth-century United States inadvertently helped to clear the path for liberal feminism by reshaping the culturally dominant ideal of motherhood. A protracted and contested process, the translation of motherhood into therapeutic terms entailed the dismantling of an ideal of "moral motherhood" that dated back to the antebellum period. By the early twentieth century, and increasingly after World War I, psychological experts began to challenge this ideal's fundamental precepts, including the notion that motherhood was an all-encompassing, lifelong identity and that selflessness was its very essence.

Associating its duties with a particular life stage, they instead reenvisioned motherhood as a source of immense personal fulfillment and a single component of a more multifaceted self. By the post–World War II era, their efforts had done much to discredit the iconic, self-sacrificing mother and to validate the young, fun-loving mom who understood the need to rein in maternal impulses and the importance of emotional autonomy.[3]

At first glance, the notion that therapeutic culture helped to prepare the way for a feminist critique of motherhood (and gender roles more broadly) seems counterintuitive. Scholars who have analyzed psychological authorities' pronouncements on motherhood in the 1940s and 1950s have understandably emphasized their often quite breathtaking sexism. According to most midcentury psychological experts, only neurotic and maladjusted women would defy their natural role by avoiding marriage and motherhood. These very same experts, however, placed little faith in women's allegedly natural maternal abilities. Harping on the dangers of both maternal overprotection and maternal rejection, they pointed to poor mothering as the cause of everything from homosexuality to autism to schizophrenia.[4]

How such critiques and prescriptive literature affected actual mothers is difficult to determine. Even when speaking of the comparatively privileged women who were the primary audience for advice literature on mothering, it would be wrong to assume that readers embraced experts' precepts in a wholesale manner. Yet such literature should not be entirely dismissed, for it both shaped and reflected cultural norms, and its influence can often be detected in women's personal correspondence and private writings.[5] Those who internalized psychological experts' contradictory messages often suffered in ways that remain difficult to articulate. Nonetheless, an overweening emphasis on the repressive aspects of postwar therapeutic culture has obscured some of its less immediately apparent implications. Because such experts viewed maternal overprotection and dominance as so pernicious, and because they placed such a high premium on the cultivation of emotional autonomy (particularly for boys), they in effect opened up cultural and psychic space for some mothers to conceptualize themselves in more individualistic terms. In other words, they promoted new ideas about motherhood that helped to make the maternal role more compatible with liberal individualism.

The women who embraced therapeutic messages about motherhood tended to be overwhelmingly white, well-educated, and middle- to upper-middle-class mothers. Prior to marriage and motherhood, many had experienced satisfaction in the workforce and had acquired skills that had earned them a certain degree of recognition. Exposure to psychological thinking encouraged these women to think of themselves as individuals as well as mothers, to value self-fulfillment, and to view their unhappiness as a problem to be solved. In this manner, it prepared them to respond favorably to the indictment of suburban motherhood and domesticity that Betty Friedan would level in her groundbreaking 1963 bestseller, *The Feminine Mystique.*

THE ORIGINS AND IDEOLOGY OF THE MORAL MOTHER

The early nineteenth century witnessed the flourishing of a veritable cult of motherhood, particularly in the industrializing North.[6] As mobility increased, extended familial networks grew more strained, and as artisanal households declined, middle-class Americans increasingly elevated the home into an arena of private retreat, removed from the corrupt worlds of commerce and politics. Clergymen and domestic writers portrayed the mother as the "angel of the house" who eschewed corporal punishment and instead used the power of her love to instill self-discipline and lead her children to Christ. A mother's duties were "time-consuming and exhausting": she had to maintain "constant moral vigilance" until that hazardous moment when her children left the parental home.[7] Even then, the importance of maternal influence did not diminish, for affective ties to the mother served as a rudder, guiding the adult throughout his or her life course.

From a contemporary perspective, several aspects of the ideology of moral motherhood are particularly striking. Foremost among these is the notion that mothers should seek to emotionally bind their children to them by forging a "silver cord." This process was deemed particularly essential with boys, since their greater freedom meant that they would eventually be exposed to the sins and temptations of the public realm. The mother's ultimate goal was to raise a son who would strive to be "the man my mother thinks I am"—a son who would never disappoint or hurt her. The popular late-nineteenth-century poem, "Like Mother, Like Son," which continued to appear in popular poetry anthologies through the 1930s, perfectly expressed this sentiment:

> Do you know that your soul is of my soul such a part,
> That you seem to be fibre and core of my heart?
> None other can pain me as you, dear, can do,
> None other can please me or praise me as you.
> Remember the world will be quick with its blame
> If shadow or strain ever darken your name.

"Like mother, like son" is a saying so true
The world will judge largely the "mother" by you.[8]

This mother was not interested in fostering her son's emotional independence or cultivating his individuality; on the contrary, she sought to impress herself indelibly upon him, so that his emerging character would incorporate her loving yet admonishing voice.

A second notable aspect of moral motherhood is its unabashed celebration of impassioned, even romantic mother-son relationships. Middle-class Americans did not perceive maternal influence as a threat to emergent manhood; instead, they viewed mother love as the substance from which manhood was forged. Thus, a mother might unself-consciously call her son "lover boy," while a son could refer to his mother as "my best girl" without fear of mockery.[9] Such practices persisted well into the twentieth century. For example, when the future Supreme Court justice Frank Murphy served overseas during World War I, he signed his effusive letters to his mother with a string of x's. "I will be home with you in a few days and we will walk and talk just like the lovers we are," he wrote in one, while in another he pined, "Tonight if I could sit near you or brush your hair or stroke your forehead or just feel your presence I would be in paradise."[10]

Murphy's devotion to his mother may have been unusual even by the standards of the time, but the cultural milieu clearly condoned such sentiments. Consider the following lines from "The Little Mother," a poem that appeared in 1918 in *Stars and Stripes*, the Army's main newspaper:

How I long for your smiles of gladness
  That are haunting my mem'ry still,
And the love in your eyes beseeching
  Even now makes my pulses thrill. . . .
The caress of your hair, soft silver,
  On my cheek how I fain would feel,
And from lips that are soft as roses,
  A sweet kiss I would like to steal.[11]

The poet could express this frank desire for physical contact with his mother because he retained a pre-Freudian sensibility, unaffected by the increasingly prevalent belief that an unusually strong mother-son attachment signaled an unresolved Oedipal crisis.

A final component of moral motherhood that marks its distance from contemporary views is the positive valuation it placed on self-sacrifice and martyrdom. Today, the mother-as-martyr is often a figure of exasperation or comic relief, the implication being that she engages in transparent emotional manipulation to gain her children's attention or compliance. But the maternal martyr did not always elicit such reactions. In the nineteenth and early twentieth centuries, countless paeans glorified mothers' willingness to sacrifice and suffer for their children, as did an 1867 *Godey's Lady's Book* when it characterized mother love as "chiefly a sorrow bearing love."[12] This conception of motherhood reflected Victorian Americans' belief in the redemptive nature of suffering more broadly, but it was grounded in an appreciation of the physical perils of motherhood. As late as the 1930s, a majority of women in the United States still endured childbirth without pain relief, and high rates of maternal death continued to shame the medical profession.[13] These realities lent weight to the religious and martial analogies that many Americans employed to describe motherhood in general and childbirth in particular.

Historians have tended to assume that the ideology of moral motherhood fell victim to the rise of "scientific motherhood" and an assault on Victorian cultural ideals that began near the turn of the century and reached full swing by the 1920s.[14] Yet traditional and modern conceptions of motherhood vied for dominance in mainstream American culture throughout the interwar period and beyond. Even as psychological experts denounced cloying and overbearing mothers, popular culture continued to draw audiences with highly sentimental dramatizations of maternal self-sacrifice. In the long run, however, the moral mother could not withstand the rise of therapeutic culture. Her martyrdom was too much at odds with the modern quest for self-fulfillment; her intense identification with her children posed too great a barrier to individuation; her sentimentality and uncompromising morality proved too easy a target for sophisticated modernists. Censuring displays of "smother love" and promoting new theories of child rearing, psychological experts led the charge to reform maternal ideals and practices.

DISMANTLING THE MORAL MOTHER

After World War I, experts of various stripes displayed an almost reflexive suspicion of maternal influence. Psychoanalysts and behaviorists alike developed a "stinging critique of American motherhood" during the interwar period that practitioners within child guidance clinics readily embraced.[15] They routinely indicted a certain type of woman: the "overprotective" or possessive mother who stymied her son's psychological development while relegating her husband to the sidelines.[16] Whereas intimate mother-son relationships had previously been thought to facilitate the development of a self-governing, manly character, by the 1920s, numerous experts identified failure to separate from the mother as the primary threat to nascent manhood.

According to behaviorists, who dominated child-rearing advice in the 1920s and early 1930s, the solution resided in strict schedules and limited physical contact. In the best-known child-rearing manual of the era, *Psychological Care of Infant and Child*, behaviorist John B. Watson depicted sentimental mother love as "a sex-seeking impulse" and shrilly decried mothers who coddled their children. "Treat them as though they were young adults," he urged. "Never hug and kiss them, never let them sit in your lap."[17] Watson's matraphobia was extreme, but most experts in the 1920s and 1930s agreed that greater distance and rationality should improve the mother-child relationship. As the psychologist and early childhood educator Ada Hart Artlitt put it, the home should be governed not by mother love but rather by the "kitchen time-piece."[18] Of course, behavioral norms change slowly, and attempts to restrain maternal affection struck many Americans at the time as quite novel. But middle-class women who fashioned themselves "modern mothers" could not easily shake off experts' admonitions. "It is to [many mothers] the most astonishing thing that mother love has been found by science inherently dangerous," noted one 1928 advice book, "and some of them grow panicky as they let the significance of the new teaching sink into their thoughts."[19]

This new wariness toward sentimental mother love is evident in society's mounting anxiety over male homosexuality. The belief that domineering or seductive mothers, coupled with passive fathers, caused homosexuality took root in a cultural landscape altered by Freudian views of female sexuality and children's psychosexual development. Acknowledgment of female desire went hand in hand with a more suspicious attitude toward impassioned mother love. As a result, maternal attitudes and behaviors that had once seemed praiseworthy began to appear disturbing or unnatural. Increasingly, a grown man's intense attachment to his mother signaled effeminacy, homosexuality, even political subversion.[20]

Finally, just as psychiatrists sought to temper effusive mother love, so they tried to puncture the ideal of maternal martyrdom. Advice literature urged mothers to "Take Off the Halo," warning that, "Self-made martyrs are unnecessary, tiresome people" who did "untold harm."[21] Psychiatrists and their allies not only jettisoned the concept of maternal self-sacrifice, they all but reversed the trajectory of indebtedness by emphasizing the fulfillment women derived from motherhood. "Every honest woman will tell you that she has been repaid in full every hour of her life for the so-called 'price of motherhood,'" asserted a writer for *Literary Digest* in 1932. "The obligation is all on the other side. How to pay the debt we owe to the young people who bring joy and hope into our lives is the mother's chief problem."[22]

The assault on moral motherhood reached its apex in Philip Wylie's 1942 best-selling polemic, *Generation of Vipers*, which introduced the word "momism" into the American lexicon. Picked up by psychiatrists and social scientists, "momism" signified both a familial and a social pathology. It referred to the supposedly archetypical American mom who henpecked her husband and dominated her children, as well as to a societal condition, in which the nation's irrational idealization of motherhood had drained it of masculine vigor. Wylie's mom was a monstrous creature determined to keep children trapped in emotional bondage. "'Her boy,' having been 'protected' by her love . . . is cushioned against any major step in his progress toward maturity," he wrote. "Mom steals from the generation of woman behind her . . . that part of her boy's personality which should have become the love of a female contemporary" and "transmutes it into sentimentality for herself."[23]

The momism critique can be viewed as an overwrought articulation of the by-then familiar arguments about maternal dominance advanced by psychoanalysts, psychiatrists, and other experts.[24] But it should also be understood as an emphatic repudiation of a maternal style that had once enjoyed widespread acceptance in mainstream American culture. By discrediting an older maternal style already fast becoming anachronistic, the momism critique helped to restrict the ways in which maternal influence could be celebrated in the postwar era.

THE THERAPEUTIC MOTHER

The political upheavals of the 1940s dramatically influenced attitudes toward mothering. Intent on curbing human aggression and irrationality, numerous experts began to focus on the mother-child relationship as the cornerstone of a peaceful and democratic order. Though their anxieties about overprotective mothers did not diminish, they increasingly turned their attention to the problems of maternal deprivation and rejection. Works such as Anna Freud's wartime studies of orphans and John Bowlby's influential World Health Organization report, *Maternal Care and Mental Health*, contributed to the growing belief that infants and young children flourished best when they received intensive, uninterrupted maternal care.[25] The scheduled withholding of such solicitude, previously regarded as a sound approach to the irrational impulses of mother and child alike, was reinterpreted as a denial of legitimate need—a denial that actually produced the dependent tendencies that it sought to prevent. Moreover, in the wake of fascism, the behaviorist view of infants as blank slates ceased to appear like a positive good; the notion that parents should "condition" their children's "reflexes" seemed all too compatible with a totalitarian agenda that sought to press individuals into a common mold.[26] Most psychological experts in the postwar era instead conceptualized the infant as an already nascent individual who would naturally develop into a reasonable, democratic citizen, so long as his or her physical and emotional needs were lovingly met.

Thus, the mother's most important role, psychological experts of various schools agreed, was to equip her children with a sense of security by providing warm and loving physical care. This particular conception of mother love privileged neither the mother's intellect—her conscientious acquisition of the knowledge and skills of a "scientific" mother, nor her personal character—her ability to use the power of mother love to ensure her children's moral rectitude. Instead, the model that emerged in the 1940s and 1950s tended to reduce maternal love to the expression of psychological and biological drives; commentators portrayed it as a force so natural that it all but secreted from the maternal body. "Mother love is a good deal like food," the psychoanalyst Margaret Ribble explained in 1943. "It has to be expressed regularly so that the child expects it; a little at a time, and frequently, is the emotional formula. When it is given in this way, independence, rather than dependence, is fostered."[27]

As scholars have shown, this new permissive child-rearing ideology—articulated most famously in 1946 by Dr. Benjamin Spock—actually intensified maternal obligations by requiring mothers to provide care "on demand" rather than following a schedule.[28] What has been less noted is that the same prescriptions simultaneously diminished the maternal role by deeming the benefits of mother love as concentrated in the earliest years of life. Take, for example, Ferdinand Lundberg and Marynia Farnham's 1947 bestseller, *Modern Woman: The Lost Sex*, a work often cited as a particularly egregious illustration of oppressive postwar gender ideology. Whereas the authors waxed lyrical about motherhood as women's natural destiny, their characterization of the ideal mother reveals that they actually sought to delimit the maternal role after a child's first few years:

> Is she so very wise? No, hers is not wisdom in the sense of intellectual knowledge. She just likes her children. . . . Being in balance, she feels no need to

> inquire into every detail of their lives, to dominate them. Instead, she watches with somewhat detached interest to see what each one takes to. . . . She does not fuss over them. If they are too cold, too hot, too wet, hungry or lonesome, they let her know it and she meets the need. Otherwise she leaves them pretty much to their own devices, although keeping a watchful eye on them.[29]

This was a far cry from the moral mother who sought to bind her children with cords of love to scrutinize the state of their souls. In fact, Farnham and Lundberg avoided any reference to love—their ideal mother merely liked her children—presumably because they regarded maternal love as potentially so fraught.

Some experts went so far as to argue that mothers should cultivate identities beyond the home to prevent them from overidentifying with their children. The woman with a "strong" personality needed "larger worlds to conquer than her home and family," wrote psychologist Anna Wolf in 1941, if only because "[h]er energies need deflection."[30] Similarly, a 1945 radio show urged listeners to guard against "too much mother love" by leading "a full, normal life" that included outside "interests" and "friends her own age."[31] A psychoanalyst quoted in *American Weekly* even argued that the woman who felt confined and depressed by homemaking should seek full-time employment. "She can't try to please friends, neighbors or relatives. She has to please herself *first*, then try to please others."[32]

Such advice suggests that the widespread discontent among white, middle-class women that informed the reception of *The Feminine Mystique* cannot be attributed solely to a gender ideology that exiled women to the domestic realm. The dilemma confronting such women is more accurately described as a double bind. Although largely denied career opportunities and still expected to view themselves primarily as mothers and housewives, these women now found themselves immersed in a therapeutic culture that emphasized the importance of fostering independence and individuation—which in turn meant viewing themselves as autonomous beings.

BETTY FRIEDAN AND HER READERS ON MOTHERHOOD

Friedan argued that the postwar feminine mystique "derived its power from Freudian thought," and she devoted an entire chapter to portraying Freud as a "prisoner of his time" when it came to women. Yet she also praised the "basic genius of Freud's discoveries," and her contempt for popularized Freudianism never translated into a wholesale rejection of psychoanalysis. As she explained,

"I question its use, not in therapy, but as it has filtered into the lives of American women through the popular magazines and the opinions and interpretations of so-called experts."[33]

This careful parsing likely reflects Friedan's own positive experiences with psychoanalysis or psychoanalytic therapy. At two crucial points in her life, therapy allowed her to affirm an independent identity that felt threatened by the intensity of the mother-child relationship. As a recent college graduate in the 1940s, it helped her separate from her own mother and renounce her mother's bourgeois values. Then, as a young mother in the early 1950s, it allowed her to acknowledge and pursue her ambitions as a writer amid the relentless demands of child rearing. In one session, her psychoanalyst, William Menaker, interpreted a dream about a male journalist not as evidence of "penis envy" but rather "as a message to take my own writing more seriously."[34] Friedan's experiences proved so positive that in 1958, after signing a contract for what would become *The Feminine Mystique*, she sought Menaker out again to propose a collaboration. Had her editor not nixed the idea, the name of an "eminent male psychoanalyst" might have graced the cover of *The Feminine Mystique*—a jarring and little-known detail that confounds her reputation as an ardent foe of psychoanalysis.[35]

Friedan's immersion in therapeutic culture is also apparent in her critique of suburban motherhood. Appropriating Abraham Maslow's theory of self-actualization, she argued that motherhood and homemaking could not serve as the basis for a mature and independent identity and that women who confined their energies to the mother-housewife role ultimately harmed both their loved ones and themselves. In advancing this argument, she cited numerous works by psychological experts and social scientists. What she did that they did not, however, was draw out the logical implications of their findings in a forceful and systematic way: if suburban mothers had become mired in psychopathology, then for everyone's sake, they should be liberated from the all-consuming demands of domesticity. "The only way for a woman, as for a man, to find herself, to know herself as a person, is by creative work of her own. There is no other way."[36]

Friedan famously received hundreds of letters from women who thanked her for writing *The Feminine Mystique*. Less well known is the fact that she also received hundreds of critical letters from women who encountered her ideas in popular women's magazines that ran excerpts of the book. Both groups of women appear to have been overwhelmingly white and middle-class; as bell hooks has observed, Friedan wrote as if working-class women and women of color "did not exist," making "the plight of white women like herself synonymous with a condition affecting all American women."[37] But despite similar demographic profiles, the two groups differed markedly on key issues, including the attitudes they expressed toward psychological expertise and therapeutic culture.

Fans of *The Feminine Mystique* frequently referred to psychological concepts and employed psychological language in their letters. Some even recounted how their feelings of emptiness and unhappiness had led them to seek out therapy. A former journalist and mother of two young children wrote,

> I had even resorted to a psychiatrist, who kept asking me if I was sure there wasn't "Another Man" involved, and whether I really loved my children! All I knew was that I had to be ME . . . but when I took time off to be myself—writing occasional feature articles or going to New York by myself for a week-end, I was enough brain-washed by the wretched feminine mystique to feel rather defiant and guilty about it. Reading your book has given me a whole new zest for life.[38]

This woman clearly received no help from her clueless psychiatrist; she needed Friedan's feminist message to realize that she should start "taking my writing seriously, instead of reconciling myself to being an amateur." But her basic therapeutic orientation—evident in the license she felt to express her need "to be ME"—had prepared her to be receptive to Friedan's feminist critique.

Women who embraced Friedan's message questioned the assumption that a "good mother" had to be a selfless nurturer, always available to meet her children's physical and emotional needs. Like Friedan, they argued that the imperatives of full-time homemaking actually prevented women from cultivating the healthy individualism that effective mothering required. "Becoming a person one's self [*sic*] is a big step in recognizing the uniqueness in others," wrote one woman. "If your only reason for living is that 'somebody needs me' this can be pretty dreadful in the family setting," another opined. "You have to shift over to 'I need me,' if you want to stop swallowing others in your need to be needed."[39] These women argued, in essence, that women had an obligation to focus on their own self-development, lest they wreak havoc on their children's emotional lives.

In contrast, Friedan's critics viewed her emphasis on personal fulfillment as appallingly self-centered and incompatible with good mothering. They did not wholly reject psychological authority; in fact, some buttressed their defense of full-time motherhood by referencing experts who claimed an association between maternal absence and juvenile delinquency. However, when they felt discouraged or restless, they did not turn to therapy; they sought sustenance in God or tried to summon a sense of duty. "It seems to me that if these trapped, frustrated women would put as much faith in God as they put in their psychoanalyst, their problems would be greatly reduced," ventured one woman. The "frustrated neurotic . . . usually has no one but herself to blame," wrote another. "She feeds her discontent by asking, 'Who am *I*?' and 'What shall *I* do with *my* life?' Never wondering, 'What can I do for my husband, family, community?' or 'How can I serve my God?' "[40] These women eschewed therapy not so much because they questioned its efficacy, but because they considered the pursuit of self-realization a frivolous and self-centered goal that diverted people from familial, civic, and religious obligations.

The disdain with which Friedan's critics regarded therapeutic culture is reflected in their discussions of the mother-child relationship. They referred more frequently to maternal "responsibilities" and "duties" than did Friedan's fans, while placing less emphasis on the importance of "enjoying" their children. They also appeared more willing to accept the notion that a child's deepest needs might sometimes conflict with his or her mother's deepest desires. Indeed, they scoffed at the notion that a child benefited most from a mother who was happy and fulfilled, even if this required her to be away from home most of the day. "A child cannot live on all this great education from his mother or appreciate her great talents," wrote one young mother. "He cannot survive without warmth, love, understanding and a secure home life. And no one can convince me that with a mother home only a few hours of the day she can provide this love and secure home."[41] Believing that children needed and deserved their mothers' loving presence, Friedan's critics argued that women should master or repress their frustrations rather than seek outside employment, especially during their children's early years.

Feminist critiques of the late 1960s and 1970s portrayed the psychological professions as such powerfully oppressive forces that one might reasonably conclude that those women most engaged with psychological thinking and practice would have been, from a feminist perspective, most in need of consciousness-raising. Yet Friedan's correspondence suggests the reverse was true: familiarity with and openness to therapeutic culture correlated closely with a willingness to criticize prevailing gender ideology. Midcentury psychological experts supported a restrictive ideal of womanhood, to be sure, but they also encouraged individuals to adopt a therapeutic orientation toward the self—toward one's private problems and needs—that would ultimately lead many women to take their feelings of dissatisfaction seriously, even when that meant violating the tenets of well-adjusted femininity.

It is instructive to remind oneself that the most ardent critics of psychiatry and psychoanalysis during the 1950s and early 1960s were not left-wing intellectuals, feminists, gay rights activists, and antipsychiatrists, as would later be the case. Rather, they were traditionalists who opposed the rise of therapeutic culture because they believed that it threatened religious authority and traditional gender roles. In regard to the cultural construction of motherhood, these critics were clearly on to something. The ideology of moral motherhood never effectively restricted white, middle-class women to the home—many in fact deployed it to exercise moral authority in the public realm through church groups and voluntary associations—but it did sharply limit how these mothers could define themselves and the activities they could pursue. The demystification of motherhood that psychiatrists and psychologists spearheaded was not without cost, but it was a necessary precondition for the rise of a popular feminist movement that would gain women greater equality by championing their individual rights.

CHAPTER 6

Confessions

Badia Ahad

Given the power that models of Victorian womanhood have wielded within the black communal sphere well into the twenty-first century, black women have historically lacked safe spaces, like the privacy of the analyst's office, in which to represent themselves as subjects that possess sexual, erotic, and/or queer desires. Historically, traditional therapeutic practices have allowed only elite white women the privilege to establish a sense of interiority within the context of the clinician's couch, making private psychotherapy and the "self-preoccupation" it signifies "seem chic."[1] But other forums designed to extend therapy to the masses did emerge. Beginning in the 1930s, the publishing world became increasingly dominated by the emergence of the confessions genre, specifically geared towards working-class women between the ages of seventeen and thirty. Specifically, confessions magazines, as George Gerbner has argued, were marketed precisely to those "persons who probably had never before read magazines, persons with little education or purchasing power, persons whom other publishers had neglected because they were not the sort that advertisers were especially interested in reaching."[2] In addition, these magazines were explicit about the social and psychical role they played in the lives of women who "never were, and never will be, the avid readers of textbooks nor the patients of psychiatrists."[3] Because of their unwillingness or inability to participate in what might be considered more conventional spaces of therapeutic culture, the confessions magazine offered a site in which working-class women without access or interest in formal modes of therapy engaged in a subversive, yet mediated, brand of self-help. Although they would never be "the patients of psychiatrists," these readers were intensely aware of themselves as subjects with interior lives and emotions worth examining, and the confessions genre provided an ideal outlet in which these women were able to establish their own brand of therapeutic culture.

During the 1940s and 1950s, black men and women were largely denied access to the psychiatrist's office. Even public mental health facilities discriminated against African Americans, offering them only cursory outpatient services or refusing to see them at all.[4] The sobering distance between black and therapeutic communities has a long and sordid history dating, arguably, back to Thomas Jefferson's 1781 assertion that blacks hid "expressions of every passion" behind "that immovable veil of black,"[5] which led to his purportedly scientific conclusion that they also lacked sentience. In the face of such persistent assumptions, the confessions magazine offered a kind of virtual community to black women, offering them a space to explore their private, emotional lives in a way similar to that of wealthy white women who were the "actual patients of psychiatrists" and a chance to affirm a psychological identity that they had been denied historically.

The idea that African Americans lacked an evolved emotional and psychological life, the exclusion of black women from traditional modes of therapy, and the consistent effort to restrict African American women to codified modes of behavior have collectively created particular silences around black women's sexuality such that, as Tricia Rose explains, "sisters have kept quiet in public for ample reasons."[6] While Rose offers "beauty parlors, kitchens, and health clubs" as private/public safe spaces in which black women have shared their stories, this essay takes a more historical turn to consider black women's negotiations with sexuality in the confession magazine, which functioned as one of the few therapeutic sites available to them. Owing to their exclusion from legitimized venues of therapeutic culture as a result of both racist practices and economic limitations, it is precisely in the space of the confessions magazine that their emotional and psychical lives acquire a greater meaning through communal sharing and exchange.

Taking its cues from mainstream confessions magazines like *True Story*, *True Confessions*, *Real Romance*, and *Experiences*, Johnson Publishing Company published its first issue of *Tan Confessions* in November 1950. Specifically addressing an African American female audience, John H. Johnson meant to create a black confessions magazine that conveyed "that part of everyday living concerning the happiness and triumphs, the sorrows and suffering of the troubled heart."[7] In his letter from the editor, Johnson makes clear the magazine's impetus to reveal to the American public another dimension of African American life, which is "ignored completely by white publications and only discussed in most Negro publications in terms of tension and violence that get into police and court records."[8] Aiming then to counter the master narrative perpetuated by popular media, Johnson Publishing Company sought to document the "emotional, intimate" lives of working-class black women in a public and accessible format.

In almost every respect the stories in *Tan Confessions*, which ran between November 1950 and September 1952 and eventually reached a circulation of nearly 300,000, mirrored those in magazines like *True Confessions* and *True Story* in that they all presented "true-to-life" narratives of scandal, sex, and intrigue from the view of the middle and working class.[9] Even the moralizing undercurrent of these stories was similar across publications, although the implications of such codes of decency proved very different for the target audience of *Tan Confessions*. While the latter offered a much needed space of therapeutic culture for black women, it also had to contend with the danger of reproducing dehumanizing stereotypes about black female sexuality—stereotypes that would jeopardize the very sense of interiority that an honest discussion of sexual desire was designed to produce. Because, as Candice Jenkins rightly notes, "the perceived inability of African-Americans to conform to middle-class understandings of family and appropriate sexual behavior has hardly diminished since its origins during the antebellum period," the insistent requisite for African Americans and black women in particular to assert and reassert rather conservative principles of sexuality and decorum has persisted.[10] In its focus on the sexual exploits of black women *Tan Confessions*, however unwittingly, normalized what might be considered more deviant sexual practices and structured a unique discourse around black sexuality that had yet to be explored in the realm of print culture. Thus, while *Tan Confessions* aimed to caution working-class black women about the hazards of being sexually loose, it also invited these women to express and share their sexual narratives, thereby allowing an open exchange around the previously silenced subject of black female sexuality.

Each issue of *Tan Confessions* contained ads asking readers to submit their stories. The advertisements informed readers that they "do not have to be a trained writer to contribute" as it "is the dramatic interest in the story that TAN CONFESSIONS is interested in rather than the style." The ads, however, also remind readers to use fictitious names and caution against plagiarizing. While it can be argued that such an open invitation leaves ample room for writers to create rather than "confess" their own dramatic exploits, it is clear that *Tan Confessions* sought to function as a space in which women, regardless of education or class status, could anonymously share their true-to-life tales of indiscretion. Although the call for contributions does not explicitly state that readers' stories should feature illicit content, there does exist an underlying pressure to produce racy narratives, especially given the magazine's existent emphasis on subjects like same sex affairs, "threesomes," infidelity, and interracial marriage. Despite the tendency of every provocative story to end with the reformation of monogamous heterosexual unions, the representation of such narratives makes visible the more "unrespectable" dimensions of black female sexuality that historically have been subject to a rather thorough and conscientious process of erasure. Readers' ability to "confess" their moral and sexual transgressions through narrative and, more significantly, to detail how they overcame their various dilemmas worked not only to further the formation of community but also to serve as a crucial point of identification for other readers.

By publishing stories written by its readers, *Tan Confessions*, like most confession periodicals, collapsed the boundary between the writer, who generally functions as authority, and reader, who passively takes in information. Instead, the confessional format, specifically its use of first-person narration, presented its stories as though the reader and the writer were one and the same (which they often were), thereby enabling the illusion of a dialogue among peers, if not friends. As Roseann Mandziuk has noted, because "the exact relationship between reader and writer lacks specificity, the first person address of the stories can promote additional empathy and recognition of correspondences."[11] Contrary to the hierarchical relationships that constitute most confessional discourses, namely, that of the priest and the parishioner and the analyst and the analysand, the confessions magazine relaxes such positions of authority to encourage instead a symbiotic relationship between reader and writer. Moreover, confessional magazines engaged a variety of textual practices like the first-person narrator, for example, to "encourage readers to approach the confessional in the therapeutic, adaptive mode."[12]

In his first letter to readers, Johnson provides a vision of the kind of collaborative dynamic he imagines between the magazine's readers and its editors, noting that "[w]e want to emphasize from the start that TAN CONFESSIONS is your magazine and we want you to join in the planning of its features. We would like you to help in its writing too for primarily our main function is to act as a forum where you and the editors can sit down and exchange true experiences for the benefit of all."[13] Although the magazine's staff of professional editors revised the contributed stories for consistency's sake and to honor Johnson's directive to "dignify" the confessions magazine by crafting such narratives as morality tales, the subject and substance of these accounts originated with articles submitted by black working-class women, thereby providing them unprecedented access to the public sphere and, more precisely, to a larger community of black women.[14]

In her discussion of the communal nature of the popular confession magazine *True Story*, Kathy Newman writes,

> *True Story*'s ads, stories, and nonfictional portions revealed . . . a world in which women worked, raised children, and supported their husbands. . . . This was a world made up of people who were on the bottom: socially, economically, racially, and in terms of gender. And, while *True Story* did not advocate collective action, it did provide them with a communal forum: a place to meet.[15]

Although the primary audience of *Tan Confessions* was African American women and many of its stories were racially inflected, it shared with *True Story* the imperative to create a cultural medium for those women who were virtually ignored by mainstream print culture. Working-class women, in particular, were drawn to the collective and cathartic imperatives of confessions magazines. Such a forum worked to assuage their feelings of isolation, social insecurity, and inadequacy. Moreover, such communality reveals the significance of the print magazine in facilitating mid-twentieth-century discussions among women about their domestic lives, their aspirations, their fears, and their innermost feelings. The impulse to confess then emerges in the print magazine as an act of therapeutic catharsis, an absolution of guilt, and a means of forming community.

Mirroring the social and psychical crossroads constituted by the politics of respectability and the politics of the erotic, *Tan Confessions* both affirmed and undermined accounts asserting what some may describe as the liberated sexual subjectivities of black women. Taken individually, the stories in *Tan Confessions* eagerly advance the social and sexual conservatism of the post–World War II era. But collectively these true-to-life narratives offer a discourse of the bizarre, the absurd, and the deviant and provide a public, social space in which African American women proffer alternative insights into black sexuality. By providing a rather schizophrenic schema of black deviance and domesticity, *Tan Confessions* presents the black female subject as an embodiment simultaneously of sexual excess and sexual lack. *Tan Confessions* epitomized this conflict in its attempt to expose the private lives and reflections of black women while at the same time advocating adherence to conventional gender roles and the institution of marriage. Although the magazine largely relied on the discourse of normalcy, it was also awash with shocking narratives of women who contemplated extramarital affairs (with men and other women), women and men who dared to marry interracially, "swingers," and young girls involved in street gangs and "shake dancing." While these stories are fascinating reads in and of themselves, collectively they offer an alternative framework of therapeutic culture especially reserved for black women whose expressions of and negotiations with marriage, sex, and sexuality emerge as a desire not only to confess but also to exist as part of a community of black women who "desperately need to hear and tell."[16]

Responses to an African American confessions magazine among the black community were mixed. The Letters to the Editor in *Tan Confessions* are especially compelling because there appeared a demand among its readers for the magazine to perform a particular kind of community work, specifically by printing stories that featured redeeming aspects of black culture. Mainstream magazines like *True Story* and *Real Confessions* could safely provide steamy accounts of white women's sexual exploits because white women's bodies had not been treated as biologically overdetermined and any deviance from sexual norms was read as individual aberration rather than genetic disposition. But *Tan Confessions* could not operate with such hubris. In the first four months of its publication, *Tan Confessions* featured letters from readers who both supported and condemned the magazine. In these correspondences readers contributed to the long-standing discourse of black respectability and used *Tan Confessions* as a vehicle to comment on their place within it. One reader, in particular, noted that "[i]t wasn't bad enough that you put all that smut into *Ebony* but now I read where you are going to have a whole magazine devoted to sex."[17] Others warned, "Let me say now—even before I see your rag in print—that I object to seeing this kind of publication aimed at the Negro market. Confession magazines exist merely to titillate the sense of unreality common to uneducated people."[18]

Responding to the mere rumor of a black confessions magazine, many would-never-be readers abhorred the very idea that Johnson Publications would print a magazine that detailed the sexual lives of black women. At the same time, supporters of *Tan Confessions* expressed sentiments like the following: "I can say with sincerity that it has made quite an impression. . . . By that I mean as I read the frank, to-the-point stories and articles about Negro love problems, sex and careers, it gave me a feeling of realness."[19] In both the letters of support and condemnation, an emphasis on the magazine's responsibility to the "community" was evident: some readers threatened to encourage a ban of the magazine at their places of employment and the public libraries, while others believed that their subscription was an act of patronage in support of a black-owned publication.

The articles in *Tan Confessions* were meant to serve as expositions of women's domestic experiences, but many of the stories were obviously designed to inform other women how to resolve their similar marital and/or sexual dilemmas. A number of the stories feature husbands who are "frigid," "docile," "insecure," and "sterile." The magazine was peppered with advertisements geared toward men for products and manuals that will help them please their wives (presumably purchased by their wives as "gifts"). One advertisement for a sex life manual reads, "many men (even those who have been married a long time) don't get half the delight because **they don't know the knack of sexual intercourse**!" (bold original).[20] The active pathologizing of the male figure in marital relationships has the effect of portraying the woman as one who must consistently make decisions and act in her own best interests. She is forced to search out and bring together the psychical, social, sexual, and sometimes economic resources necessary to resolve a given problem.

"Do Good Husbands Make Unhappy Wives?" aptly illustrates some of the burdens that were placed upon black women during this period. In the piece, Gussie recounts the experience of her courtship with her husband, Ralph. Reproducing a classic psychoanalytic scenario, Gussie theorizes that as a result of her "tyrannical" father, she "vowed that when she got married, [she] would marry a man who was willing to grant [her] a lot more authority than Dad allowed Mother."[21] Gussie found a willing and submissive partner in Ralph, although the story is framed around her tendency to question her decision to be the "boss" of the family. Gussie's assertiveness is read as a disturbing reordering of conventional gender roles and as part and parcel of a psychological problem Gussie must work to overcome. She attempts to "cure" her domineering ways by "reading articles," "consulting books," and "talking with a friend who had some marriage counseling."[22] As part of her research, Gussie independently consults the Institute of Family Relations and finds that the "happiest unions are those in which full democracy is practiced between husband and wife. The next happiest marriages were those where the husband ran the family . . ."[23] The essay, while advising all women to appreciate their husbands' kindness and not to mistake it for "weakness," has a lot to say about the strategies the writer employs in order to come to terms with her own self-admitted superiority complex.

Gussie's attempt to work through her authoritarian ways by consulting psychological "texts" in the form of books, national institutions, articles, and friends in therapy, reveals a great deal about the therapeutic process that black working-class women, without means and access to traditional forms of therapy, underwent in order to resolve psychological and social problems. By extension, the readers of such texts become the beneficiaries of the writer's therapeutic process. Moreover, the narratives in confessions magazines are strategically meant to engender a sense of sympathetic identification among its readers, particularly among the nouveau middle-class who, as Gerbner notes, "find the white collar world strange, uncomfortable."[24] The "new women" who are "often bewildered in their new roles . . . have a burning interest in 'reading how other women—like themselves—solved their problem.'"[25] This mode of identification is important because it positions the reader as one who consumes confession narratives not solely for their entertainment value but also for the life strategies these narratives offer, thereby demonstrating the magazines' therapeutic impulses. According to Gerbner,

> obviously, "in the good confessions story the reader does not escape from life. She doesn't want to. She wants to read about an emotional life-experience that could have happened to her (and maybe did), or might happen to her next door neighbor." . . . This then is the mission of our writers: to give readers what they want plus constructive instructions on how to be happy.[26]

While many stories in *Tan Confessions* focus on conventional marital difficulties, others, like "Do Mail Order Marriages Work?" offer women alternative and unconventional strategies for finding love. Initially the narrator admits her skepticism about the process of meeting a man through the mail after having received a letter from a marriage correspondence club: "I should have been amused about the letter. I thought it the most idiotic thing with its sentimental phrases about 'curing those long hours,' 'drying up those tears on your pillow,' by allowing the club to send you for $1 a list of twenty-five eligible bachelors who had looks, in some cases money or thriving businesses."[27] But the author's position eventually shifts from doubt to receptiveness once she begins to receive letters from Sidney who will later become her husband. While the anonymity of the narrator suggests the larger social stigma around meeting men "virtually," the piece nevertheless emphatically recommends that women experiment with unorthodox methods in order to find the love they desire. Although the narrative still follows a neat trajectory leading towards a heterosexual union, it also quite daringly pushes the boundaries of black female respectability and invites readers to rethink the normative rules that ordinarily govern gender relations. The divulgence of intimate details about women's sexual and marital life distinguishes *Tan Confessions* as a public document of black women working out and working through matters of the heart that is both complicit with and antithetical to dominant "expert" discourses of sex and sexuality. The audience's ability to bear witness to and learn from their experiences demonstrates the extent to which the magazine allowed for a conversation around psychosocial and psychosexual norms, even in their complicity with the conservative impulses of the moment. In addition, stories like these serve as keen examples of how black women writing for *Tan Confessions* actively produced an alternative to the more traditional therapeutic cultures from which they had been excluded.

While most stories in *Tan Confessions* served to help their readers attain and maintain all of the accoutrements associated with middle-class respectability, specifically through an adherence to proper heterosexual unions, the magazine did contain stories in which the imperative to adhere to normative gender roles was more fraught. While the ability to challenge sexual norms and even have sexual problems has in fact historically been a signifier of middle-class privilege, it is important to note that this privilege has always been racialized. Because black sexuality has been pathologized historically, *Tan Confessions* risked validating cultural and scientific narratives of black deviance by publishing stories that detailed nonnormative sexual relations within black communities.

In the Letters to the Editor section of the December 1950 issue, a reader praises the magazine as "wonderful" but insists that "one story, 'Strange Love,' should have been stricken from the book."[28] He goes on to write that, "a story such as that is not accepted in our society, even if the facts are true." Such a response to "Strange Love" and its subject of homosexuality intimates the extent to which *Tan Confessions* tested the boundaries of social respectability by exploring sexualities deemed deviant, immoral, and inappropriate. "Strange Love" recalls the budding illicit love affair between Willa, a lesbian, and Yvonne, a married woman. In describing Willa, Yvonne notes, ". . . there was something about her—something intangible—that attracted me to her, something yielding and at once compelling . . . when I told her that I thought she was one of the most beautiful woman I had ever met, I felt easy saying it because she was."[29] The narrative makes consistent references to Yvonne's interest in Willa, referring to her as "arrestingly beautiful," a "strange beauty," and "entrancing." While, on the surface, such flattering references provide a rationale for Yvonne's attraction to another woman, the language of the narrative alternatively condemns Yvonne's feelings. While Willa's beauty is undeniable, it is also "haunting." Her eyes "sparkle bewitchingly" when she smiles, and though she is "effeminate enough to be charming," she has "features so delicately chiseled she was not at all unlike an extremely handsome man."[30] Like most stories featured in *Tan Confessions*, the narrative concludes with a "happy ending," that is, the woman's resolution to be a faithful and devoted wife. Thus the story serves as a cautionary tale for heterosexual women, alerting them to the potential dangers of acting upon their homosexual desires. Yet, in detailing the evolving friendship between Yvonne and Willa, the narrative also suggests that such same sex attraction can develop as a rather organic and natural process. Even though the writer attempts to undermine this desire by masculinizing Willa, Yvonne's attraction to her is undeniable.

A more progressive reading of the story could interpret Willa and Yvonne's relationship as only thwarted by the threat such a union would pose to Yvonne's comfortable domestic and social position. During the course of a weekend vacation with Willa, Yvonne gives in to her feelings and the two women have an intimate encounter. Yvonne explains that it "might have been the drinks or it might have been the enchantment of the night but I suddenly felt helpless, weak, and at once aroused."[31] After the trip, however, Willa distances herself from Yvonne, which effectively ends the burgeoning love affair:

> After [the vacation] Willa and I saw each other less and less. For her I had been a quest. I had been teased, tantalized, and cleverly won in the game she played. I was wrong—I know that now—stupidly wrong. I had been selfish, blind to all the things that had brought me real happiness—Claude, the hours he spent trying to earn enough to make me happy, even his stuffy old office. My conscience bothered me.[32]

Never in the story does Yvonne disavow her sexual attraction to Willa; nor is it Yvonne's decision to end their relationship. Once she believes that Willa has betrayed her, she then feels guilty and remembers her obligations to Claude, her hardworking, devoted husband. Ultimately, Yvonne regrets her adultery, but not her same-sex desire, and it is this element of the narrative that exemplifies the ways that *Tan Confessions* simultaneously undermines and advocates conventional modes of sex and sexuality. By transgressing the normative boundaries of gender and sexual relations *Tan Confessions* produces a discursive therapeutic culture that acknowledges black women's unique historical position within sexual discourses.

The conflation of sexual norms and "deviant" sexual exploits in *Tan Confessions* underscores the publication's fundamental tension, specifically its impetus to reinforce social and sexual standards through the expression of social and sexual acts of transgression. Ironically, in its attempt to instantiate a kind of sexual conservatism among its readers, *Tan Confessions* inadvertently created a productive space in which the politics of black female sexuality were addressed, debated, negotiated, and challenged and in which black women were able to freely articulate their own sexual lives. While these women's stories may have been deemed deviant within conservative black social and cultural spheres, it is noteworthy to consider how their confessions may have reflected a more popular and liberal idea of feminine sexuality outside of this space. Given the abundance of stories detailing the illicit affairs of white women made fashionable in mainstream confessions periodicals, black women's retelling of personal scandals oddly aligned them with those same women featured in publications like *True Story* and *Real Romance.* Ironically, while W.E.B. DuBois sought to equate black women with white women through the instantiation of Victorian notions of womanhood, *Tan Confessions* accomplished such equivalence through the very articulation of sexual desire and agency.[33]

Even when black women assumed the conservative stance put forth by previous dictums of black respectability, as many stories in *Tan Confessions* demonstrate, they were not incorporating these ideas wholesale but reconceiving them in ways that addressed the specificity of their racial and gendered subjectivities. Rather than being coercively shaped by the normative impulses of the black social order, the stories in *Tan Confessions* prove that therapeutic discourses are remarkably mobile and versatile—capable of functioning and assuming relevance within all kinds of communities, even those that they have historically marginalized and repressed. The confession narrative, in many respects, provided an outlet for and antidote to black women's "longing to tell" and, in the process, allowed for an expressive power that affirmed and validated their own psychological identities, all within the unlikely space of the print magazine.

CHAPTER 7

Radical

Michael E. Staub

In the course of the late 1960s and 1970s, members of the counterculture and New Left established alternative community therapy groups and "rap centers" across the United States to deal with all sorts of emotionally intense consequences of life in a messed-up world. These centers theorized and practiced a "new kind" of counseling and psychiatric treatment, dedicated (as the Radical Therapist [RT] Collective wrote in 1971) to the development of "a therapy that serves the people." The RT Collective motto announced, "Therapy means change not adjustment." To which the collective added with caustic bluntness, "When people are fucked over, people should help them and fight it, and then deal with their feelings."[1] In its manifesto, the RT Collective identified the many ways persons were being "socially traumatized" by their circumstances: by the chemical destruction and pollution of the environment, by the barrage of the mass media, by the tediousness of public education, by the war machine in Vietnam, and by the haunting gloom that hung over humanity from the threat of nuclear annihilation. The RT manifesto concluded, "Unless we as therapists and people can look beyond 'professional' issues and approach the social and political roots of suffering, we act as unknowing agents for the established order."[2] The influential Radical Psychiatry Center (RaP) in Berkeley, directed by psychotherapist Claude Steiner, espoused a similar philosophy toward mental problems: "People's difficulties have their source not within them but in their alienated relationships, in their exploitation, in polluted environments, in war and in the profit motive."[3]

This essay investigates how members of the counterculture and New Left radicals sought to use various forms of therapy to combat the emotional ills wrought by a society they believed had itself gone insane. Across the United States—from Seattle and Portland, Oregon, to Chicago, Ann Arbor, and Atlanta, to Manhattan, Brooklyn, and Cambridge, Massachusetts—radicals established "counterinstitutional" therapy rap centers by 1970. As a way to break down the power hierarchy between client and counselor, these centers emphasized the group encounter—which was also identified as one important key to the processes of making progressive social change.

As the editors observe in the Introduction, it is a central aim of this volume to "denaturalize" therapeutic culture. In this contribution focused on the radical therapy movement of the 1960s and 1970s, I seek to offer precisely this sort of denaturalization through a reconstruction of the cultural and historical circumstances that led to a passionately felt sense that such a new movement had to be established in the first place. But it is important as well to understand that those who called for such a new and explicitly radical therapy often had no clear roadmap for how to adapt and reformulate (or jettison entirely) normative therapeutic methods. Much of what radical therapists said and did was more a reaction against what they disliked and less a definite program for what they wanted to see accomplished in their own therapeutic encounters. As a result, there were likely as many ways to do radical therapy as there were radical therapists and radical therapeutic group settings.

RaP in Berkeley, for instance, operated workshops as well as discussion groups and training programs for radical therapists. It offered any number of group therapeutic exercises, such as the Trust Circle, which was intended to help the anxious individual "learn to trust the whole group in close contact."[4] It provided young people a place to crash for a couple of nights in case of emergencies, and it provided free drug counseling. Counselors came with training in law, psychiatry, and psychology and were dedicated to helping others "get their heads together." The aim in all instances was strictly to avoid the conventional (and always disingenuous) "games" that radical therapists were convinced were typically being played in more mainstream therapeutic relationships—games that denied the existence of both power and politics. What radical therapists sought "should be an end to therapy programs as they now exist," pronounced Michael Glenn and Richard Kunnes, cofounding members of the RT Collective. As they also proclaimed: "Everyone therapeutic, no one a therapist!"[5]

Yet such efforts inevitably led to further questions, such as, Could radical therapy really work to eliminate the psychic ills caused by a sick society? Or were therapeutic interventions just another means to "adjust" to that sick society—and thus inherently depoliticizing? Was it necessary first of all to treat the illness of the individual? Or was the initial step to change the social environment? What were the mechanisms of interaction between individuals and their social environment? And what should the direction of social change be? Radical therapists agreed that mental illness was socially produced and that madness was a political phenomenon. Nonetheless, radicals ultimately remained hopelessly confounded on the core question of how best—or even if—the many varieties of radical therapy they began to propagate could ever result in meaningful social change. However, and as this essay contends, the impact of radical therapy on mainstream therapy would be profound.

*

The 1960s and 1970s remain well remembered as the era when the hippies of the First World romanticized the rebels of the Third World, and Argentine guerrilla leader Che Guevara, Caribbean psychiatrist Frantz Fanon, and Vietnamese revolutionary Ho Chi Minh were heroes in the West. Historians of the era acknowledge the sixties as a moment when white styles mimicked black ones and an essay called "The Student as Nigger" (written by a white student) resonated powerfully with a generation of white middle-class progressive youth. Such were the political and emotional processes of cross identification. But there were other important—and no less complex—cross identifications in the sixties that have been largely erased from history: many radicals and members of the counterculture identified with those labeled mentally ill, arguing either that madness represented a sane response to life in an insane society or that those who claimed to be sane were actually the crazy ones.

A preoccupation with madness intensified as the Vietnam War escalated. The war made it appear as though the world had turned upside down, with the categories of "normal" and "abnormal" entirely inverted. The idea that dropping napalm on a civilian population could exemplify sanity anguished radical critics of the war; they were no less stunned that they frequently were the ones pathologized as unstable and deviant by war promoters and by the US government. Yet many antiwar protesters also came firmly to believe that going crazy could be a way to achieve greater mental and emotional health and well-being—and that breaking down might also be a potential means of breaking through. There were, in short, many reasons for "the insanity trip" (as cultural critic Susan Sontag would later sardonically term it) to acquire such prominence during the Vietnam War era.[6]

At times the argument was that true sanity meant resistance to the war and institutional racism and poverty. At other times the point was that what counted as sanity was evil, and craziness was the only appropriate moral response. Or, in yet a third variation, the contention was that society was making people crazy. As radical psychiatrist Joseph Berke wrote in the early 1970s, "We're up against a whole society that is systematically driving its members mad."[7] By this logic, those individuals who had been officially diagnosed as insane by psychiatric professionals could be recast by young radicals less as objects of pity or disgust or fear and more as object lessons. As Mitch Snyder, head of the Community for Creative Non-Violence in Washington, DC, put it in his passionate advocacy work on behalf of the homeless, "A psychotic episode is a socio-political event and not a medical event."[8]

As radicals politicized the category of mental illness, they increasingly began to identify mainstream psychiatrists as insidious defenders of a nefarious status quo. By the early seventies, for instance, it was taken to be simple truth by radicals that also many mental health services advocated and supported by more conventionally liberal therapists were not beneficent but repressive. Key instances of this were community mental health programs. Liberals championed these programs as the desirable outcome of federal efforts under President Kennedy to deliver psychiatric and counseling services directly to poor and underprivileged neighborhoods that had traditionally little or no access to such services. Radicals disagreed, however, increasingly seeing in community mental health programs just more subtle forms of social control. Professional therapists who worked with young people had only been trained to "depersonalize them, adjust them, change them against their will, or blackmail them by withholding achievement."[9] Social workers and psychologists as well as psychiatrists and educators in these communities served as "soft police" who helped to enact "a form of oppression far more destructive than that of the armed occupier." Brute force alone would never be enough to suppress political dissent because law and order tactics were not politically expeditious as a means to win the hearts and minds of the people. Kinder and gentler approaches were also required. The aim of psychiatric interventions in underprivileged communities was to weaken militant action, often by channeling the fervor and rage of the militants towards more individualistic goals—such as personal advancement. "Therapy" meant "co-opting" militant action.

From the radical perspective, mainstream therapeutic tools served to trick oppressed individuals by suggesting offers of material and psychic rewards if they abandoned their activism. This was the "psychologicalization of discontent," as a radical psychologist said to the Annual Meeting of the American Orthopsychiatric Association in San Francisco in early 1970. He concluded, "The problem of the ghetto is not one of psychopathology. To convince an individual in an oppressed community that the root of his problem is intrapsychic is to mystify him, pacify his legitimate and healthy anger, and surely, to oppress him."[10] For radicals, therefore, it became common sense to see the mental health industry in general as an enterprise which needed strenuously to be resisted.

In 1970, for instance, Howard Levy, a military doctor locked up in a federal penitentiary for refusing to train Green Berets in medical techniques (on the argument that it violated medical ethics and furthered the war effort), wrote from his prison cell that "psychiatrists play an essential role in, firstly, defining standards of behavior which serve the needs of repressive institutions and, secondly, in enforcing adherence to these standards."[11] Or to state the matter more generally, as radical psychiatrist Richard Kunnes put it self-critically, "Psychiatric services help, allow, or force people to adjust to an often repressive system." And it was the *system* that was the problem: "Staying within his licensed, professional role, the psychiatrist may seldom consider that the economic and social system is 'sick,' instead of the individual patient."[12] Likewise, when the American Psychiatric Association held its annual convention also in 1970, a radical newsletter distributed to attendees clearly linked the diagnosis of mental illness to larger political issues, noting that "we should be aware that we are serving to pacify our patients, and not to liberate them." Here again the war was never very far from anyone's mind. The statement added, "Pacification in the sense that the word is used in Vietnam—keep the natives quiet, keep the natives supporting the existing power structure, keep the natives apart and isolated."[13]

Madness, in short, became a crucial thematic obsession within the broader sixties move to theorize "the social"—structures, institutions, interpersonal relations. Many came devotedly to believe that the principal causes of mental illness could be unhealthy familial dynamics or socioeconomic stresses. Mental illness might also be traceable to the emotional debilitations of racism, militarism, or patriarchy. A great many cultural commentators (both inside and outside the psychiatric profession) argued with increasing fervor how crucial it was to understand that environment played a decisive role in the etiologies of mental disturbances and that it was the environment that needed to be changed.

*

Considerable energy in radical therapy centers went into attempts to politicize the deeply alienated persons who came through their doors. This too was in keeping with ideas promoted by Claude Steiner, who wrote the equation like this: "Oppression + Deception = Alienation." To which Steiner added a second equation: "Oppression + Awareness = Anger."[14] Feeling alienated was bad and lonely, but it could also potentially be turned into something positive and political when it was understood as stemming from societal dilemmas. Spreading the news about a sociopolitical diagnosis was itself part of the healing process; breaking down boundaries between individuals was also essential. The formula Steiner emphasized was this: "Liberation = Awareness + Contact," where "contact" meant interpersonal relations that fostered inner strength and bonded persons together in communal opposition to their oppression.[15]

In this way, mental health came to be understood by many radicals as directly linked to political activism as well. An African American woman in the 1960s succinctly informed an interviewer, "Black power is my mental health."[16] The story was similar for disaffected white students. Seymour L. Halleck, director of psychiatric health services at the University of Wisconsin at Madison in the sixties, also recommended that depressed or anxious teens and young adults help themselves heal by becoming more politically active and working on behalf of social justice.[17]

At the same time, another immensely influential offshoot of radical therapy began to emerge: feminist self-help groups and clinics sprang up everywhere in the course of the 1970s. In the Boston area alone, more than a dozen feminist therapy organizations were established. New groups like the Feminist Psychology Coalition in New York and the Feminist Therapy Collective of Philadelphia were organized "to provide individual and group therapy services promoting the growth of responsible, autonomous individuals who are able to choose and create options for living which transcend the traditional norms and boundaries of sex roles."[18] The Association for Women in Psychology—founded in 1969 to combat sexism within the ranks of the American Psychological Association—repeatedly called for a nationwide referral service designed to help women connect with feminist therapists wherever they might be. Feminist therapists came to be seen as vital to the process of overcoming the debilitating effects of society and social expectations on women's lives. As an early feminist therapist wrote, "The feminist-oriented therapist will have a sensitive awareness of what it means subjectively to be a woman in a male-dominated society, to be bewildered by the conflicting stereotypes and hounded by a sense that she's damned if she does (assert herself) and damned if she doesn't."[19]

Women's consciousness-raising (CR) groups, established already in the late 1960s, continued to flourish during the 1970s. The aim here too was to rewrite the traditional rules of psychotherapy so that women would be allowed to "stay in touch with our feelings," as Kathie Sarachild, who helped to originate the concept of CR groups, wrote in 1968. Sarachild added, "In our groups, let's share our feelings and pool them. Let's let ourselves go and see where our feelings lead us. Our feelings will lead us to ideas and then to actions."[20]

Feminist therapists adopted a potpourri of analytic techniques. Many turned to the holistic approach of Gestalt psychotherapy as promoted by Paul Goodman and Fritz Perls.[21] Gestalt emphasized the taking of responsibility for the choices one has made in one's life. The idea was that it was not particularly useful to muck around in a patient's childhood; what needed to be addressed was what was evident in the here and now. Gestalt feminist therapy encouraged women to understand their "personal power" and to "use more powerful and assertive language."[22] Others utilized the concept of a client-centered therapy developed by psychologist Carl Rogers, a key early progenitor of the human potential movement. Client-centered therapy posited that the therapist should not direct therapy toward a definitive end or interpretation but rather should function more as empathic facilitator and gentle guide. It further argued that each person had the capacity to control his or her own personal growth and that such personal growth was necessarily good.[23] Still other feminist therapists adapted concepts promoted by psychologist Abraham Maslow, who believed that self-actualization was the aim of all human beings. Maslow's popular *Toward a Psychology of Being* (1962) might well have been addressed directly to the future women's liberation movement: "The thing to do seems to be to find out what *you* are *really* like inside, deep down as a member of the human species and as a particular individual." Maslow also argued that mental illness was socially produced: "Sick people are made by a sick culture; healthy people are made possible by a healthy culture." He urged that "we must not fall into the trap of defining the good organism in terms of what he is 'good for' as if he were an instrument rather than something in himself, as if he were only a means to some extrinsic purpose."[24]

Feminist therapists were often drawn to the transactional analysis (TA) of psychiatrist Eric Berne, author of the hugely successful *Games People Play: The Psychology of Human Relationships* (1964). Berne had argued that individuals inevitably engaged with one another by playing roles. In Berne's view, these roles prevented people from achieving meaningful intimacy and authentic relationships. For feminists theorizing their own alienation from their marriages, their sexuality, and their lives, the focus of TA on "role playing" became a powerful and intuitively compelling strategy. Berne had said very little specifically about women in society; it had not been his purpose to reflect on the oppressive conditions confronted by women. But this did not prevent the wholesale adaptation of TA by feminist therapists.

The Radical Psychiatry Center in Berkeley, for instance, promoted women's problem-solving groups whose techniques were often derived from TA and based on methods elaborated by Berne in *Transactional Analysis in Psychotherapy* (1961) and *Games People Play*. Among other things, Berne had coined the concept of "stroking," which he had defined as one person's validation of another person's "*recognition-hunger*."[25] All persons needed strokes in social transactions—which meant that they needed to be heard and acknowledged; so in women's groups at the Radical Psychiatry Center, when two women paired off they were encouraged to ask for and provide affirmation from and to each other. A participant wrote in *Radical Therapist*, "The group observes closely, making sure that strokes are given openly and received in like manner."[26] As Berne had proposed, and his disciples elaborated, persons who received sufficient strokes in life were capable of greater spontaneity, awareness, and intimacy, but far too often individuals suffered from "stroke deficit." According to TA, individuals who did not receive enough strokes tended to play more games in life—and thus became more manipulative and difficult in their human interactions. And women suffered unduly from stroke deficit.

From a feminist perspective, mainstream (and overwhelmingly male) psychiatrists were agents of adjustment whenever they stated the answer to women's problems in terms that were private and individual rather than social and interpersonal. "The prevalence of psychotherapy in American life is another force working to stabilize oppression by reconciling women to their condition," several radical feminists wrote in 1971. They added, "All of us—women in particular—are encouraged to believe that our individual 'hang-ups,' although they are the results of objective social conditions, are to be treated as isolated, idiosyncratic cases."[27] This represented a constant refrain from feminists. "I am tired of thinking of myself as Crazy," a woman in 1970 wrote in an open letter to her psychiatrist. "The whole psychological thing is based on the premise that there are INDIVIDUAL problems rather than a social problem which is political."[28] On this many feminists could agree.

Feminists could also agree that the entire cultural project of assigning sharply distinct gender roles to men and women was laughable. Activist Meredith Tax wrote in a widely circulated pamphlet, *Woman and Her Mind* (1970), that women were quite literally "made stupid by the roles they are pushed into" and added (building explicitly on antipsychiatry guru R.D. Laing's view that schizophrenia was a madness produced by unhealthful interpersonal relations) that "this remorseless stifling of a girl's intelligence and ego, this socialization into a life of service, this continued undermining of any possibility of independent achievement outside of the prescribed realm, all constitute a condition one could describe as female schizophrenia."[29] Or as psychology professor Michele Hoffnung Garskof wrote in 1971, "A woman who feels dissatisfied with her suburban home and family, a young wife who does not want children, or a woman who is sexually aggressive is likely to be labeled 'disturbed.' The definitions of who is 'sick' and what constitutes a 'cure' have similar built-in biases."[30]

No one did more to dramatize the means by which the psychiatric profession came systematically to crush the hopes and dreams of independent-minded women than psychologist Phyllis Chesler. As Chesler summarized it in the bestselling *Women and Madness* (1972): "Women are seen as 'sick' when they act out the female role (are depressed, incompetent, frigid, and anxious) and when they reject the female role (are hostile, successful, sexually active, and especially with other women)."[31] In short, the daily operation of a supposedly sane society worked to psychically cripple its women.

*

All did not always run smoothly for feminist therapy, however. Historians of American feminism have gingerly acknowledged that the power-sharing therapeutic strategies adopted by women—not unlike the similar strategies used in mixed-gender radical therapy groups—often led to severe internal conflicts within groups and to countless hours of self-examination that yielded painful paralysis rather than practical insight or effective action.[32] The aim of "structurelessness" within women's groups, as Jo Freeman tactfully pointed out in 1972, may have been "a healthy counter" to an "over-structured society," but it was also "becoming a goddess in its own right."[33] Moreover, as feminist therapist Hogie Wyckoff wrote, women were just as capable as men of playing the "Lefter Than Thou" game in which some participants professed "to be more revolutionary or more radical" than other participants.[34] Wyckoff herself experienced this in late 1971 when "the New Radical Psychiatry Group" broke with her group, the Berkeley Radical Psychiatry Center, over charges that she and other RaP leaders had "become anti-creative as a result of the power structure."[35]

There were further problems—some intrinsic to the nature of therapy itself, some to the inevitable impotence of therapy in a fundamentally unjust society. It was not proving enough for women to separate themselves from men and reject the heterosexist and male-dominant paradigm that so often accompanied the profession of psychotherapy. Women-only facilities or women-focused therapies had their own homosocial problems. Women who worked in therapeutic settings with female (as opposed to male) professionals found that this did not necessarily mean that everything suddenly got better. In her poem, "Ode to My Analyst," a woman mocked the notion that female therapists were somehow automatic improvements over male therapists ("on your way out tell my secretary to double your dosage she says dryly /thanks see you thursday I say" concluded the poem).[36]

Even feminist therapy, some of the most radical commentators contended, was its own kind of adjustment. Perhaps all feminist therapy could offer was "a catalyst not a cure," as the feminist journal *Off Our Backs* concluded in 1973.[37] Or as a lesbian psychology student at Berkeley noted in 1975, while feminist therapy was helping some lesbians "grow strong inside ourselves," feminist therapy "can never by itself be effective for mass revolutionary change."[38] And some leading feminists rejected the usefulness of therapy (feminist or otherwise) altogether. Marxist feminist Shulamith Firestone, for example, argued that since therapy had historically "proven worse than useless," it needed to be replaced "with the only thing that can do any good: political organization."[39] Psychologist Dorothy Tennov was even harsher, dismissing psychotherapy in 1971 as "a kind of opiate."[40] She considered feminist therapy to be no better than the generic masculine variety, rhetorically inquiring: "*What is feminist therapy?* I find the two terms mutually contradictory." Tennov tersely stated, "Feminists do not practice *therapy* on their sisters."[41]

The concept of changing the roles women played in society saturated the movement's goals of psychological transformation and political liberation alike—but what was the relationship between these two goals? Could psychoanalysis and other forms of talk therapy be properly retooled to incorporate a feminist ethos? As feminist psychiatrist Carol Wolman observed in 1975—quite evidently disagreeing with the kinds of views espoused by Dorothy Tennov—"Feminism is intrinsically therapeutic and all good therapy whether done by and for men or women, must be feminist—in other words, it must include a feminist analysis of the clients' thoughts and behavior patterns and an effort to help the client overcome his or her own internal sexism, which is so self-crippling." But Wolman also acknowledged that feminist therapy should not be considered an end in itself. "As women working for the mental health of women, we have an important job—to heal our battered sisters and strengthen each other for the fray," Wolman wrote. "But we must remember that therapy only helps individuals, it doesn't change the system. In order to do that we must work together—collectively and politically."[42] Thus while some groups were overtly political—and especially those self-designated "consciousness-raising" groups—others confined themselves to the task of mutual assistance in personal problem solving.[43] Both kinds of groups were understood by many feminists as crucial to social transformation. Women's lives would not change if the roles they were forced to play did not change, and these roles would never change until women freed themselves from the games in which society had trapped them.

Such considerations may have seemed circular, but the yearnings that lay behind them were profound. Feminists felt deeply—as a group of psychologists put it already in 1970—how frequently women had been expected to suppress the human urge "toward self-actualization, toward mastery of the environment, and toward fulfillment of one's potential" and to become "adjusted to a social environment with associated restrictive stereotypes."[44] But knowing this did not mean knowing what to do about it. And it did not alter the simple fact that women too often experienced existence much like Alice did in Wonderland, when she asked, "Who am I then? Tell me that first, and then, if I like being that person, I'll come up: if not, I'll stay down here till I'm somebody else."[45]

*

Were radicalism and therapy, then, entirely at odds? On the contrary, many sixties radicals—though certainly not all—believed that radicalism and therapy were inseparable. Many believed that the individual had to work principally on his/her own self before societal change would successfully be effected. Others brought political issues (discussions of economic injustice, militarism, or racism and/or sexism) directly into individual or group therapy. On the other hand, there were those radicals (to paraphrase Dorothy Tennov) who did argue that friends did not let friends do therapy on one another; this radical camp posited that therapy was wholly antithetical to the process of transforming society.

It would be accurate to conclude that radical therapy and conventional therapy had much in common—although this depends as much on what one means by "conventional" as it depends on which aspects of radical therapy one means. If we take the insights of popular sixties psychologists like Abraham Maslow or Carl Rogers or psychiatrist Eric Berne as "conventional," for instance, we can definitely see how the ideas and perspectives put forth by these (and other) "conventional" therapists were routinely utilized by both radical therapists and feminist therapists. For instance, Berne's emphasis on role playing in human interactions had a profound impact on a good deal of radical therapy—since radical therapy often placed a high premium on authenticity and directness in interpersonal exchanges. Radical therapy rejected the "games people played" and sought to rebuild social relations around more "honest" modes of interaction.

Yet it would also be accurate to conclude that radical therapy represented a rejection of many of the mainstream styles of therapy that prevailed in the 1960s and 1970s—and with some very good reason. Conventional modes of therapy were male dominated and often deeply misogynist and homophobic—as were conventional modes of psychiatry and psychoanalysis. There were also strong racist strands within conventional psychiatry as well—for instance, when psychiatrists sought to diagnose civil rights and Black Power activism as a pathological or narcissistic reaction formation (rather than a legitimate response to societal ills).

Yet it would finally be accurate as well to conclude that radical therapy had an incalculably positive impact on conventional therapy over the course of the last half-century, as conventional therapy absorbed many (if not most) of the lessons and arguments put forth by the radicals in the 1960s and 1970s. It is far less common to find open misogyny and/or homophobia in the therapeutic community today than it was fifty years ago—just as it would be inconceivable in the twenty-first century to find overt racism within mainstream psychoanalytic circles. What are often seen today as the finest aspects of therapeutic culture—its democratic impulses, its nonhierarchical aspects, its emphasis on individual self-reflectiveness and overall wellness—may all be interpreted as stemming in large part from the advances sought by radical and feminist therapists more than a generation ago. In a definitive sense, therefore, radical therapy succeeded beyond its wildest dreams by revolutionizing American therapeutic culture. Nonetheless, radical therapy certainly failed to effect the sorts of societal changes it had also imagined were essential to the long-term mental health of the United States' citizenry.

CHAPTER 8

Narcissism

Elizabeth Lunbeck

Narcissism is inescapably part of the critique of therapeutic culture. In the 1970s it became a purportedly newly ubiquitous condition, providing the occasion for critics to issue stinging indictments of the American nation's sorry state and the American people's characterological decline. As Christopher Lasch put it in his landmark 1978 book, *The Culture of Narcissism: American Life in an Age of Diminishing Expectations*, a "narcissistic preoccupation with the self" had overwhelmed the "the culture of competitive individualism" that underlay the country's freedom and prosperity. Self-indulgence had displaced self-control, nurturing "a state of restless, perpetually unsatisfied desire." The ascendancy of a commitment to "psychic self-improvement"—evident in the appearance and flourishing of a range of new consciousness movements and their allied therapies—was tearing apart a once robust social fabric, prompting a mass retreat to interiority and what journalist Tom Wolfe, in an essay that christened the 1970s the "Me Decade," skewered as a culturally sanctioned, unceasing "analysis of the self," a "dwelling upon *Me*."[1] Alongside Lasch's book, a host of titles such as *Generation of Narcissus, The Narcissistic Condition: A Fact of Our Lives and Times, ME: The Narcissistic American*, and *The Self Seekers* collectively made the case that narcissism was becoming endemic in the population, portending the disappearance of the disciplined, independent, and fully realized bourgeois type and the rise of the empty, dependent, and vacuous consumer—of everywhere abundant material goods and therapies alike.[2]

Since the 1970s, the category of narcissism has remained in the service of comprehensive cultural indictment and used as an alluringly simple explanation for all variety of political, social, and psychological ills. And yet an examination of the term's genealogy and its redeployment within various popular and scientific debates reveals a rather complex, even contradictory, set of meanings. Americans have understood narcissism in competing ways, consistently manifesting profound ambivalence about the narcissistic tendencies whose newfound omnipresence Lasch and his fellow critics lamented. Not least because their lament continues today, this essay maps the intellectual genealogy of narcissism, examining the term's migration from the analytic into the popular realm and seeking to understand both its enduring appeal and its sometimes contradictory meanings.

Narcissism was new to cultural criticism and popular debate in the 1970s but not to psychoanalysis. From the time of the appearance of Freud's landmark 1914 essay, "Narcissism: An Introduction," the condition had figured importantly in psychoanalytic thinking. From the 1920s on, psychoanalysts used the term to denote self-esteem and to discuss its regulation in individuals, and in the 1930s Freud's Viennese colleague Paul Federn coined the term "healthy narcissism" to refer to the general well-being, self-assurance, self-assertion, satisfaction with oneself, and inner resources that sustained individuals' capacities to weather the challenges of daily life. Healthy narcissism was libido turned outward, towards engagement with the world.[3] Positive feelings about the self were "narcissistically gratifying" but also indispensable supports to normal functioning—and, it might be noted, to worldly success. Echoing Alexis de Toqueville's observations of the relationship between American individualism and industriousness, Federn noted that "mentally healthy and normal people enjoy their narcissistic satisfaction, if at all, only after the act. They are so preoccupied with the object and the overcoming of difficulties that they have no libido left for self inspection."[4]

Though it was long present in analytic discourse, it took half a century for narcissism to become the center of creative and contentious analytic debate. The publication of paradigm-shifting works by the eminent émigré analysts Heinz Kohut and Otto Kernberg in the 1970s prompted analysts to refocus their discipline around narcissism and sparked animated public discussion of the contours of the condition. Both analysts described the narcissist as a particular type of person, characterized by grandiosity, a fantasized omnipotence, interpersonal manipulativeness, and fears of dependency linked to an unacknowledged but insatiable need for others' admiration as well as, more subjectively, feelings of inner emptiness and despair. But their stances toward narcissism also differed in critical ways. In *The Analysis of the Self: A Systematic Introduction to the Psychoanalytic Treatment of Narcissistic Personality*

Disorders (1971), Kohut celebrated what others condemned, rejecting the pejorative attitude toward narcissism he saw both in his disciplinary colleagues and in the culture more generally. He proposed that narcissism—here referring to our preoccupation with and love for ourselves—was a necessary dimension of a self engaged with its environment, one that fueled individuals' ambitions, creativity, empathy, and fellow feeling. Kohut thus reframed narcissism as a desirable rather than pathological dimension of mature selfhood, and introduced to a popular audience the notion of "healthy narcissism."

Kernberg, in contrast, highlighted narcissism's darker side, detailing narcissists' destructiveness, in particular the rage and aggression they directed at the hapless victims they so masterfully exploited and enslaved. Charming and seductive, the narcissists described in *Borderline Conditions and Pathological Narcissism* (1975) could imagine themselves blissfully independent of normal human needs, and they often enjoyed a measure of material success—in part by performing an enviable but illusory self-sovereignty. Although maddeningly unwarranted, their success suggested that the culture not only tolerated but rewarded narcissistic traits, enabling those skilled at manipulating interpersonal relations and deft in sustaining the illusion of their own limitless possibilities to prevail within the drab conformism that was the bureaucratic world of business, politics, and government.[5]

Several generations separated Kohut and Kernberg from Freud and Federn, and both the institutional and intellectual cultures of American psychoanalysis had changed significantly. Clinical conditions no longer needed to be parsed through the narrow metapsychological schema of ego and id, libido and cathexis. There was room in the analytic encounter—perhaps even a mandate—for consideration of the individual's relationship to the social, especially to the workings of power. Narcissistic personality disorder was assimilated easily to the image of the "one dimensional man" delineated in Herbert Marcuse's 1964 best seller of that title and provided a useful heuristic through which to explain America's changing geopolitical strategies. The result of this combination of a more accessible and public clinical language and of diagnostic categories attuned to more facets of human existence was a psychoanalysis that could explain not only the psyche but also the world. As a diagnosis with clear social as well as personal ramifications, narcissism was ripe for appropriation by cultural critics.

The Culture of Narcissism skillfully wove the insights of Kohut, Kernberg, and other analytic thinkers into a narrative of national decline that had already been made familiar by, among others, David Riesman in his 1950 best-selling work of sociology, *The Lonely Crowd*, and the analyst Allen Wheelis in the popular storybook account of characterological decline and national malaise he offered in *The Quest for Identity*, published in 1958.[6] Following in their footsteps, Lasch looked at America's increasingly "other-directed" culture and found both the individual and the state wanting. As he saw it, the former had been fatally weakened as the latter enhanced its powers and reach and usurped many of the functions formerly the province of the family—child rearing and character formation foremost among them. The result was an overall decline in what Lasch called "the moral climate of contemporary society," especially its nurturing of dependencies and its obliviousness to the dangers of a rampant consumerism.[7]

Skeptical critics suggested there was nothing new in Lasch's account. Feminists objected to his barely concealed celebration of a lost masculine autonomy and undisputed patriarchal authority.[8] Psychoanalysts faulted him for his nostalgic view of the past and for seeing narcissism as the source of every conceivable social ill.[9] And commentators from the left accused him of "humorless hectoring" and of delivering "a jeremiad for yuppies."[10] Yet none of this detracted from the book's popular appeal or lasting impact. It spent seven weeks on the *New York Times* best seller list and received the National Book Award for Current Interest in 1980.[11] Ironically enough, Lasch, the dour critic of celebrity culture, was featured in *People* magazine, declaiming on the dangers of gratification and indulgence and promoting the lost virtues of restraint and self-control. He admitted to being bewildered by his book's popularity: "I thought the book was difficult, even somewhat forbidding," he told the *People* interviewer. Among the many readers persuaded by his argument, perhaps the most influential was President Jimmy Carter. After reading Lasch's book (reportedly his favorite of the several works of sociology he read), Carter delivered a radio address in 1979—the so-called malaise speech, considered the most important of his presidency—charging that Americans' worship of "self-indulgence and consumption" had displaced their historical commitment to hard work, close-knit communities, and faith in God and arguing that "owning things and consuming things" was inadequate to "fill the emptiness of lives" devoid of meaning.[12]

Carter's embrace of Lasch's broad-stroke portrait of what one reader called "an ailing society heading toward disaster" ultimately did little to help his popularity: in the 1980 election, Ronald Reagan successfully campaigned against Carter's "defeatism" with the slogan "It's Morning in America."[13] But more than thirty years on, Lasch's dour diagnosis continues to have remarkable traction. That we live in a "culture of narcissism" is by now an unexceptionable claim, and the term shoulders a heavy moral burden in public discussion across the intersecting realms of popular psychology, mass media, and policy formation. A new set of critics has carried on the task of documenting its pernicious spread, and it still serves as a site for overheated condemnations of the present, to which nostalgia-tinged portraits of a mythical, prenarcissistic past serve as a useful foil.

Consider, for example, *The Narcissism Epidemic: Living in the Age of Entitlement*, a 2009 book by psychologists Jean M. Twenge and W. Keith Campbell. As seen by Twenge and Campbell, narcissism is dangerously on the increase, testified to by the ubiquity of what one reviewer calls "ego-addled spoiled brats" and evident in our inflated self-esteem, shallow values, and materialism.[14] According to the authors, earlier works (Lasch's among them) documented a cultural shift to the individual and a concomitant, corrosive celebration of self-admiration. But these works appeared before "any serious research" into the issue had been carried out. Having undertaken such research, we are told, Twenge and Campbell know that the situation is far more dire than previously believed.

As social psychologists, Twenge and Campbell stress they are interested in narcissism not as a clinical diagnosis but as it is found in "normal" populations: not in Kernberg's, Kohut's, and psychiatry's Narcissistic Personality Disorder but in the "extraverted, outgoing, and exhibitionistic folks" with narcissistic personalities who score high on the Narcissistic Personality Inventory (NPI). While not officially pathological, these narcissists "cause plenty of trouble for the people around them."[15] Here the development of an objective "scientific" instrument for the measurement of narcissism (in contrast to a diagnosis decided upon by a mental health clinician, one on one) facilitates seeing narcissism everywhere. Developed in 1979 by psychologists Robert Raskin and Calvin Hall, the NPI is a forty-item test that psychologists claim predicts narcissistic behavior based on choices subjects make between paired statements. For example, test takers must decide between agreeing with the statement "modesty doesn't become me" or "I am essentially a modest person"; "I think I am a special person" or "I am no better or worse than most people"; and "I like to have authority over other people" or "I don't mind following orders." (This question, intended to measure deference to authority, is particularly odd, as the second, nonnarcissistic option is strangely oblivious to the post-Eichmann resonances of following orders.) Choices on the NPI are starkly cast in black and white, offering test takers none of the gray in which most of us live our lives. Additionally, the person whose score on the NPI is low is more than likely quite cautious, insecure, unassertive, easily embarrassed, inattentive to his or her presentation of self, and meekly accepting of the status quo—in all a characterological caricature of the personality an earlier generation of social psychologists had seen as particularly open to the charisma of the powerful fascist leader.

For Twenge and Campbell, however, cross-generational analysis of responses to the NPI provides indisputable evidence that narcissism is reaching epidemic proportions. Ignoring any clinical niceties, they extrapolate the diagnostic category beyond even Lasch's imaginings. "Feeling special is narcissism," they assert, warning parents that telling children they are special will lead to frustration as well as antisocial habits like cutting in line and, more generally, treating others poorly. They do note that "children are of course very special to their parents" but suggest that while it is okay to tell children you love them, "don't tell your kids they are special." But they take no account of widely accepted developmental stages and associated tasks: is the four-year-old's feeling of specialness the same as the Wall Street trader's, and are the behavioral consequences equivalent? And they collapse any distinctions among thoughts, fantasy, and reality, proclaiming simply that "it is logically impossible for everyone to be special." To the assertion of one reader that it would be "just creepy if 7-year-olds walked around saying, 'I'm not special,'" they offer a big dose of reality's harsh message, to be drilled into children by parents and society: let them know "that the world doesn't revolve around them."[16] Narcissism is a cultural problem, but the fight against it begins at home.

Like "the triumph of the therapeutic," Philip Rieff's lapidary 1966 term for the ascendancy of self-fulfillment over religiously mandated renunciation, "the culture of narcissism" has taken on the status of a truism. Both catchphrases were generated within and, as a result, summon up an especially fraught moment in American cultural history, when intellectuals took stock of the political ferment of the Vietnam-era years—assassinations, urban riots, Black Power, student protests, nascent second-wave feminist agitation, and claims for gay liberation—to collectively warn of the unraveling of Western society and the undermining of its most cherished ideals. Freud as a prophet of gratification and liberation from society's constraints figured prominently in their indictments, as did a generalized version of psychoanalysis, one that brushed off Freud's well-known pessimism as to the possibility of reconciling society and desire and promised that you could, actually, get what you wanted from life. Narcissism entered the popular realm in the 1970s linked to hedonistic consumption, with the narcissist figured as the exemplary shopaholic. The apparent excesses of the countercultural young, whom their elders believed reveled in an Elysium of instantly gratified desires of every type and variety, came under especially sharp scrutiny; hippies, for example, were cast as "total narcissists," and their peers were more generally characterized as the most narcissistic generation in history.[17] Critics like Rieff and Lasch promoted old-fashioned self-restraint as a counter to hedonism, gratification, and the personal quests for self-realization and self-exploration that they saw convulsing the culture. Whatever their positions on the political spectrum, they wove together emotional and material indulgence to caustically maintain that the cultural revolution was but the occasion for hedonistic consumption and ultimately "a terrific thing for American capitalism."[18] Significantly, the more ascetic impulses of the young—their rejection of their elders' aspirations for a house in the suburbs, two cars in the garage, and (for men) a regular ascent up the corporate ladder—were altogether missing from the critics' portrait of the American character gone amok.

Since the appearance of these canonical indictments, the narcissism of popular commentary has been, for the most part, a distinctively American malady associated with affluence and abundance, an endlessly commented-upon characterological failing, and a temptingly easy occasion for critics to lambaste their fellow citizens while referencing a lost Eden superintended by self-restrained, powerful patriarchs. That the aspiration to self-realization is part and parcel of the American national ethos and that the capitalist system—aligned in the minds of the critics with the values of hard work, individual initiative, and entrepreneurial courage—depends for its vitality on ever-expanding consumer demand is an inconvenient fact mostly ignored. As a result, the stunning irony that the critics' narcissist might be seen not to reject, but to perfectly embody, the critics' own vaunted America-in-the-good-old-days values, has remained largely unexamined.

An exception to this tendency was Daniel Bell, on this issue the most brilliant star in the 1970s critical firmament. His book of 1976, *The Cultural Contradictions of Capitalism*, saw clearly capitalism's Faustian self-destructiveness even as it lamented the culture's abandonment of a once allied asceticism. Were the sources of the narcissism epidemic extrinsic to defining aspects of American culture, as Lasch would have it, or were they perhaps located in the culture's own unfolding political and economic dynamic? Bell's judicious answer was "both"—which was itself exemplary of the category's extraordinary, and extraordinarily useful, ideological plasticity. But few popular narcissism critics have shared Bell's insightfulness.

Instead, for the last thirty years, readers of the popular press and magazines have been reminded of the existential loneliness of the child raised by narcissistic parents, of the joyless narcissists desperately seeking admiration from others to stave off despair, and of the narcissistic grandiosity that all too often eventuates in scenarios of self-destruction. In part because the narcissist entered the public realm tied to the critique of consumerist indulgence and abundance, in public commentary her plight has been cast less as a tragedy than as a willful spurning of the imperative of self-control, a deliberate glorying in the "plenitude of option" that, according to Philip Rieff, was the hallmark of the modern order.[19]

There has been no place in this public-sphere narcissism for the positive, even necessary-to-life, dimensions of the concept that had long been a minor note in analytic discourse and that were at the center of Kohut's theorizing. The healthy narcissism he brought to the center of the analytic conversation, the celebration of the self's potentialities and "the ideology of personal growth" that characterized life in a modern democracy, has drawn from Lasch and later critics only withering criticism.[20] Nowhere has this been more apparent than in the decades of derision heaped on the public school system's attempts to educate students in "self-esteem," as healthy narcissism was rebranded in the 1980s. Born of California assemblyman John Vasconcellos's experiences with human potential therapies at the Esalen Institute, in the mid-1980s the California Task Force to Promote Self-Esteem and Personal and Social Responsibility spent nearly three-quarters of a million dollars touting self-esteem as both a key to personal success and a prophylactic against a host of social ills, including "crime, drug abuse, teen-age pregnancy and welfare dependency."[21] What began in California became a national trend, despite the fact that the movement was lambasted as "mindless psychobabble" by critics from both the right and the left. To conservative critics, self-esteem education is an exemplary excrescence of the Me Decade moment and a repudiation of the nation's heritage of hard work and strenuous effort. (As Twenge and Campbell put it, life is about "fitting in and getting things done rather than admiring yourself."[22]) Paradoxically, progressives argue that the self-esteem education's focus on the self overemphasizes personal responsibility, and claim that it smoothed the path for the current regime of high-stakes testing.[23]

Regardless of their place on the political spectrum, such critics may flatter themselves Kernbergians as they slight narcissism's positive aspects. But Kernberg himself, when asked in a 1978 interview whether we weren't all narcissists, secretly loving ourselves, enjoying "feeding and grooming ourselves . . . soliciting the admiration and approval of others," replied that in fact we were not. The "normal narcissism" such activities sustained was unproblematic, he maintained, even necessary to exist effectively in the world.[24]

Since healthy narcissism proved difficult to conscript into the critics' narratives of decline, they chose to construe the condition narrowly, capturing but one stream of a complex conversation about the phenomenon and offering implausible antidotes designed to stem its spread. The result is a flat and far more reproving vision than that of analysts, one that offers an impossibly straitened vision of individual liberty and possibility, as well as an unrealistic assessment of community and society. That vision has rested uneasily alongside critics' celebration of market capitalism's ability to foster the personal freedom that allowed the individual, in Daniel Bell's words, "to 'make' of himself what he willed."[25] It is but a thin, ideologically freighted line that separates this critic-approved self-realization from the self-exploration, self-expression, and self-gratification that drew—and continues to draw—critical censure.

Increasingly, however, the ways in which popular critics find themselves boxed in by the logic of their own arguments is more clearly on view. While Twenge and Campbell's *The Narcissism Epidemic* continues the Laschian tradition of defining narcissism in wholly pathological terms, in an academic article asking "Is Narcissism Really So Bad?," Campbell wonders if research on narcissism has overemphasized the negative. (Without a trace of irony, he suggests that the popular understanding of the condition engendered by books like Lasch's has unduly influenced the scholarship.) He admits that high scores on the NPI may in fact indicate healthy narcissism.[26] Indeed, he acknowledges that narcissists, with their high self-esteem, may in fact be happier, more satisfied, and more successful than their nonnarcissistic peers and points out that research shows that social psychologists' narcissists are happier than clinicians,' who conform more to Lasch's fragile, empty, and depressed modal type. It may be, Campbell writes, that the narcissists who end up in psychiatrists' offices and on analysts' couches are *failed* narcissists, those "not doing their 'job' correctly"—the job consisting in "achieving and winning." "Narcissism may be a functional and healthy strategy for dealing with the modern world," he concludes, invoking Freud's 1931 sketch of the narcissist as a larger-than-life personality striding confidently across the world's stage as an attempt to "create a theory of normal personality types."[27] Other commentators in effect agree, with one, for example, arguing that some of the statements indicative of narcissism on the NPI "sound like pretty normal personality features" and citing number 10, "I see myself as a good leader," as a case in point.[28]

Such critiques suggest a scrambling of the categories that have structured our understanding of narcissism, and the sense that the condition is indeed deeply contested is borne out in the liveliness and complexity of the discussion about narcissism in books, in the press, and on the web. It is possible, for example, to go online and find websites offering nuanced, sophisticated discussions of narcissistic pathology, as well as advice from both experts and their autodidact counterparts on how to identify, deal with, recover from, and—most useful of all—altogether avoid narcissists, whether at work or in intimate relations.[29] Much of this advice channels a Kernbergian vision, characterizing the narcissist as an interpersonally enticing but dangerous figure who snares unwitting victims in his charismatic net while callously draining them dry. Ordinary people wounded by narcissists offer wrenching testimony to the confusing allure of the narcissist as well as to the devastation that often follows in its wake, drawing on the writings of professionals but also on readings in the popular literature. But the healthy narcissism of psychoanalysis, and its benefits, can also be found on the web: "Healthy Narcissism Can Help You Succeed," reads the title of one recent piece; "Sex Addicts Need *Healthy* Narcissism," proclaims another.[30]

What these popular conversations document is neither a hapless submission to nor a radical independence from expert knowledge but rather a rough mastery of the positions articulated by both Kernberg and Kohut as well as a general—and inconsistent—assent to those of social psychologists such as Twenge and Campbell. "Narcissism" as seen and used by the general public is thus complex and paradoxical: a vernacular construction, it nevertheless resonates as much with clinical portrayals of narcissism in the professional literature as with the updated, social versions promoted by Lasch and his inheritors. This suggests that both Kernberg and Kohut have been appropriated by those trying to make sense of the many ways we exist in the world as well as of the puzzling (and often infuriating and inexplicable) things we do to one another.

One of the chief tenets of the therapeutic culture critique is the claim that the expertise of professionals—in particular of the psychiatrists, psychologists, and social workers who appear as "helping" professionals in standard accounts—has overwhelmed the intuitive and customary knowledge of ordinary citizens, opening the most private aspects of their lives to prying inquiries and regulation. We have been rendered dependent on experts, advice, and institutions in our efforts to do what had formerly been governed by custom—raising our children, managing our emotions, governing our homes. It is assumed that the flow of disciplinary knowledge and power moves in one direction, from the expert to the benighted citizen, who may or may not resist or enact a measure of diminished agency, but who in any case emerges a reduced version of her former robust self.

Narcissism as currently used by the general public as a diagnostic or explanatory category both confirms and upends this truism. The culture of narcissism as denominated by Lasch in the 1970s still usefully conjures up a narrative of national decline that seems intuitively right to many people. Indeed, it would be possible to argue that, in the case of narcissism at least, it is the critics of therapeutic culture, rather than the therapists themselves, upon whose "expertise" we depend for our understanding of the clinical term and for instructions on how to use it as a heuristic for making sense of the world. But dig deeper, and the conversation about narcissism becomes more nuanced, less certain. The social critics' narcissism does not carry the day. The more clinical meanings of the term still resonate and are used both to diagnose the failings of others and to talk hopefully about our complex selves. A survey of the career of narcissism within both professional and popular circles reveals both a general consensus on the utility of the term and an utter lack of consistency insofar as its meaning is concerned.

This strange state of affairs certainly challenges the argument, central to the therapeutic critique, that the rise of experts creates a docile citizenry, devoid of self-will and agency. If we recognize this complexity, we can perhaps see the maturing of the therapeutic culture critique, its evolution into something that treats the cultural formation of "the therapeutic" as still special but not singular and that is free of the limitations—the shrill simplifications and reproachful attitudes—that marked the critique's painful birth.

CHAPTER 9

The Left

Beryl Satter

What is the relationship between therapeutic culture and the US left?[1] Does therapeutic culture undercut the left, as therapeutic culture critics insist? Or are the two compatible, as the post-1960s "therapeutic left" assumed?

The answer is complicated, in part because of the left-wing roots of the classic therapeutic culture critique. Therapeutic culture, which holds that emotional expression is beneficial, dates to the nineteenth century. The classic therapeutic culture critique emerged much later, in the 1960s, as part of an internal debate between old left and New Left perspectives. As will be detailed below, the "old" US left of the 1930s and the New Left of the 1960s regarded emotional expression very differently. Older leftists generally viewed emotional expression as childish and irrational. In contrast, many New Leftists believed that emotional repression created irrational behavior. In order to think clearly, they claimed, people needed to break through social conditioning and access their "true" emotions.

We can evaluate these competing perspectives by examining one expression of left-leaning therapeutic culture, Re-evaluation Counseling (RC).[2] RC claimed that its unorthodox counseling methods would eliminate damaging biases and liberate innate rationality, thereby enabling people to solve the problems of exploitation and injustice. Commentators on the right have mocked RC as an example of the therapeutic silliness of the left; commentators on the left have ignored it. Its history enables us to sort through the old left and New Left positions on the value of emotional release and its relationship to political radicalism. RC challenged an older left tradition that ignored the psychological costs of social oppression. Therapeutic culture critics were indifferent to psychic damage caused by racism, sexism, classism, and homophobia, damage that groups like RC were correct to address. RC adherents' activism demonstrated that attention to emotions need not undercut political engagement. Yet RC's simplistic understanding of human psychology encouraged practices that could trigger the solipsism and emotional excess that therapeutic culture critics warned against. Psychological harm caused by social oppression is real and deserves investigation by those on the left—but not with the simplistic tools offered by therapeutic organizations such as RC.

THE OLD LEFT, THE NEW LEFT, AND THE THERAPEUTIC CULTURE CRITIQUE

Early therapeutic culture critics were leftists attempting to warn fellow radicals against the "therapeutic sensibility."[3] For example, Christopher Lasch begged his readers to focus on the real danger—monopoly capitalism—that deskilled workers through mind-numbing subdivisions of labor, and then used consumer goods to bribe them into accepting their deadened condition. As this volume's introduction indicates, these critics interpreted therapeutic culture as a new, more dangerous form of consumption. It was more harmful than stockpiling goods because it encouraged narcissistic self-involvement while undercutting the emotional control needed for struggle against the real enemy, capitalism itself.[4]

Lauding the nineteenth-century white male, the canonical therapeutic culture critics claimed that his stoic, self-denying character was a critical resource in the fight against bureaucratic control. They criticized forces that undercut nineteenth-century patriarchs, from Progressive-era child welfare services to the New Deal welfare state, since the resulting bureaucracies rendered Americans passive and dependent upon experts. They saw the faddish therapies of their own era, such as rolfing, bioenergetics, and Reichian therapy, encouraging self-involvement and emotional dependency, weakening the critical thought needed for resistance, and strengthening the hold of monopoly capitalism. In Lasch's words, they "discredit[ed] authority, especially in the home and the classroom, while leaving domination uncriticized."[5]

Lasch and his cohorts highlighted the power of corporate bureaucracies while trivializing the domination of whites over blacks or of men over women. They attacked black liberation, feminism, and gay and lesbian liberation as emotionally regressive movements that threatened what remained of the morally grounded, emotionally circumspect, self-denying American character. Lasch derided the Black Power movement for demanding "programs in black history" instead of focusing on the supposedly more fundamental issue of "the expansion of the educational bureaucracy." Interest in women's history was motivated by a "desire for an intellectually undemanding curriculum."[6] In his view, feminism and Black Power encouraged narcissistic self-involvement and infantile rage against authority. They were emblematic of the undisciplined, self-involved therapeutic ethos itself.[7]

Such attacks on feminism and Black Power were partially an expression of a generational divide between a 1930s "old left" that hoped for a revolt of industrial workers and a 1960s New Left that had a more complex understanding of oppression—and of the steps needed to overcome it. Their disagreements could also be traced to their competing understandings of the relationship between rationality and emotional repression. Therapeutic culture critics believed that emotional repression enhanced rationality, while many in the New Left believed that the one distorted the other.[8]

The New Left's understanding of rationality and emotion had its roots in the 1950s, when beat poets, abstract expressionist artists, and other cultural rebels attacked American's embrace of technological rationality. These artists argued that our terror of emotion created soul-killing conformity. We could restore our health and vitality if we loosened self-control and embraced our emotions.[9] Building upon this critique, many 1960s-era hippies and New Left activists attacked conformity, environmental destruction, and the "death culture" producing the Vietnam War as examples of cultural madness rooted in sexual repression and fear of emotion. They opposed the "roles" that warped human relationships—especially interactions between social unequals such as men and women or whites and minorities. They applauded instead the authenticity of groups that were excluded from the mainstream, and thus exempt from the deadening conformity of mainstream America.[10]

Rather than admiring moralistic and emotionally and sexually controlled individuals, some in the New Left cast such people as bundles of repression whose neuroses had profound political effects. They hoped to break through psychological blocks that fueled racism, sexism, homophobia, and other dangerous bigotries. They argued that socially constructed biases penetrated the individual psyche, becoming entwined with the repression of frightening emotions. Such repression produced arrogance and damaging aversions among those in power and shame and self-hatred among those excluded from power.

Some New Leftists tried to interrogate the psychological blind spots of the powerful, as well as their own internalized feelings of shame and self-hatred. Mainstream midcentury psychotherapy was saturated with misogyny and class bias. Therefore, some who sought the liberation of marginalized populations embraced humanist, Gestalt, and other pop therapies as tools for challenging internalized bigotries, hoping they could undo racist and sexist socialization and enable honest interaction across differences.[11] To the therapeutic left, the critics of therapeutic culture embraced an oddly celebratory attitude towards the unexamined life: they denied that the psyche is a political space, conditioned by societal as well as familial experiences.

But to Lasch and his cohorts, lauding emotion and loosening sexual repression could only be signs of infantile regression. As this volume's introduction explains, they insisted that emotional openness damaged the formalities that made civilized social interaction possible. Valorizing emotional expressiveness created an obsessive focus on the self that sundered older bonds of community, "liberated" individuals from their obligations, and made civic participation nearly impossible. Practices that encouraged emotional vulnerability before strangers undercut the independence, clear thinking, and integrity that was the best defense against political hysteria. It rendered Americans passive in the face of bureaucratic conformity. Therapeutic activities, they insisted, were emotionally regressive, intellectually vacuous, and damaging to those who embraced them.

RE-EVALUATION COUNSELING (RC)

Re-evaluation Counseling, a therapeutic practice based upon the idea that emotional catharsis enhances rationality, has clear affinities with New Left culture and a history of presenting itself as a means of achieving left-wing goals.[12] According to RC literature, "co-counseling" was developed in the early 1950s by Harvey Jackins, a labor organizer who was blacklisted for his activism. One day Jackins was approached by his friend Merle, who was distraught over losing his job and his wife. Jackins sat with Merle for weeks while he recounted his traumas, physically manifesting his feelings as he spoke. For the first week, he wept. Then he began shaking, then yawning, and finally, laughing. By the end of a few weeks, Merle had recovered his emotional equilibrium. He rejoined his wife and became a happy, rational, well-adjusted person. Jackins had cured Merle simply by listening to him and allowing him to physically "discharge" his emotional pain.[13]

In his manifesto entitled *The Human Side of Human Beings*, Jackins concluded that painful experiences from childhood created rigid patterns of behavior. Adults behaved irrationally because of unintentional restimulation of early emotional distress. However, "chronic distress patterns" could be "discharged" if another person listened in a focused, nonjudgmental way as one recounted one's traumas. This would trigger a catharsis of weeping, shaking, sweating, yawning, or laughing. Once traumas were discharged, individuals would be liberated from rigidity and regain their natural wisdom. They could then reevaluate their experiences with a rationality and flexibility previously clouded by old patterns of emotional distress.[14]

RC accounts of Jackin's breakthrough omitted a crucial ingredient—his time as a follower of Scientology founder L. Ron Hubbard. Scientology, originally known as Dianetics, originated in the early 1950s, and online documents of RC history suggest that Jackins helped establish Hubbard's Dianetics Auditing Center of Seattle in 1952. By the mid-1950s, the two men had a falling out, and Jackins apparently then changed the name of his Dianetics Auditing Center to Personal Counselors, Inc., and later, to International Re-evaluation Counseling Communities. He also replaced Hubbard's terms with new jargon.[15]

RC's organizational structure bears little resemblance to Scientology's. Nevertheless, the overlap between the groups' belief systems is obvious. Hubbard claimed that people were stunted because of forgotten emotional traumas he called "engrams" (Jackin's distress patterns). Engrams could be discharged with the help of an auditor (Jackin's co-counselor). Auditors could also audit each other. Once individuals were "cleared" of their engrams, they would exhibit immense inherent intelligence (Jackin's reemergence).[16]

Jackins trained people to co-counsel: pair off and take turns listening to each other's traumas to enable discharge. Although he presented himself as bringing free therapy to the masses, RC was highly profitable. Leaders recruited new adherents through six- to fifteen-week "basic courses" on the "Fundamentals of Re-Evaluation Counseling." Costs were low—ten to twenty dollars per class—although weekend workshops ran considerably more. All teachers were required to send 15 percent of their earnings to Jackins's headquarters. Jackins also profited from the sale of his books, printed by his Rational Island publishing house (so named to connote RC adherents' self-image as islands of rationality in a sea of emotional distress).[17]

Scientology, which provided the theoretical basis of RC, is hardly a left-wing movement. Its view of the relationships among emotional pain, catharsis, and healing is a rehash of nineteenth-century pop culture ideas about how repressed traumas create illness.[18] Yet Jackins targeted his Scientology-tinged therapy to progressives, arguing that distress was triggered not only by personal traumas but by sexism, racism, xenophobia, and "adultism."[19] The wealthy were just as emotionally damaged by social injustice as the underprivileged were. Both sides needed to acknowledge the other's pain.[20]

Since bigotry was aggravated by "distress patterns," those who had been co-counseled were best situated to eliminate those patterns, first in their own psyches and then through promoting RC in social movements (or what RC called "the wide world"). RC practices (sometimes disguised, or "naturalized," as workshops on topics such as confronting racism) taught people to reject internal blocks. Their resulting rationality would empower them to resolve all personal, community, and international problems.[21] Once the world embraced RC, what Jackins called the "great irrational threats" of war, suffering, and bigotry, would become "historical curiosities."[22] Fueled by missionary zeal, RC spread throughout the United States in the 1970s. By the early 1990s, it was an international movement, although strongest in the United States, followed by the United Kingdom.[23]

What was problematic about RC? Its underlying assumption that psychological and political perspectives are interrelated and that distortions in the former can lead to rigidities in the latter does not push credibility. And RC members' political activism undercuts the therapeutic culture critics' assertion that attention to one's psyche hurts civic life because it funnels time into navel-gazing pursuits. Instead of encouraging atomization, RC's proponents argued, it brought people into close communities.[24]

Instead, RC's weakness lay in its basic understanding of the psyche. Like Scientology, RC's premise was that physical discharge of emotional pain led to heightened rationality.[25] RC asserted that human nature was flexible and wise, blessed with the ability, in Jackins's words, "to create and use brand new, unique responses to each new, unique situation we meet."[26] RC's goal was not maturity but the liberation of a "childhood self" supposedly characterized by natural rationality. As one former RC leader recounted, members were encouraged to retrieve their lost innocence. Thus overnight workshops, in which six to nine people slept in one room, became adult pajama parties in which participants giggled, cuddled, and spent the whole night whispering to one another.[27] In addition to encouraging regressive behavior, RC also insisted that emotional outbursts heal pain and cure conflicts, rather than add to them. This lent additional credence to therapeutic critics' concerns about the valorization of infantile rage over concern for others.[28]

As therapeutic culture critic Elisabeth Lasch-Quinn observed, RC is based on "a severely impoverished notion of the human mind that lacks *any* acknowledgement of the role or complex workings of the unconscious."[29] Thus RC posited that regression to childhood perfection would be achieved through the public airing of intimate experiences and elevated emotional catharsis over analysis.[30] As Thomas J. Scheff, a sociologist who spent years in RC, explains, the RC counselor "refrains from interpretation, advice, comparison, or classification of any kind. . . . His only function is to facilitate discharge. Other modes of counseling are seen as interfering with this process."[31]

How typical of New Left therapeutic practices was RC's privileging of childishness, lauding of emotional display, and rejection of analysis? Despite some therapeutic critics' claims, RC had little in common with other ostensibly therapeutic activities embraced by New Left movements.[32] Take feminist consciousness raising. Like RC, consciousness raising (CR) assumed that private experiences mattered. It encouraged individuals to discuss personal experiences in a group.[33] The similarities end there, however. In the CR model, the group used information gathered from women's usually hidden experiences to construct an analysis of how sexism functioned. These analyses informed political actions designed to raise awareness and offer solutions. In contrast, RC asserted that emotional testimony was valuable not because of its content but because the physical signs accompanying it (laughing, weeping, etc.) were magically curative.[34] Although RC members supported the goals of the left-oriented groups they joined, their aim was to encourage activists to co-counsel, since this would create the rationality needed to solve social problems. In practice, since emotional outbursts were believed to be curative, provoking them became the goal of many RC activists.

"ANY PLACE WHERE THERE'S A FOOD CO-OP AND LEFTIES, YOU WILL FIND RC."[35]

Participation in RC waxes and wanes, and the organization has historically been unwilling to disclose membership figures. There does seem to be a consensus, however, that from the late 1970s onwards, RC spread its influence on the left. As Elisabeth Lasch-Quinn argues, the group's ideas were congenial to institutional demands for "political correctness" and "sensitivity training" during the 1980s. Members participated in everything from dissertation support groups to union-organizing meetings and used all such organizations to promote RC. They offered workshops at high schools, colleges, church groups, community centers, workplaces, and law enforcement agencies on topics such as "overcoming sexism" or "unlearning internal racism."[36] But as one workshop participant recalled, "They melded together two models that didn't make sense—the antioppression model and the express-your-feelings model."[37]

While analyzing sexism or internalized racism can be useful, this was not the underlying goal of RC practice, which promotes emotional discharge as the only damage-repair process that can restore people's inherent rationality.[38] Instead of exploring, say, the barrage of cultural imagery that encourages men to belittle women or whites to denigrate blacks, participants in RC workshops were encouraged to publicly recount their earliest and most disturbing encounters with sexual or racial misconduct. They were then paired off for further sharing of intimate experiences. As one woman who attended an RC "coalition building" workshop that was unwittingly sponsored by the Unitarian Universalist church recalled, "We were told that this was a new, egalitarian method for dealing with difficult emotions." The goal was to get individuals to laugh, yell, shake, or cry. Yet while some may have experienced the desired catharsis, others who "testified" were left in a state of confusion and vulnerability. "The inauthenticity and inappropriateness of it was stunning," noted a minister who observed an RC workshop at his church, in which a woman was encouraged to describe a terrifying sexual assault to a group of people she had just met. "It was so dangerous and irresponsible."[39]

Respected academics who have described the positive effects of their experiences in RC, including historian John D'Emilio, psychologist Phyllis Bronstein, and sociologist Thomas Scheff, are proof that RC need not reduce its participants to a childish, narcissistic state.[40] Yet its baseline is deeply anti-intellectual, and its haphazard practice of eliciting strong emotions could damage already fragile people. Some former RC members speak bitterly about how they were pushed to co-counsel with people who were clearly unstable. They describe breaches in the confidentiality of co-counseling sessions. They confirm that by demanding the public airing of intimate information, RC sometimes undercut its members' intellectual independence and emotional maturity.[41]

As RC expanded its influence, its chances of damaging individuals and progressive organizations increased. In 1984, for example, RC leader Cherie Brown formalized the organization's ties to what Lasch-Quinn calls "the diversity training movement" by creating the National Coalition Building Institute (NCBI), which offered workshops aimed at reducing prejudice and intergroup conflict.[42] Clientele were easy to find. As one observer noted, the NCBI "made a fortune when Louis Farrakhan inflamed black-Jewish tensions" in the mid-1980s, thus increasing demand for the mediation of such conflicts.[43] By 1996, the NCBI had fifty city chapters, all earnestly attempting to induce discharge around feelings of race- and class-based shame.

To increase their reach and influence, RC adherents seem in some cases to have identified groups whose mission seemed in line with RC values, joined them, and pushed them to address the root cause of bigotry and injustice—

undischarged emotional pain. Since most left-wing organizations have more concrete agendas, an influx of RC members could be harmful. Their incessant focus on discharging psychological biases could weaken or destroy the groups' political efficacy.[44]

This troubling dynamic was at play in the New Jewish Agenda (NJA), an organization founded in 1980 to be "a Jewish voice among progressives, and a progressive voice among Jews." The opening conference brought together a broad spectrum of politically engaged individuals. According to a recent history of the NJA, RC, described only as a "therapeutic and consciousness raising community," exerted disproportionate influence. "The RC crowd was . . . well-versed in specific detailed group-process that was frustrating to other attendees." As a result, NJA founder Gerry Serotta explains, "we were badly hamstrung by very silly fights about process that had to do with a jargon . . . that was coming from co-counseling." Those lacking a "high tolerance" for debates about process fled the organization. As Serotta delicately puts it, this influenced "the quality of people who were willing to continue" on with NJA. Avi Rose, an RC member who was active in the NJA, gives the situation a harsher spin. RC members sought

> to influence the direction of the organization, so the distressing thing was that there was an effort to do that and then a simultaneous denial that that's what people were doing. . . . [A]s a result . . . non-RCers were wondering, . . . "Is there this cult . . . that's . . . trying to run the show . . . ? Why don't they identify who they are? And why do they go in the corner and laugh inappropriately?" It was just really destructive. . . . [P]eople got the hell out of there.[45]

When RC commandeered movement agendas, the results could be disastrous. One example is RC's influence on a Brooklyn branch of the National Black Women's Health Project (NBWHP). The organization was founded in 1984 to address the health needs of African American women, who suffer high rates of heart disease, stroke, and diabetes. Cofounder Lillie Allen had participated in RC groups in graduate school and incorporated some RC insights and techniques into the workshop "Black and Female: What Is the Reality?" at the project's first national conference. Incorporated into a larger black feminist and womanist discourse, RC techniques shaped the distinctive self-help component of the NBWHP, which focused on helping black women understand and overcome their internalized oppression. During the 1980s, the NBWHP's self-help addressed personal, political, and public health concerns simultaneously, if unevenly, as Evan Hart notes: "though the self-help program had a basic structure and common goals . . . individual self-help groups adapted [it] to meet the needs of their members."[46]

As a result, one woman who joined the Brooklyn chapter of the NBWHP in 1991 recalled that by that point, the group had stopped engaging in community organizing or discussing the economic roots of black women's poor health. Furthermore, they did not offer services such as blood pressure screening or sickle cell anemia testing. Instead, meetings were devoted to introducing black women to RC. Women were told that RC was a form of "radical praxis" that grew out of the 1930s labor movement and was devoted to empowering the poor through free therapy. In the context of the multiple traumas of early 1990s Brooklyn, including the spread of crack, an AIDS epidemic, deindustrialization, a decaying infrastructure, and high rates of homelessness, many responded with enthusiasm to this promise of healing.[47]

What paraded as healing, however, turned out to be harmful. First, an emotive woman would describe her sexual victimization in front of a gathering of fifty or so. Then the audience would pair off. Each person would recount her most painful memory while her partner listened. After five minutes, the roles switched. It created a "false intimacy," a participant recalled. "They sold me on the idea that it was a radical form of activism," but in fact it was "like having the sutures of a wound ripped open" in an unsafe environment. "I finally realized it was abusive," this woman recalled. "I don't think it was a good example of building community." Instead of encouraging discussion of a range of experiences as a foundation for analysis, as in the feminist CR model, organizers told members that their self-understanding was flawed—unless they dredged up and publicly purged their hidden trauma. If they did so, they would be rewarded by the attention of the group—though at the price of embracing a new identity as a victim. In the end, it is unclear if women purged their pain or simply reexperienced and reinforced it. As a result of RC members' dominance of this particular branch of the NBWHP, an organization that promised desperately needed health care, emotional healing, and political empowerment to its members instead left some members further traumatized.[48]

RC's influence has waned in recent years. Starting in the late 1980s, numerous national and international RC affiliates broke with Jackins because of evidence that he had pushed sex on hundreds of women in the guise of counseling them about sexual distress. They also rejected Jackins's insistence that homosexuality was a "distress pattern" and his call for a "quarantine of people with AIDS."[49] Jackins's death in 1999 left the group without a charismatic leader (although his son Tim has taken over as head of International Re-Evaluation Counseling Communities).

Yet even in its weakened state, RC continues to introduce its odd version of therapeutic culture to progressive organizations. For example, some RC members have joined US Jewish organizations that oppose Israel's post-1967 occupation of former Egyptian and Jordanian territories—land which, they argue, should become the basis of a Palestinian state. When one such group, Brit Zedek v'Shalom, faced a leadership vacuum in the early 2000s, Cherie Brown, Diane Balser, and other RC activists assumed the organization's leadership positions and immediately instituted the RC policy of "no attacks on leaders"—a policy derived from efforts to defend Jackins from hundreds of carefully documented accusations of sexual misconduct.[50] This, along with their insistence that emotional pain was at the root of all conflicts, including political differences, effectively silenced opposition within the organization. "They waged a war on facts," recalled one woman who left Brit Zedek after Brown and Balser took over. "If you strongly expressed a political opinion, they ignored your argument and insisted you had to deal with your emotions instead."[51]

The new leadership retained Brit Zedek's original agenda, although the group's mission shifted from broad-based education about Israeli occupation and the organization of US Jews to oppose it to an arguably narrower agenda of encouraging individual Jews to lobby their congressional representatives. They also promoted activities addressing what they saw as the core of the Israel-Palestine conflict—unresolved emotions. To the horror of Brit Zedek's founders, the group organized ventures such as the Listening Project. This involved setting up a booth at Jewish cultural festivals in which individuals were invited to speak for five minutes about the Israeli/Palestinian conflict. Their words were not recorded or analyzed. It was simply assumed to be "salutary" for Jews to express their feelings on this emotionally charged topic.[52]

In 2009, Brit Zedek entered into a cooperation agreement with J Street, a lobbying group of US Jews devoted to a two-state solution to the Israel/Palestine conflict. J Street accepted Brit Zedek's self-representation as a grassroots organization.[53] It seemed unaware or unconcerned about the perils of embracing an RC-dominated group, although perhaps it should have been. In articles published in *Tikkun* magazine between 2009 and 2011, Brown (identified not as an RC leader but as the founder of the NCBI and board member of Brit Zedek) argued that Jews have never "un-numbed" from the grief and terror they hold from past persecutions and have passed their fears to their children. She proposed support groups in which Jews listen to one another and vent their emotions, promising that if they did so, their "rigidified" attitudes would melt away. They would learn to "think with greater, relaxed clarity about social justice issues" and "face what is really needed for a long-range, viable solution for Israel and the Palestinian people" (a solution Brown left unspecified).[54] There are signs that Brown's perspective has been embraced by J Street, probably the most active American Jewish organization opposed to Israeli occupation. At J Street's 2012 conference, most of a student training session went to pairing students off so they could share their feelings. I asked a participant what she thought they were doing. "Dialog?" she responded. Perhaps—or perhaps they were unintentionally engaging in co-counseling.

THE LEFT AND THERAPEUTIC CULTURE

The authors of the therapeutic critique denigrated progressive movements. They viewed activists' anger at injustice as symptomatic of an implosion of an earlier, largely mythical culture of responsibility, respect, and restraint—a respect and restraint that never extended to the treatment of racial minorities and others lacking social power. They mocked emotional introspection and examination of feelings about social difference, neither of which is inherently negative. Indeed, even an organization as extreme as RC could be beneficial in these regards. As a former RC youth leader recalled, "RC opened my eyes to the experience of people of different backgrounds." The initial attraction of RC, she added, was that "someone was paying attention to my mental and emotional well-being."[55] Clearly, therapeutic culture critics' neo-Victorian valorizing of emotional repression is no answer to the human need for emotional care, much less to progressives' desire to challenge bigotry and internalized self-hatred.

Yet, as another, more cynical observer noted, such needs and desires can be easily exploited. "Women are suckers" for RC, she said, because "they are vulnerable to people who claim to care about their feelings."[56] And as RC shows, all antiracism workshops are not alike. We have a responsibility to examine the premises of organizations claiming to challenge bigotry and to reject those whose premises are absurd and whose practices put individuals at risk.

One should distinguish between therapeutic culture critics' denigration of the left's legitimate interests in the interplay between the psychological and the political and their insights into the perils of trumpeting the healing power of raw emotion. The odd history of RC's pursuit of discharge makes this distinction clear. Feminist CR showed how attention to personal experience, accompanied by analysis, led to positive transformations in women's lives, from the rewriting of sexual assault laws to the relative opening of job markets. Emoting for its own sake is another matter. Yet because the therapeutic culture critique dismisses all attention to personal experience and emotional pain as narcissistic and infantilizing, it denigrates real suffering. It remains too ham-fisted to make distinctions between sophisticated treatments of the psychological costs of social oppression and simplistic, cultish ones.

Yet despite therapeutic culture critics' biases and limitations, their critique of public emotional expressiveness remains relevant to the left. Progressive movements champion groups who experience cultural and economic marginalization. Such groups long suffered at the hands of experts who categorized them as ill instead of angry. They have reason to reject such authorities and hence are particularly vulnerable to organizations such as RC that present themselves as empowering and egalitarian. Therapeutic culture critics' admonitions to marginalized people to suck it up and carry on is no remedy. But RC's encouragement of public venting as the solution to all problems, personal and political, can have negative effects, which we would be wise to address.

The therapeutic promise of intimacy answers a real need. Institutions that supposedly provide caring and community, such as churches and families, have been oppressive to some in the left, such as lesbian, gay, bisexual, and transgender people and women who reject conventional behavior. But as RC's history shows, false intimacy and pressure to publicly reenact private pain can damage already fragile individuals. The result is the opposite of what RC and other therapeutic cults promise—and close to what therapeutic culture critics predict. Left-wing organizations that attract adherents of therapeutic movements like RC can be weakened. Those fully embracing such approaches can experience a dangerous combination of emotional weakness and rigid righteousness, rather than the personal empowerment and analytic clarity needed for the difficult task of social change.

CHAPTER 10

Pills

David Herzberg

THE PHARMACEUTICAL APOCALYPSE?

You don't have to be a doctor to know what everyone knows about pills: we use far too many of them, and they are killing us. And not just us. Our whole culture is dying, maybe even civilization itself. Hear it from historian Christopher Lane, one of many who makes this argument, in his prize-winning book *Shyness: How Normal Behavior Became a Sickness.* "We've narrowed healthy behavior so dramatically that our quirks and eccentricities—the *normal* emotional range of adolescence and adulthood—have become problems we fear and expect drugs to fix," he laments. "We are no longer citizens justifiably concerned about our world. Our worries [are] chemical imbalances that drugs must cure. . . . The sad consequence is a vast, perhaps unrecoverable, loss of emotional range, an impoverishment of human experience." This wasn't always the case: Americans used to savor "the wisdom that ensues from deep reflection," and their culture produced the likes of Emily Dickinson, Henry David Thoreau, and Nathaniel Hawthorne. "Today," Lane notes mordantly, "psychiatrists offer us a pill."[1] It's like a pharmaceutical version of *Invasion of the Body Snatchers,* with deep thinkers replaced by anxious conformists eager to avoid social engagement and existential contemplation.

This vision belongs to a dynamic new literature of pharmaceutical exposé, and it shares many of that genre's strengths and weaknesses. At their best—which is very good indeed—books like Lane's expose how corporate and professional self-interest has influenced scientific research, transformed the medical marketplace, and even redefined such basic concepts as "illness" and "therapy," all on the way to vastly expanding drug use, enormously increasing pharmaceutical company profits, and utterly degrading American psychiatry.[2]

This is a very important story, full of shocking revelations and perceptive arguments about our medical system and its founding myths. Everyone should read at least one of these titles. Probably more.

There is one thing, however, that diligent readers of this literature will generally not find: a politically meaningful portrait of the people who use all those medications. On this topic analytical sophistication gives way to relatively simple depictions of pill takers as manipulated and powerless victims of avoidable drug-induced tragedy. Or worse, as pleasure-hungry enablers of drug company perfidy, willfully blinded by their own eagerness for quick fixes and at least partly to blame for the coming pharmaceutical apocalypse.

Lane's *Shyness* is a good example. It implicates the public in the coming disaster by suggesting that "we" have willingly narrowed our conception of healthy behavior and given up justifiable concerns about the world. At the same time, however, it strongly implies that the public is actually impotent—after implicating "us" in its dramatic opening claims of cultural loss, it never mentions "us" again. (Even the sense of loss fades from the story, perhaps for good reason, cultural decline being notoriously difficult—or perhaps notoriously easy?—to prove.) Instead *Shyness* focuses on the psychiatric professionals and pharmaceutical companies who have worked the cultural disappearing trick. Cultural change, in other words, happens at the hands of psychiatric authorities and drug marketers, unaffected by the decisions of ordinary people—unless one counts the venal decision to accept easy fixes for existential suffering.

I don't mean to pick on Lane; he's an insightful historian and a wonderful writer. More to the point, *Shyness* is hardly alone in its tendency to give short shrift to ordinary pill takers. Take Charles Barber's *Comfortably Numb: How Psychiatry Is Medicating a Nation*, which describes a "Serotonin Empire" wherein pill takers "come to inhabit an inauthentic and less challenging existence and come to embrace a uniquely American form of emotional sanitation."[3] Or Melody Petersen's *Our Daily Meds: How Pharmaceutical Companies Transformed Themselves into Slick Marketing Machines and Hooked the Nation on Prescription Drugs*, which pairs a devastating critique of drug industry duplicity with a similarly harsh (if extremely brief) slap at ordinary people: "We expect instant gratification of our desires and a quick fix for whatever bothers or distracts. Americans are eager to believe in the panaceas offered in the six drug commercials that regularly accompany each evening's news."[4] And the list could go on.[5]

Such portraits will sound familiar to anyone who has read other critiques of therapeutic culture and its mindless, depoliticized minions, with one notable caveat: the new pharmaceutical critics are much more firmly grounded in a muckraking tradition of exposing corporate criminality. Medications can, and do, kill, injure, and otherwise harm the people who take them; pharmaceutical companies can, and do, obscure these risks in the pursuit of profit. This situation cries out for close scrutiny by intelligent and able researchers. So it can be unnerving to raise questions about pill takers' agency, which risks playing into the hands of drug industry "democrats" who claim that widening access to pharmaceutical goods is automatically empowering and that people choose to take pills simply because they work. And yet, as with the therapeutic culture critique more broadly, one cannot help but be skeptical of a politics that casts millions of pill takers, most of whom just happen to be women, as dupes perpetrating their own oppression and destroying American culture along the way. There is rich territory between the false optimism of drug marketers and the dark vision of cultural critics, and in this essay I would like to suggest a few ways we might begin to take stock of it.

POWER TO THE PILL POPPERS!

One clue that psychiatric medicines may not be harbingers of political and cultural apocalypse: if they were, then we have been living in a postapocalyptic world for some time now—at least since the late 1960s and early 1970s, when prescriptions for Valium topped 100 million annually in a much smaller population. And yet that era was hardly known for political or cultural somnolence, even among the most rabid pill takers. The vast majority of Valium users were women, and one of the most radical rebellions of the era was—that's right—feminism. If those women were soma-eating zombies, how did they stage a political revolution? Of course we do not want to join drug marketers in calling the pills women's great emancipators (or, as Peter Kramer said of Prozac, "feminist drugs"[6]). Pills had no more power to cause feminism than to prevent it. Indeed, one of the signal accomplishments of the women's health movement was to dramatically reduce the prescribing of Valium and other psychiatric medications, precisely because—feminists agued—they were sedating, conformist, and individual ways to resolve problems that were fundamentally social and political and could only be "cured" through activism.[7]

The story of feminists and pills is complex enough to raise suspicions about simpler tales of either the pills-are-the-apocalypse or the pills-are-liberating variety. But where can we turn to find the kinds of nuanced and multivalent stories we need? One good place to look for models is beyond pharmaceutical history to the more developed vein of scholarship that examines the politics of popular culture and, more specifically, of consumerism.[8]

It is, of course, common sense that patients are not consumers and that health care is not a consumer good. This is the logic behind the establishment of the Food and Drug Administration and prescription-only laws: patients do not have the knowledge and expertise required to make good choices about health care consumption, so they need expert protection. And yet the divide between medications and other consumer goods can be overstated. Pharmaceuticals were among the first brand-name goods sold nationally in the nineteenth century, and drug companies have been influential pioneers in modern marketing all the way through to the present day. Nor are pharmaceutical markets the only ones to incorporate expert guidance: protective intermediaries can be found all over the place, from the Federal Trade Commission to *Consumer Reports*, from interior decorators to countless boycotting activist groups.[9] Further, while "prescription only" is an unusually strong form of intermediary, it is far from infallible. There are countless ways to get a prescription if you want one. So it is not unreasonable to think that the history of popular consumption might provide useful insight into pharmaceuticals.

Interestingly, consumer culture scholars used to sound a lot like pharmaceutical critics. Influenced by Frankfurt School Marxists, who saw mass culture as a fascist tool for securing the tacit consent of the masses, scholars in the 1940s and 1950s dismissed the progressive political potential of consumerism. Commercial goods, they argued, only entangled their consumers ever further into conformist acceptance of the capitalist status quo. They could not be liberating.[10] Beginning in the 1980s, however, scholars began to reconsider commercial culture, in part because what counted as "political" had begun to change as academia absorbed the lessons of the civil rights and feminist movements. Some of the first revisions focused on working-class ethnic leisure activities in the early twentieth century, as historians found that saloons, dance halls, amusement parks, trashy novels, cheap fashion, radios, cinemas, and brand-name goods could be used to sustain oppositional cultural values while also creating spaces for young women to challenge familial control.[11] Other historians looked at boycotts and similar kinds of formal consumer activism, which, they noted, were forms of political action unusually welcoming to women and nonwhites.[12]

The most valuable scholarship for our purposes began to come out in the 1990s, in work that explored how acts of consumption could provide building blocks for radical identities even as they also entangled consumers in oppressive economic relationships. One of my favorite examples of this approach came in Robin D.G. Kelley's "The Riddle of the Zoot," which argued that Malcolm X's early years as a "conked" and zoot-suited criminal were more politically significant than Malcolm himself was willing to admit in his *Autobiography*. The young Malcolm Little may have accepted racist notions of appearance (straight hair) and fun (consumer goods) while spending his money in an oppressive economy. But he was also insisting on a right to joy and pleasure in defiance of racist social values that held him unworthy of these fine things and that limited his approved role to serving whites—especially during the "total war" against Germany and Japan. This type of defiance, Kelley suggests, was no false consciousness. Radical in its own right, it was also an important part of Malcolm X's political journey.[13]

Kelley thus challenged scholars to explore the resistance that poor and marginalized people undertake with the limited and sometimes even self-destructive tools available to them. The resulting victories may be partial, contingent, and accompanied by even larger defeats. But so are many, if not all, political achievements. This is certainly true in the case of pharmaceuticals. Given the power disparities within pharmaceutical culture and the undeniable risks that pill users are exposed to, the stories we are looking for are unlikely to be uncomplicated triumphs.

A good way to find these stories begins by acknowledging a not-so-hidden secret running through much of the new pharmaceutical history: despite the enormous waves of drug marketing that have crashed over America for the past more than one hundred years, there has probably been as much (and sometimes more) cultural pressure not to use mood-altering medications. Christopher Lane's *Shyness* and other modern antidrug manifestoes are nothing new; rather, they are only the most formal articulations of a long moralizing tradition. Take tranquilizers, for example; for every glowing, tranquilizer-friendly article placed in *Cosmopolitan* magazine by industry public relations men in the decades after World War II, there were five or ten articles elsewhere—or even in a different issue of *Cosmo* itself—warning about toxicity, addiction, and cultural traditions under siege.

If you can believe surveys, these articles captured widely held attitudes of unease or outright opposition to use of psychiatric medicines. Drug skepticism was so common, in fact, that a cottage industry of psychiatrists and pharmaceutical industry spokesmen produced a bulging literature specifically devoted to debunking it and warning about underuse of helpful medicines. It was even given its own dismissive name, "pharmacological Calvinism," by influential psychiatrist Gerald Klerman in 1972.[14]

In light of all this, we might well wonder why so many people have continued to use psychiatric medications, despite deep skepticism, bordering on the paranoid, about the intentions of physicians and drug companies. The implicit explanation in many pharmaceutical histories, as I noted earlier, is none too flattering: at best, pill takers are desperate and powerless and thus have little choice but to accept what they are offered; at worst they are gullible and eager for quick fixes. There is probably some truth to these arguments. There are, for example, compelling correlations between drug advertising and sales.[15] But correlation and causation are notoriously fickle bedfellows, and claims about consumer gullibility are particularly suspect in pharmaceutical markets, where consumers can only buy what physicians prescribe.

A better way to characterize pill takers might be by likening them to the young Malcolm X: negotiating from a position of weakness among powerful contending forces. They are met at every corner by drug companies, purveyors of powerful but dangerous substances who are motivated more by profit than concern for individual drug takers. They must navigate the complex and occasionally baffling protections of drug regulators, who can sometimes be too weak and sometimes too strong in safeguarding the public.[16] They must negotiate, too, with their physicians, who can heal but who have also often served as agents of gender and race politics inimical to individual patients' best interests. All this takes place amidst a cacophony of unsolicited advice from cultural authorities castigating medications as an easy way out or—alternately—praising them as technological wonders. And of course, at the center of this maelstrom is their own very real suffering, be it emotional, social, political, or some combination of all three. In choosing to accept or even demand particular pills—or to refuse them—ordinary people make clear political choices that, almost by definition, defy some authorities even as they follow others. The benefit to drug companies, in other words, does not exhaust the political ramifications of a decision to use psychiatric medications, any more than the benefit to the clothing industry is the last word on Malcolm Little's purchase of zoot suits.

To illustrate this, let's take a closer look at one of the seminal texts in the feminist campaign against Valium in the late 1970s: television producer Barbara Gordon's memoir of addiction, *I'm Dancing As Fast As I Can*, later made into a movie starring Jill Clayburgh. At the beginning of the story, Gordon is wrestling with anxiety and panic despite her successful career. Politically unenlightened and respectful of sexist medical authorities, she accepts her psychiatrist's prescription for Valium, a decision for which she castigates herself. "I wasn't that weak, goddammit," she remembers thinking as she filled the prescription. "I wasn't. Someday I'll learn what's behind all this [anxiety] shit, I promised myself. But right now I'll get more Valium."[17] The dangers of her medical docility become even sharper when her psychiatrist tells her to stop taking the pills "cold turkey," which she does. Withdrawal effects cause a psychotic break and land her in a mental asylum, where her political consciousness is raised through terrifyingly hard talk therapy and increased self-knowledge. When she is finally released she no longer yearns for the easy way out and is ready to teach other women about the need to become skeptical—and political—patients.

This was a powerful story, and evidence is abundant that it resonated with many women, helping to stir an anti-Valium drug panic.[18] But if we read this memoir against the grain, the way Kelley read Malcolm X's *Autobiography*, a very different picture emerges. There is plenty of evidence that Gordon was no political naïf at the beginning of the book, for example, no matter how she may have later described herself. She was a pioneering woman in the male-dominated world of television. She won awards (including an Emmy) and had successfully negotiated a remarkable degree of artistic freedom from CBS to produce documentaries on politically charged subjects like slumlords, mental patients' rights, and the plight of Vietnam War veterans. As she puts it in the book, "I was a lucky lady, lucky to be able to merge my politics, my passion . . . my private self, with my career."[19] Meanwhile she was living with a man to whom she was not married, much to her parents' aggressive dismay. This was no timid woman afraid to challenge gender orthodoxies.

More specifically, there are hints that even her Valium use was not simple passive obedience. For example, her lover hated the drug—and hated her psychiatrist too. Foreshadowing the violently controlling person he would turn out to be, he insisted that she could better cure her panic attacks by marrying him: "If you'd only marry me, babe, I'd make sure they went away."[20] Maybe taking Valium wasn't only timidity but also a strategic choice to help her handle the stress of being a professional pioneer with an unconventional romantic life. Valium might not have been good for her, any more than a conk or a zoot suit was good for Malcolm Little, but it may have helped her to continue withstanding significant social and cultural pressures to back off from her more politically risky life choices. Maybe it even helped her to enjoy them—although she is not willing even to hint at this possibility in the memoir. Valium may not have been a perfect strategy, but that does not mean it was a perfectly bad one. And if you read between the lines of Gordon's own self-criticism you can see that she recognizes at least some degree of agency—she describes it as culpability—in the decision to take the drug. As she told *People* magazine, she was part of "a silent conspiracy with the psychiatrist [to replace] therapy with pills. For that I am as accountable as he, but he should have known better."[21]

Does this mean that Valium was politically empowering? Not at all: it means that Gordon was politically empowered, in a contingent and conflicted way, and Valium was one of the imperfect tools she reached for, probably because corporate and medical forces made it so available to her (and not, admittedly, out of concern for her). But if she had quit the drug slowly instead of cold turkey, and thus avoided the calamitous withdrawal syndrome, her book might have had a radically different political moral at the end. Her critique of her earlier self as naïve rang true in some ways, just as the broader critique against shoveling Valium at unhappy women undoubtedly carried truth. But it also robbed those women of their agency, however partial, misdirected, or even (in some cases) self-destructive it might have been.

In the end, feminism probably did have more to offer than a pill—at least, most of the time. But the two were not necessarily mutually exclusive. (Indeed, Valium was one of many shared experiences that formed the basis of "consciousness raising" for some second-wavers.) More important, if we bestow the term "agency" only on those who pick what we judge to be the purest form of political resistance, history will provide us with precious few "agents."

Casting our political net so widely takes us into even riskier territory for rethinking: illicit or nonmedical use (i.e., abuse) of prescription drugs, a practice that has been surprisingly widespread throughout the twentieth century. Prescription drug abuse has often been attributed to the combined power of drug marketing and the gullibility of the American public.[22] These factors may play roles, but such critiques tend to ignore the rich and extensive global history of recreational drug use and abuse. Drugs have been commercial items for much of that history, true, but it would strain credulity to argue that this thousand-year-old tale has been driven by criminal masterminds continually preying on an endless series of innocent publics.[23] Cultural biases invite us to favor the privileged social groups associated with pharmaceutical drug abuse and see them as victims, not culprits. Otherwise why would we assume that people who pop pills have been snookered by a pharmaceutical-industrial complex, while street drug addicts are morally suspect?

A better way to think of prescription drug abusers can be found in Caroline Jean Acker's *Creating the American Junkie*, a study of the relationship between addiction researchers and addicts in the early twentieth century. Acker argues for an ethnographic model of addiction, which, she says, assesses addicts' decisions "in the context of [their] life course, identity, and social environment . . . allowing reconstruction of the addict's life in terms meaningful to the addict him- or herself." The "addict career" is no simple, unchanging portrait of pathology or victimization but a life story complete with "such issues as making a living" and choices "facilitated or constrained by structural factors such as law, social custom, . . . drug markets, and so forth." Both judgments and sympathy take a back seat in such analyses to exploring the strategic decisions addicts make to sustain, further, or quit their careers.[24]

Seen from this angle, using a brand-name version of a chosen drug instead of the street alternative can be understood, in some circumstances, as a rational move. Because of various legal and market mechanisms, one can know a great deal more about prescription medications than street drugs; criminal penalties have often been lighter for the same reasons. Indeed, where markets make them available and affordable, at least some addicts prefer branded drugs.[25] Again, such a strategic preference highlights the terrible trade-offs that can be involved in consumer politics; few people see drug abuse as a good route to empowerment. And yet it is possible to see decisions made within the context of addiction, limited as they are, as meaningful efforts to make the best choices possible in highly constrained circumstances—efforts that are themselves a defiance of sorts against a culture that reads addicts as dangerous ciphers, utterly dominated by mindless need.

Returning to licit use of medications, we can also find this kind of contingent agency in Internet chat rooms like crazyboards.org, a forum where drug users, would-be drug users, and former drug users share information, stories, and sophisticated analyses of physicians and pharmaceutical companies. Posts are typically skeptical but not paranoid about drug companies and physicians. The site's tone suggests cautious consumers, aware of their vulnerability and of the power differentials they face, who are helping each other maximize benefits while avoiding risks.

It's worth quoting at length from one thread, begun by "Daisy," to give an idea of how crazyboards.com looks in action. The thread began with this post:

> My pdoc [psychiatrist] gave me a sample today of Aplenzin, which was just released for sale. I couldn't find a lot of information on it. He said that it would likely have less side effects than my Wellbutrin XL, but from what I've read, the only differences are that alcohol will not affect the release of the drug and that those who take 450 mg of Wellbutrin a day can now only take one pill. I've google searched and that's all of the info I can find. Anybody know about this? What makes it so different from Wellbutrin XL? Anybody else going to be a guinea pig?[26]

After being told that "It's the same active ingredient as the Wellbutrin your [sic] were taking with what appears to be a slightly different way of delivering the medication," Daisy announced that she was "willing to try something new," even though she was skeptical that it would do any good ("it sounds like Biovail just wants to make some money," she wrote). She promised to "keep y'all updated on how it goes."

Daisy's experience with the new drug was inconclusive, but she appreciated a reduction in side effects. Her final report to crazyboards.com gives a good sense of what it means to make choices from within the modern pharmaceutical landscape:

> My doctor only gave me a 7 day sample, but I think I'll call and see if I can get another 2 or 3. I need to call my insurance company and see how much it will cost. I found out it will also cost me more to get a different Wellbutrin generic. If this begins to help and continues to give me a lack of side effects, I'll compare the cost difference and see which is a better deal. I'll likely stick with the Wellbutrin and just get a different generic, but it would be great if I could get a few more free samples from my pdoc. I'll just tell him I want to make sure it works before I go spending a ton of money on a new med when I JUST bought the Wellbutrin! He's pretty cool, so hopefully he'll agree.

One could certainly make an argument that "Daisy" and her interlocutors have been coopted into the worldview of biological psychiatry, accepting their diagnoses and believing that medications are the route to health.[27] But they are also critically examining their responses to those medications, valuing the expertise of their own experiences within a system that typically assigns merit only to medical and pharmaceutical authorities. They are skeptical of physicians and drug companies but believe that good things can be extracted from them if they are handled correctly, that is, on the patients' own terms. Crazyboards is designed to soften the great disparities of power and knowledge that patients face. (Many posters write, with varying degrees of satisfaction or irritation, that they know more about the drugs under discussion than their doctors.) Given the realities of the pharmaceutical landscape as described by the new pharmaceutical histories—of great dangers lurking behind the latest miracle pills—this may not be an unreasonable aim.

CONCLUSIONS

It is important not to counter ridicule of therapeutic culture with Pollyanna praise of it. As I hope my examples have made clear, even at their best, pills are imperfect tools. Drug critics are not wrong to focus on the health risks posed by Prozac, Dexedrine, Valium, Quaalude, Adderall, and the rest, nor is it wrong to eviscerate the corporate or medical malfeasance that allows the public to be exposed—or overexposed—to those risks. I have no quarrel with these narratives. In fact, I would argue, this sort of pushback against the harms and injustices perpetrated by a pharmaceutical-industrial complex is itself a good example of the politics of therapeutic culture. The experience of being helped, or harmed, by medications is personal and individual, but, thanks to the marketing-driven fascination with all things pharmaceutical, it is also highly public and social—a basis for collective action. Far from politically neutering America, psychiatric drugs have galvanized a wide range of activism, from oppositional medical research, bureaucratic crusades, and investigative exposés, to grassroots campaigns to treat Valium addicts with a dose of feminism. The activism of present-day "psychiatric survivor" groups such as MindFreedom International, for example, powered by "those labeled with psychiatric disabilities," aims to "challenge abuse by the psychiatric drug industry" and "support the self-determination of psychiatric survivors and mental health consumers."[28]

Defending the drug industry (and professional psychiatry) from such challengers is not my goal. Instead I want to add another dimension to the story: the decision making of ordinary pill takers, who are sometimes victims but who are also political actors whose agency we should not ignore or deride. I would like to suggest that rethinking pills leads us to two kinds of oppositional politics. In the first, pills are an example of a therapeutic culture, much disparaged but also endowed with unrecognized political salience. The act of consuming pills can be a strategic (if risky) choice to assist in pursuing personal goals in the face of steep cultural pressures—to use drug companies' power, in effect, to resist control by other social authorities. The pursuit of health, especially for women, may involve creatively working around, not succumbing to, medical authorities. In the second kind of politics, pills are not part of therapeutic culture themselves; instead, they are the harm that people need to recover from. In this case, some kinds of antipharmaceutical activism can be a sort of openly political "recovery movement" tackling an enormously powerful American institution.

On the surface these two pharmaceutical politics seem contradictory. One sees liberatory potential in pills, and the other sees oppression. But people do not live in a world with the contradictions ironed out; to live in a "pill-popping culture" means to participate in both stories, for better and for worse. We have seen a great deal of terrific scholarship on why we should oppose pills. A full accounting of the place of pharmaceuticals in American culture should also reckon more seriously with the reasons people use them anyway.

CHAPTER 11

Testimony

Stevan Weine

When survivors give accounts of the events of political violence that they themselves have endured or witnessed, they often do so through stories referred to as testimonies. These are modern narratives for modern atrocities—for what psychologist Robert Lifton called "an extreme century"—and they shift the focus of classical psychoanalysis: rather than addressing the subject's interior, they speak instead of the experience of war, nuclear weapons, and genocide.[1] In the 1960s and '70s, Lifton's work with Holocaust survivors and Vietnam veterans affirmed that survivors of historical extremity possess valuable and potentially powerful moral knowing.

Survivors' stories were also central to the Chilean mental health professionals Elizabeth Lira and Eugenia Weinstein, who introduced the idea of the "testimony of political repression as a therapeutic instrument" in the early 1980s.[2] Since then the survivors of many other types of traumas have given testimony in diverse political and mental health settings, and the narrative form has become central to contemporary culture and its therapeutic ambitions.

There are good reasons for this. As anthropologist Michael D. Jackson has observed, "A story enables us to fuse the world within and the world without. In this way we gain some purchase over the events that confounded us, humbled us and left us helpless. In telling a story we renew our faith that the world is within our grasp."[3] Testimony's seeming ability to "fuse" or create a shortcut between the private and public worlds, combined with its considerable redemptive promise, have given it a unique therapeutic and cultural power.

But testimony has its critics. In his sweeping intellectual history *Thinking the Twentieth Century*, Tony Judt indicts testimony along with other forms of personal memory as "all feeling" and "of necessity partial, brief, selective." He warns that in testimony, "memory is keyed to public, non-scholarly purposes," unlike history, which "becomes ever more open to the perspective of third parties." For Judt, the risk of "allow[ing] memory to replace history" is less that the memory of atrocity will be forgotten than that it will be misremembered, or deployed in the service of power,[4] as in the George W. Bush administration's manipulation of fears generated by the 9/11 attack as a pretext for the United States' war in Iraq.

Judt's concerns about testimony are more than the parochial concerns of a professional historian. They echo concerns from the fields of human rights, journalism, conflict resolution, and psychiatry that testimony, the unadorned story of the trauma survivor, could unintentionally loose something powerful upon the world that will do more harm than good—to personal well-being, institutional stability, or the public interest.[5] These criticisms in turn channel the anxieties of midcentury therapeutic culture critics like Robert Bellah and Richard Sennett, who worried that "we have come to care about institutions and events only when we can discern personalities at work in them or embodying them."[6] By taking a shortcut from the private to the public, in other words, testimony may distort the public.

Ambivalence about testimony runs in the other direction as well. Some mental health and human rights professionals argue that rather than being cathartic, retelling the trauma story can be retraumatizing for survivors because it reminds them of events they want to forget and can thereby make their suffering even worse.[7]

Testimonies keep being told and retold in all kinds of private and public spaces, and despite the growing critical discourse on testimony's nature, purpose, and impacts, central questions about the practice remain unaddressed. For example, what are the benefits and risks of testimony for individuals, communities, and society? What impacts, both positive and negative, have the expansion and institutionalization of testimony had upon the act of testimony and its meaning for the testimony giver? And most broadly, what are the roles of testimony in therapeutic culture?

The first of these questions is the most clinical. Trauma theorists in the 1980s took the psychoanalytic axiom that keeping secrets was unhealthy as their jumping off place. In the context of repressive and nontransparent political regimes, this insight seemed unimpeachable. Lira and Weinstein described the aims of testimony as "documentation," "purification," and "deprivatization"; their work produced documents that were used to challenge the Pinochet regime in Chile. Similarly, in her work with refugee survivors of trauma and torture, Danish psychologist Inger Agger argued that when the survivor "told her private story about a common oppression" it "nurtured the feeling of fellowship, or communitas." Through integrating the practices of psychotherapy, human rights, and feminism, Agger devised a testimony practice that aimed to empower women and give them a public voice.[8]

This logic fueled the development of testimony theory and practice during the 1980s and '90s. It was complemented by survivors who wanted to live another day if only to be able to "tell the world" about the injustice or injury done to them.[9] And it was further abetted by the form of testimony narrative itself, which often resonates with unusual intensity, beauty, truth, and power. For these powerful cultural reasons, claims such as Achille Mbembe's "I can tell my story, therefore I am"[10] have made testimony an accepted clinical practice within trauma work, even though little scientific evidence exists about whether or how giving testimony helps to achieve positive outcomes in the complex real world conditions where refugees and other survivors of political violence live. This is an important shortcoming because often in the clinical realm, what at first seems helpful turns out to be either not so helpful, helpful only under certain circumstances, or perhaps even harmful.

Several studies of testimony given to the South African Truth and Reconciliation Commission, for example, found no relationship between testifying and improved mental health, and one study observed that low forgiveness was associated with poorer psychiatric health.[11] As in South Africa, women who testified in the Rwandan Gacca Courts did not report healing but traumatization, ill-health, isolation, and insecurity. And when Phoung P. Pham et al. observed surviving victims' participation in the trial of Kaing Guek Eav, alias Duch (Case 001), at the Extraordinary Chambers in the Courts of Cambodia, they found that while survivors viewed positively their overall experience of participating and testifying, those whose claims were denied felt anger, helplessness, shame, and worthlessness. Pham's team concluded that public testimony is important but alone is unlikely to bring about healing, closure, and reconciliation for the trial victims.[12] These findings are echoed by peace psychologist Brandon Hamber, who argues that "the long-term ability of a once-off statement or public testimony to address the full psychological impact of the past is questionable."[13]

To address this gap in the clinical literature, when refugees from Bosnia-Herzegovina resettled in the United States in the mid 1990s, my colleagues and I conducted an investigation of testimony as a psychotherapeutic intervention with adults who had survived ethnic cleansing and/or siege. Using a clinical trial research design with statistical methodologies, we found that giving testimony significantly reduced the symptoms of post-traumatic stress disorder and depression in a group of Bosnian refugees. Telling their stories helped them to feel better, and this lasted for at least the six months we observed them. One survivor said, "When I speak to someone who listens to me, and who respects me, and when I can tell my story to such a person, than I feel good. I don't feel like a zero."[14]

This study taught us that under the right conditions (for example, some individuals with severe clinical forms of traumatic stress or depression may benefit first from psychopharmacological treatment), giving testimony could be beneficial to some refugee survivors of genocidal violence. Unsurprisingly, a great deal depends on the relationship between the teller and the receiver of the testimony. Unlike psychoanalysis and some psychotherapies, testimony work is brief, one or a few meetings. Yet as in psychoanalysis the listener inhabits a position of power in the relationship, even if it is a healing power. Therefore any concerns that the survivor has about confidentiality or safety must be thoroughly addressed before proceeding; the relationship must be safe, trusting, and caring. The survivor must be fully told about the aims and procedures of testimony, including the issues of who has access to their testimony. Most of all, it is essential that the person want to tell his or her story and not feel coerced. Our study was suggestive, but definitive work evaluating the effects of testimony upon individuals has still not yet been conducted.

Considering not only the clinical but also the cultural dimensions of testimony is crucial, since the practice has been significantly expanded and institutionalized over the past twenty years. Testimony has emerged as a key concept not only in mental health but also in human rights; it grounds narrative approaches to trauma work in situations of mass violence and has come to be seen as a practice in its own right that transcends traditional disciplines. Survivors giving testimony were once lone wolves but now are part of a chorus of voices organized by academics, media, nongovernmental organizations, and governments. Turn on CNN or open up the *New York Times* and someone is telling their trauma story. A website that advocates for female victims of sexual trafficking features several survivor videos. One begins, "I am a survivor of slavery in America."[15] These stories carry an authenticity, truth, and humanity that registers with readers and listeners because they are more than mere sound bites. They can set the agenda and tone for public discourse on very difficult to talk about topics like war, disasters, and social and family trauma. Testimony invites survivors' memories to rewrite not only individual but also collective history.

Although injustice and suffering are nothing new for humankind, the phenomenon of testimony as we know it today is in many respects a product of modernity. Its central ambition—"If I tell my story, I may remake not only myself, but others and perhaps even the larger public"—is literally "self-centered," and broadly therapeutic. Its narrative form and its growing prominence in everyday life have fueled the therapeutic critics' complaint that investment in the personal can come at the expense of the social or, as Richard Sennett claims, "obsession with persons at the expense of impersonal social relations . . . discolors our rational understanding of society."[16] For Sennett, specifically, the potential power in the act of remembering social traumas is undermined by the cultural logic of modern capitalism, which lends itself to a kind of mythmaking centered on private empowerment. The "memories" produced within this logic do not actually correspond with lived experience and thus undermine the potential for true understanding and meaningful resistance. In other words, Sennett notes, memory "can become a detour rather than a confrontation with capitalism's current pains."[17]

Thus if we wish to understand the role testimony plays within therapeutic culture, we must speak not only of the testimony giver's therapeutic ambitions or of the ways that the act of testifying may reiterate the centrality of the self. The cultural context in which testimony is produced must be acknowledged as well. Many persons are involved in testimony work, not as tellers, but as producers, mediators, and receivers. These agents in the testimony industry bring to it their own ambitions and power relations. While they aim explicitly to shape the "rational understanding of society," they are not necessarily committed to facilitating the diverse voices speaking in healthy conflict in shared social space—the utopian vision of memory sharing that Judt and Sennett posit as the possible antidote to mythmaking.[18] While guidelines have been developed to protect crime victims in the media, it remains uncertain who is looking out for the interests of the testimony story itself as it enters into the public realm.[19] Who assesses its correspondence with lived experience, with history?

The growth of both the testimony industry and its specifically social ambition can be seen clearly in the expansion of the institutions devoted to collecting, preserving, and circulating the stories of Holocaust survivors. These testimonies were initially collected by individual documentarians like the psychologist Henry Greenspan or groups like the Holocaust Video Archive at Yale University.[20] According to the Yad Vashem website, testimony works to promote awareness of the Holocaust by (1) rehumanizing the victims, (2) making the inconceivable more tangible, and (3) delivering moral messages.[21] The voices of survivors stand as a corrective against white-washed accounts of the Holocaust that sought to downplay its moral atrocity. Recordings ensure that survivors' voices persist across time, countering the silence or untruths of the deniers. The collection of Holocaust testimony grew exponentially when, following the success of *Schindler's List* in 1994, filmmaker Steven Spielberg established the Survivors of Shoah Visual History Foundation.[22] More than 52,000 video interviews, with survivors from fifty-eight countries, are now digitally alive and accessible for widespread public use, particularly for outreach to youth and for adults unfamiliar with the Holocaust. At some point soon, the Shoah Foundation hopes to exploit the speed of modern communications and gather testimonies of "those experiencing exclusionary and genocidal ideology in real-time, and using their voices to warn those who have the ability to intervene."[23]

Drawing on but also differing from testimony work with Holocaust survivors, the South Africa Truth and Reconciliation Committee (TRC) was undoubtedly the most socially and politically ambitious effort to use testimony to reshape the public sphere. In the TRC, wrote Fiona Ross, "Individual experiences of suffering were harnessed to the imaginative work of forging a new public imaginary and sociality."[24] Testimony was linked with legal justice, quasi-legal justice, and identity. Although the commission did not mention healing as an official aim, the widespread assumption was that the TRC would lead to the healing of individuals and the collective body. "The testimonial form," Ross explains, "became a means in the ongoing work of fashioning the self in relation to changing social circumstances . . . reshaping their understandings and seeking acknowledgement."[25] To facilitate this work, the TRC insisted that the hearings be broadcast on radio and television. As Catherine M. Cole notes, "the cameras were witnesses. They gave recognition to victims." By making their experiences real to the nation, they also remade the nation along the lines of the victims' experiences.[26]

In the years since the TRC hearings, Fiona Ross's observation that "the problems of vulnerability in the face of large-scale social processes such as global information flows has not been much addressed" has come to seem increasingly insightful.[27] Advocacy organizations often use testimony as a prompt to social action, even if not action against the exact violence that injured the testimony giver. Humanitarian aid or social justice groups may present survivor testimonies in public relations or fundraising campaigns. For example, the Rwanda Survivors Fund sponsors a reading of survivors' testimonies in Trafalgar Square each year to remember the survivors of genocide and raise awareness for the fund's other campaigns—for example HIV/AIDS prevention.[28] The voice and face, tears and courage, of survivors can get their message across far better than statements by professional leaders.

In addition to such face-to-face appeals, video testimony, begun with Holocaust survivors, has become increasingly popular. It conforms to the demands of contemporary media, which call for brevity and focus, not longer format storytelling. New possibilities for the spread of testimonies, both mediated and unmediated, have emerged with the Internet, which has created flexible ways of delivering content, with shorter interviews broadcast on news programs and longer format testimonies available on the program's website. These new channels for disseminating testimony mean that the professionals who transmit, rework, study, interpret, reframe, and restage testimonies have also multiplied. Their role is not secondary but primary, shaping how testimony enters into and does work within society and therapeutic culture. (Cable news interviews with George Clooney visiting Sudanese refugees at the height of that nation's decades-long civil war come to mind.[29])

Unlike testimony work in the clinical setting, professionals with their own agendas serve as brokers and producers, incorporating testimonies into advocacy work, packaging and staging them to be shared as widely as possible. The justification for this promotion of testimony has remained constant: education about and action against atrocity. But increasingly the self-reaffirming aims of testimony appear to merge with both celebrity and advocacy journalism, and the impact of offering testimony within this mass-mediated web remains unknown. We have come to demand that trauma survivors step forward to tell their story for the public good, but we remain unclear about what cultural work testimony can perform. Just as clinicians assume that individuals achieve some degree of personal resolution through testimony giving (which may be very difficult if not impossible to achieve in real world circumstances as complex and difficult as those faced by survivors), the testimony industry assumes that because testimony narratives are gripping, they are educational and facilitate social change.

As if this were not complex enough, consider the global and cross-cultural dimensions of testimony work. Given that many testimonies concern violent conflicts unfolding outside of the United States, testimony has become a key instance of the global circulation of information, knowledge, and practice. On the one hand, testimonies flow in, both through the media representations described above and, more literally, through refugees and immigrants repatriating to the United States. But they also flow out. Representations of testimony like Claude Lanzman's *Shoah* (1985) or Roman Polanski's *Death and the Maiden* (1994) spread and legitimate the genre around the world. Similarly, testimony has become part of the globalizing apparatus of mental health and human rights, which the United States and other Western countries attempt to export to low- and middle-income countries with very different cultures. Whether testimony can successfully cross borders without committing any grave errors of social and cultural misunderstandings has emerged as one of the most important points of tension in testimony work. For example, how well does testimony work in cultures that do not prioritize the self and confession as much as the West? Or in cultures that enjoy a stronger sense of collective participation? Or where freedom of speech is threatened or forbidden? Cultural differences call for careful efforts to adapt the testimony approach for socially, culturally, and politically diverse situations.[30] That calculus may be difficult to execute given the immediacy and power of the testimony form, but that does not mean it cannot or should not be done.

I have described testimony as a potent shortcut that makes the private public and vice versa: stories usually not told are shared, emotions usually not revealed are expressed. But the shortcut can break different ways. It can benefit individuals and groups, institutions, and societies. Or it can be neglectful, shortchanging either public or private reality. Its potential in both regards is linked but not reducible to what Sennett calls the "tyranny of intimacy"—the belief that human-to-human relations are the source of all meaning and that the impersonal workings of social power are irrelevant and beyond our reach.[31] Private "empowerment" may come at the expense of engagement with the social.

The unique dimensions of testimony mean problems may arise when people attach high ambitions for both private and public change to it but do not pursue it with commitment and care. For individual testimony givers, telling their story promises validation, understanding, consequence, and perhaps healing. For testimony receivers, it promises authenticity, truth, and inspiration. For groups, organizations, and government, testimony promises social change. It does not seem unreasonable to attach such high ambitions to the work that testimony can do with respect to the private and the public. But it may be naïve to assume that testimony's shortcuts between the private and public will be simple or achievable. Balancing these interests will always be imperfect, and constant critical vigilance should be at the very core of testimony work.

Ironically, the reverential attitudes often directed toward testimonies may themselves create obstacles. Testimony stands in contrast to many of the words that enter into public discourse. It possesses qualities of emotional intensity, authenticity, morality, and diversity that may be wanting in other parts of the culture. Critics like Sennett and Judt are correct that our society values these characteristics, and because of that we want to believe in the testimony, to encourage those who give and receive it, and to draw upon its unique strengths. But our investment may at times exaggerate testimony's potential benefits, or simplify its processes; we believe too much that it will simply help us wake up and get better, rather than seeing it as a risky but potentially productive path into larger and more complex social questions.

This is particularly true when testimonies reify either the survivor or the testimony receivers or handlers. We can see evidence of this in the practices of testimony receivers, managers, and interpreters as they make deliberate efforts to shape testimony so that it serves strategic aims. The greater the deliberate attempt to put the narrative to the service of "healing," "education," and so on, the more that testimony is asked to fit a particular narrative structure or speech genre. For example, in the testimony method of psychotherapy, clinicians deploy particular characteristics of narratives to bring about the types of changes that trauma psychotherapy deems worthwhile. They construct trauma stories to respect or facilitate the survivor's need for a plot. By establishing a sequence of events over time, trauma stories offer a means to include disparate and extreme experiences, memories, and emotions, which may otherwise be nonarticulable, incoherent, or inconsistent into one coherent narrative. They convey a point of view and actively attempt to represent the individual's subjective interpretation of events. The trauma story may not be a formula, but it can be formulaic, reflecting the fact that as testimony becomes more institutionalized, key narrative principles such as openness are often not adhered to by practitioners and purveyors.[32] As testimony gets put to more and more uses, the risk increases that it stops being an authentic expression and starts being an object for manipulation. When this happens, testimony's potential as a shortcut between public and private has failed. The testimony becomes just another commodity, and we have indeed reached the debased state Sennett fears, in which "people are working out in terms of personal feelings public matters which properly can be dealt with only through codes of impersonal meaning."[33]

This tendency to engineer the testimony is encouraged by scholarship that focuses more on production than reception. The difficulty in conceiving of testimony's reception may arise from—or reflect—our reluctance to shift our focus from individual truth telling to shared production and reception, which is entangled with community, cultural, and societal discourses, or to move from talking about healing to talking about resilience or resistance. To achieve this type of trauma work, so necessary in situations of disaster or mass violence, we need to go beyond a clinical trauma perspective and draw upon narrative approaches from literature and philosophy that explicitly connect individual to social experience.

I argue for the need to treat more seriously the narrative dimensions of testimony, including reception, in *Testimony after Catastrophe*, which demonstrates how often the professional, not the survivor, is given the power of authorship to shape, interpret, and communicate testimony. In clinical mental health settings, for example, the foundational assumptions of trauma often are not questioned, so the testimony is framed as a clinical trauma story, which foregrounds traumatic memories and the damaged self. Although many aspects of the survivors' unique local perceptions come through, others do not, and that can pose limitations in a narrative truth sense.

The narrative philosophy of Mikhail Bakhtin offers a way to revise the dichotomous thinking that has polarized the mental health field, where trauma either exists or does not exist and where the focus is either on the individual or on the collective. In my own work I have found that there is no singular "trauma story." Instead testimony is many kinds of stories, told for multiple purposes, towards different outcomes, in different contexts. In this it reflects Bakhtin's claim that "catastrophe is not finalization. It is the culmination, in collision and struggle, of points of view (of equally privileged consciousnesses, each with its own world). Catastrophe does not give these points of view resolution, but on the contrary reveals their incapability of resolution under earthly conditions."[34]

With this in mind, the survivor works with a trusted receiver to create a testimony that offers that survivor an enhanced sense of completeness and responsibility over his or her experiencing of violence that is both personal and political. Neither the choice to give testimony nor the act of giving it is by any means simple, and both involve considerable risk; there can be no guarantee that testimony will not inflict or exacerbate injuries on the one who gives it. Awareness of this, and concern with potential harms, has influenced efforts to manage the risks inherent in testimony by controlling what can or should be said. But testimony's capacity to effect change depends upon risk. As Sennett notes, "the cautionary, hard work of recall is active when narrative is unstable, but fades as narrative crystallizes and comes to rest."[35] Testimony's efficacy depends upon its properties as a polyphonic and dialogic narrative—not a closed and predetermined genre—that actively facilitates the survivor's struggles concerning individual consciousness and socially or community-based ethics. Whether it helps to make such changes, and whether this diminishes suffering, is always difficult to assess, by no means certain, and sometimes not even achievable; but under the right conditions, for the survivor, testimony can provide a hopeful act like none other.

In the present so-called age of testimony, scores of persons give testimonies, and receiving them and reflecting on their meaning is central to the culture itself. Critics like Tony Judt and Richard Sennett before him, are right to ask questions about the kind of work testimony accomplishes. But sometimes it seems as if they too want to wipe out the complexities that surround testimony giving, transmitting, and receiving—complexities that surround all narrative and rhetorical forms that move between private and public. The therapeutic ambition central to testimony remains strong: If I tell my story, I may remake not only myself, but others too and perhaps even the larger public. However, taking personal stories and making them public in order to achieve healing, truth telling, or social change is fraught with myriad complexity. It may invite us to deeper understandings of suffering, vulnerability, and injustice and the emphatically social conditions that create them. To address these complexities, more and better scholarship—particularly interdisciplinary scholarship that engages many diverse voices—is needed concerning testimony, scholarship that digs deeper than mere intellectual position taking.

This discussion of testimony's risk and benefits, its expansion and institutionalization, and its place in therapeutic culture concludes without closure. Testimony is an act that guarantees no results but is sometimes worth trying. Testimony is an imperfect balancing of the individual and the social, the local and the universal, the private and the public, but it just might be good enough. Testimony does not belong to any one discipline, and no discipline is right for testimony if it is not centered on stories.

Even though there are more questions than answers surrounding testimony, many survivors still want to tell their stories, and many others still want to preserve or further develop testimony's healing and/or liberatory potential. Testimony has a remarkable power to reshape who we are, what we believe in, and what we choose to do. It can also spread untruths and inflict harm. Testimony can either obliterate, remake, or affirm the self. Because not every testimony guarantees positive outcomes, ambivalence about testimony is necessary, and critical inquiry should be encouraged. As a prerequisite for better managing the form's challenges and opportunities, testimony givers, producers, and receivers should approach the project of testimony critically and learn how to better rely on one another to get beyond the fixed universal notions of testimony that threaten to undermine its potential.

CHAPTER 12

Heart

Tanya Erzen

A vital organ, one that signifies a person's core, interior, and capacity for love, the heart is a simultaneously powerful and diffuse symbol with myriad associations. It generates platitudes in abundance: you can break a heart, have a change of heart, give your heart to someone, proclaim from the bottom of your heart, and be accused of heartlessness. Christians talk of having a "heart for God," "a prayerful heart," or a "heart for helping." There are suggestions to guard your heart and to open your heart. You can, as one Christian prison ministry promises, have a "makeover" of the heart. Belief in the heart's centrality to human being and, more specifically, in the idea of a heart change that is a total metamorphosis in a person's life motivates the existence of a range of faith-based programs in prisons throughout the United States.

During several years of doing ethnographic research in prisons in Florida, Ohio, Oregon, California, and Washington, I have observed the language of "heart change" in numerous such programs. Within them, volunteers assert that heart change is an inner revolution that remakes prisoners into new human beings. Drawing on a tradition of prison reform that dates back to the first penitentiaries of the early 1800s, such faith groups argue that men and women in prison are not incorrigible and irredeemable criminals, but sensible (in the nineteenth-century sense of that word) beings who always have the potential to be reformed. Heart-change programs dispute the well-worn adage, "once a criminal, always a criminal," and promise instead that incarcerated criminals can rediscover their true selves, their true hearts, and thus be remade.

As they pursue heart change, such programs call into question a central plank of the conservative critique of therapeutic culture, namely, that therapy has replaced religion as the most salient moral discourse of our time.[1] The dominant discourse of prison ministries stresses the old-fashioned message that it is ultimately God, Jesus, or the Holy Spirit who transforms hearts and that such transformation requires unwavering faith in God's power. In a recent newsletter, Jim Liske, the director of Prison Fellowship Ministries (PFM), a national organization that runs evangelical programs in hundreds of state and federal prisons, recounted the difficulty researchers faced when they tried to statistically measure the intrinsic motivation for someone in prison to change. "They were having a hard time," according to Liske, "because they were trying to analyze the supernatural—the unique power of God's Holy Spirit to transform hearts [and renew] the spirits of men and women from the inside out."[2] Heart transformation exists outside human intervention in this model, and Liske's juxtaposition of petty social science and God's mysterious and all-powerful ways is a reminder that there are large swaths of contemporary culture in which the therapeutic has not fully triumphed. Despite the dominance of an old-fashioned gospel language (not to mention overt skepticism about contemporary commercial self-help), faith-based prison programs promulgate a hybrid message in which therapeutic tropes and techniques serve the age-old Christian purpose of rebirthing the self.

Another dimension of heart-change ministries poses a second, probably more profound, challenge to a classic critique of therapeutic culture, one mentioned in this volume's introduction: this is that it fails at and/or inhibits progressive politics. While socially conservative, such programs offer a serious challenge to the assumption of "incorrigibility" that underlies the contemporary carceral state, which has largely abandoned any pretense at prisoner reform. Liske and others like him believe no one is inherently criminal and that Christians owe a duty to aid the incarcerated in changing their hearts, emboldened by the biblical injunction in Matthew 25:36, "I was in prison and you visited me." They believe that by so doing, prisoners can transform not merely themselves but also their families, communities, and the nation.

This commitment runs counter to the logic of mass incarceration that has led scholar Jonathan Simon to call the US prison industrial complex a "waste management system"[3] for the poor and socially marginalized. In 1973, there were 300,000 people in prison; today we have 2.5 million, almost one in every one hundred Americans, and the United States has the dubious distinction of incarcerating 25 percent of the world's prisoners despite having only 4 percent of its total population.[4] A constellation of economic, social, and political factors has fueled this growth, but the key driver since the early 1990s has been the War on Drugs and tough-on-crime sentencing laws that deploy the image of the "superpredator," a pathological and violent inner-city youth whose moral sense is so degraded that rehabilitation is not a possibility.[5] These historical factors have tipped the penal system's always precarious balance between reform and punishment toward the latter. The result, as Robert Perkinson notes, is a systematic attempt "to segregate offenders from free society, subject them to extended controls, and, ultimately, relegate them to a permanently subordinate class of citizenship as defined by conviction status."[6] Prison ministries do not always challenge the political economy or structural racism and classism that have underpinned the growth of the American prison system, but their focus on heart change mounts a strong challenge to the logic of incorrigibility. Their work cannot be easily assimilated to the left critique of the prison industrial complex, but this does not mean it cannot overlap with and, in some places, complement it.

The tension between inherent criminality and individual redemption, or between punitive and reformative impulses, haunts the history of American incarceration. The newly constructed prisons of the early 1800s were designed to replace brutal physical punishments like lynching and the stockade. As religious scholar Jennifer Graber writes, rival prison reformers, including Evangelicals, Presbyterians, Quakers, and Methodists, debated prisoners' inherent sinfulness versus more hopeful pronouncements about character change.[7] From the colonial model in which all crimes were sins and imprisonment was almost nonexistent, reformers and ministers came to see incarceration as the means to treat crime and the punishment itself. More importantly, they believed prisons must have a reformative goal and that Quaker silence, Presbyterian prayer, and Methodist discipline were methods for fostering a redeemed life.[8]

Gradually, the arguments for individual reformation were superseded by the belief that punishment was an end in itself, especially at the end of the Civil War when the criminalization of rural African American spaces resulted in record imprisonment of black men in the Reconstruction and Jim Crow–era South.[9] As the crime rate declined in the early twentieth century, however, these attitudes softened and rehabilitation again became the public's dominant intended goal for prisons. By the 1960s, most prisons had college programs due to the Higher Education Act of 1965. California governor Ronald Reagan signed an inmate bill of rights into law in 1968. However, as the prison population has skyrocketed by 700 percent since 1970 as a result of mandatory sentencing laws and drug legislation, educational, vocational, and other programs have been stripped out of the system. In 1994, the Violent Crime Control and Law Enforcement Act banned financial support for higher education inside prisons, and roughly 350 college programs in prison closed. Just as prisons terms across the country lengthened, most rehabilitative programs disappeared.[10]

By the turn of the century then, mass incarceration in the United States had resolved the schizophrenic and uneasy contradiction between reform and punishment in favor of the latter. As of this writing, millions of people are warehoused in abysmal, overcrowded conditions without even the pretense of rehabilitative programming—except for labor that can be extracted for private profit. Over half are incarcerated for nonviolent drug offenses.[11] Michelle Alexander calls this penal behemoth "a new Jim Crow," in which black men are imprisoned at three times the rate of white men and in which women are the fastest growing segment of the prison. Even if prisoners are inclined to transform the self, overcome addiction, or turn their lives around, the brutality of prison ensures that many who enter prison with nonviolent offenses become more violent and likely to commit crimes in the future.[12]

Americans by and large seemed to favor the growth of the prison system in the last decades of the twentieth century, but more recently the Federal Bureau of Prisons and individual states have come under intense political pressure to tighten budgets in a time of economic recession. National organizations like Right on Crime, with prominent Republican conservatives at its helm, advocate economically responsible solutions to mass incarceration.[13] Reentry and rehabilitation, despite the lack of infrastructure to support them, have become fiscal imperatives. Faith-based programs had grown as a result of policy initiatives—particularly under George W. Bush's presidency—but economic constraint helped to solidify their hold on prison culture.

Faith-based programs allow Christians to enter the prison in massive numbers and proselytize to those desperate for any lifeline amidst the collapse of even the veneer of rehabilitation. According to the Office of Justice Programs, almost all US prison systems offer faith-based worship services and 93 percent also offer prayer groups.[14] These statistics include the vast numbers of religious volunteers, working under the supervision of primarily Christian chaplains, who regularly conduct worship services, Bible studies, individual counseling, and small encounter groups throughout the day in prison chapels.[15] This corps of free labor drawn from conservative nondenominational faith-based groups has helped to fill the void created by budget cuts. Religious volunteers who administer everything from AA groups to public speaking save the state money. And in the prison, where boredom and lethargy reign, they also provide some of the only available programs. As access to educational, vocational, and recreational programming that is secular, non-Christian, or even mainline Protestant has diminished, heart-change programs like PFM,

Kairos, and Horizons, as well as those sponsored by local Christian churches and prison ministries, have flourished within American prisons. The punitive regime of the prison system coexists uneasily with the rationale of faith-based programs that redemption and transformation are possible with heart change.

One such program is Pathways, a nondenominational Christian prison ministry that provides Bible studies, support groups, worship services, and individual mentoring for incarcerated women seeking heart change.[16] Pathways operates in a women's prison in the Pacific Northwest where for a year I have taught college classes, conducted interviews, and observed faith-based programs; religious organizations comprise 85 percent of the volunteers working there. The premise of the program is that each meeting is part of a long and arduous pathway designed to remake a broken individual by transforming her heart and opening her to God's influence, so that she can eventually leave prison a law-abiding citizen. Pathways volunteers come from a variety of local nondenominational Christian churches but agree on several theological precepts: a Christian can and must know God intimately, the Bible is the living and literal word of God, and one has a duty to evangelize this good news to whomever will listen. Heart-change ministries often adopt the hard-line antitherapeutic stance articulated above by Jim Liske: they eschew twelve-step work, cognitive efforts to rebuild self-esteem, and traditional worldly schemes for improving the self in favor of leaving all hope and expectation for change with God. But often, and seemingly unwittingly, their faith in God's grace combines with a belief in the malleable and fixable self and, with that, the importance of individual self-improvement. Pathways is one of many ministries that believe a heart must change through God, but that it will do so only if individuals take specific steps and exert effort and will to recreate their identities.

Overtly evangelical practices then—like prayer, Bible study, and worship—dominate Pathways. All cultivate the belief that every individual is inherently good and that people should not be discarded and locked away in prison. The ministry also resists a notion of punishment as ordained by God and manifested in incarceration, promoting instead the ideals of grace and transformation. If prisoners work to transform their own hearts, and to allow God to do the same, they will encounter their unblemished, pure selves, separate from their crimes. As one Pathways student articulated it, "I found myself in myself."

The gloominess of the prison chapel where Pathways meets is alleviated by a large stained glass window perched high in a corner. Sometimes thirty or more women attend Pathways classes, but numbers fluctuate. Volunteers show up three nights during the week and on Sunday mornings and evenings. Margaret and Jeffrey, members of a local nondenominational Christian church, run the Thursday night ministry during the few hours when women are free to attend classes and other programs. The temporary release from restrictions during the fifteen minutes of movement results in boisterous clusters of people. Then the buzzer blasts through the omnipresent speakers indicating that everyone must be at their destination or incur an infraction or disciplinary measure.

For the past month, the theme of Thursday night has been "Disgrace and Grace" with a specific emphasis on overcoming histories of violence. The preponderance of women inside the prison who have been the victims of abuse, rape, and domestic violence is astronomical. A study conducted by the mental health staff at the prison indicates that 65 percent of the inmates there report experiences of domestic violence and 47 percent have histories of childhood sexual abuse.[17] Darlene, a group regular, greets the theme with the skeptical comment that "Everyone here has been abused or raped. Show me one person who hasn't," as if such violence were so commonplace that it hardly merits further discussion.

Nevertheless, Darlene is present along with nine other women at this Thursday night's meeting. The premise of "Grace and Disgrace" is that heart change ensues from relinquishing the will to heal, the will to transform, and the will to overcome. It is in submission that healing and transformation occur. The group has been reading 2 Samuel 13, the biblical account of Tamara, who is assaulted by her half-brother Amnon. The story is supposed to illustrate the necessity of heart change, and Pathways leader Margaret guides the group in an interpretation that explicitly critiques therapeutic culture. Grace, she notes, is "one-way love" from God, and only this love will transform them—just as it did Tamara. She explains that survivors of sexual assault are normally expected to heal through support groups and conscious attempts to change their thinking. But grace "does not come from reading Oprah's latest book," Margaret admonishes (a calculated jab since many of the women revere Oprah Winfrey). A transformed heart will not be found in this month's women's magazine. Instead, "grace floods in from the outside when hope to change oneself is lost," Margaret explains. "One-way love does not command 'heal thyself,' but declares 'you will be healed.'" God's love and grace purportedly work on the women's hearts, replacing self-love and guiding them on the "true path to healing." Margaret warns the prisoners that trying to heal themselves through their own efforts is at best a temporary solution, at worst, a delusion. Healing "only comes by laying down your life and picking up His. It comes by saying, 'God, I am tired of doing things my way. I need you. I want you.' It comes by surrendering your heart to the one who can heal it." Self-help techniques will succeed only on a superficial level, and the individual's failure to overcome the repercussions of violence entirely through her own efforts will ultimately produce more shame in a never-ending downward spiral.

Whereas the punitive discourse of the prison is focused on the individual as criminal, Pathways removes this burden by emphasizing that God can take over responsibility for your life. Participants read Jeremiah 17:14, which promises, "Heal me, O Lord, and I shall be healed; save me and I shall be saved, for you are my praise." At Margaret's urging, they pray together to heal from the disgrace of sexual assault. "I am not damaged goods. I was sinned against." The alleviation of shame, what most women report as the overwhelming emotion that both incarceration and sexual violence engender, resonates deeply for the group.

Allowing one's heart to open is the key to being remade as a person. The prisoners bow their heads in prayer: "Simply ask Him to be the Lord of your life," Margaret reminds them. "Invite Him to sit on the throne of your heart." The loving and sexualized nature of some of these prayers reflects how Jesus or God becomes a repository for longing and desires that cannot be fulfilled by human love. One woman tells us that she has a heart "head over heels in love with the Lord, completely focused on Him and His will for my life." There is also a measure of safety in their desires. God's love, unlike many of their real relationships before and during imprisonment, is condoned and without risks. One woman talks of completely abandoning herself to his love. Another, Patty, a fervent Christian with a life sentence, reads from her journal: "I promise, it is a WILD ride—the greatest adventure you will ever have. It is joy unspeakable—impossible to find the words to express it. He will fill you with such love, such joy, such HOPE, such peace. Ask Him to be the Lord of your life today. Open your heart to Him. Let Him in." As part of the Pathways prayer, Margaret says, "Yes, He will ask you to change. But, He gives you the grace and the power to do it." By abandoning themselves to God, the prisoners unleash their pain and open their hearts to transformation.

Margaret disparages twelve-step programs and Oprah and entreats women to dissolve their wills, since heart change requires faith in something beyond the self. And yet, while assuring them that God will spark the revolution within, Pathways reminds prisoners that a changed heart also emerges from the effort of the self. A necessary set of actions and disciplines is required. "Even God is not willing to mend or repair a heart that you have corrupted or messed up with your evil desires," Margaret reminds her charges. Thus the program also relies on traditional self-help strategies to promote personal change, such as taking a self-inventory, maintaining bodily discipline, exploring one's life history, listening to other testimonies, and revising one's identity according to a coherent narrative of transformed hearts and personhood. Women have to apply themselves to Bible study, come to services, and pray as hard as they can.

Nowhere is the program's self-help dimension more evident than in the Pathways sessions led by Diana, a volunteer from a local church who also runs an online ministry for women. We live, Diana explains, in an age of makeovers and "extreme makeovers," and we are always looking for ways to transform ourselves. Since women particularly are not satisfied with staying the same, and are searching for ways to improve, their concentration often focuses on outward appearance. Diana chides the group for this, reminding them that the Bible says to concentrate on our inner beauty by paraphrasing Peter: "Your beauty should not come from outward adornment, such as braided hair and the wearing of fine jewelry and fine clothes. Instead, your beauty should be that of your inner self, the unfading beauty of a gentle and quiet spirit" (1 Peter 3:3–4).

In her introductory welcome packet, she urges women to have a "makeover of the heart" that is the key to such beauty:

> If you are like me, I didn't even realize I needed to change my heart! I thought, "My heart's OK. I'm a good person. I love God." But, over the years, I have had a total transformation of my heart. My heart has opened to a new Truth, a new joy, a new love, and a new way of life. I have had a complete MAKEOVER of my heart! I want you to experience the ultimate makeover—to become a new creation in Christ starting with your heart.

From here, Diana breaks down the process, in which each week is devoted to a different heart theme: delightful hearts, healed hearts, committed hearts, and prayerful hearts. First, the heart transplant occurs, and women relinquish their fear, selfishness, and stubbornness. Diana compares her heart premake-over to a spoiled two-year-old throwing a temper tantrum "who wants what it wants and wants it now," and many women laugh in agreement. They analyze Ezekiel 36:25–28, in which God speaks, "I will give you a new heart and put a new spirit in you; I will remove from you your heart of stone and give you a heart of flesh."

But while God will transplant women's hearts, the makeover requires prayer, participation, focus, and effort as well as a relentless and constant self-inventory of the familial dysfunction and moral failings that led inexorably to prison. They learn practical ways to incorporate prayer into daily routines, including "praying Scripture into your life," which means inserting your own name into generic prayers as part of personal devotion time. For instance,

"I pray that God will give me (or your name here) a Spirit of wisdom and revelation."

Individualizing the Bible as a self-help manual promotes the goal of what Diana calls "growing closer to the heart of God. The Bible says, 'Draw near to God and He will draw near to you.'" Another Pathways class with the clunky title "How to Choose Your Own Change" exhorts women to follow the "TACT" formula in order to alter their thoughts, actions, and ways of speaking until the person is habituated into a specific mode of biblical living. Discipline is required for the task of enacting these principles in everyday life. It means compelling yourself to forgo girlfriend drama, fighting, drugs, and the dayroom where all of the above are most likely to occur. Diana expounds the steps: search through the Bible for verses related to what you want to achieve. Memorize and repeat them to yourself. Run from anything that tempts you. God hears us, she reminds the group, so pray regularly and without ceasing.

To help retrain the mind and body in these new paths, Diana encourages a practice similar to that of many secular and New Age therapies: journal writing. Embossed with a heart clasped between two hands, the journals she donates are cherished commodities, given the prison's restrictions on notebooks with metal binder rings, which are viewed as potential safety hazards. She gives the group writing prompts intended to shore up and strengthen their new hearts, encouraging them to ponder: What are the desires of your heart? How do you want God to change you? What are your personal expectations?

Sharing their writings solidifies their commitments to change. As one woman reads, "I believe God is taking me on a transformation where Lisa diminishes and Jesus increases. I'd love to get to the place where there is nothing left of Lisa!" Alyssa, a young woman who is serving a ten-year sentence, articulates a typical mix of cognitive and spiritual goals when she reads of her desire "to love and be loved with an unconditional love with no strings attached or controlling issues with humans the way that Christ loves me . . . to not let emotions rule my life or ruin it. To break free from past and walk in that freedom not just talk about it!" Sharla, another participant, reads,

> My personal goals are to be transformed and to stay transformed. I want to be rid of my selfish heart. I guess all of my "hang-ups" could be attributed to my childhood. I could put the blame on my broken childhood, the absence of a father, abuse by a stepfather. These things created a longing in me, **but instead of turning to God, I turned to the world to satisfy me.** I was seeking my identity and my worth in these things. Instead of filling the emptiness I

> felt and giving me a lasting satisfaction, these only created more of a longing, a deeper hole to be filled.

Writing and sharing such stories not only prepare the spirit but retrain the mind and discipline the body; in Diana's ministry, all three activities are necessary for a makeover of the heart.

When the self that was criminal is renounced, a person transformed from the inside out by God's grace appears. Whether they rely exclusively on the power of God to transform hearts or adopt a more eclectic approach, heart-change programs intimate that prisoners are not constituted by a rotten core of criminality but instead have been adversely affected by their circumstances. Their transformations recover their true selves, free of criminality and sin. Although this intervention targets the individual, the Pathways group, like many self-help and therapeutic models, has social implications: transformation does not occur alone but with others who have already changed themselves or can potentially change along with you. Once they open their hearts to God's will, individuals become selves in relation, animated by conscious mutuality and joined in a broader community. This promises the individual an escape from social isolation; at the structural level, it offers a theory of self and society in which the two are mutually constitutive and absolutely necessary. This challenges a punitive model that holds individual prisoners solely responsible for their actions and seeks to isolate them from the larger society that they have wronged.

To back that theory, many heart-change programs offer material forms of structural and social support to prisoners seeking parole and reentry—a marked contrast to the prison-industrial complex's neglect and disregard for prisoner and parolee well-being. The narratives of change that prisoners adopt as part of their heart makeovers are particularly legible to the parole and clemency boards to whom they express remorse for their crimes and prove that they have become newly restored. Often, whether a prisoner's sentence is lessened and parole and work release are granted can hinge on the verbal or written support of a volunteer. As economic constraint has made reentry more of a priority (and rehabilitation, job training, and transition services even less of a priority), Pathways volunteers aid prisoners with the practical challenges that attend release from prison: preparing a life plan, writing a résumé, arranging for housing, and repairing relationships with family members. After prison, Margaret, Diana, and others coordinate job placement, housing, drug treatment, and medical care and then match inmates with a mentor. These concrete social services are unavailable to most people who leave prison after long sentences, the majority of whom are simply deposited at a bus stop with a modest sum of "gate money" and the clothes on their back.[18]

Because they are volunteerist and culturally and morally conservative and avoid discussion of systemic and structural inequalities, heart-change programs are easily dismissed as new forms of neoliberal governance under which the individual bears the responsibility for reforming herself while serving her sentence.[19] Yet Pathways fosters social networks within and outside the prison and builds connections that restore authentic versions of community—the very community that some critics like Robert Bellah believe therapeutic culture supplanted. In the same prison where I observed Pathways volunteers at work, inmates have created an organization called "The Women's Village." The genesis of the organization was a group of women who asked their Pathways leader if they could start their own Bible study as a space to address violence, mental health, mentoring, education, and other pressing issues either ignored or underserviced by the prison. Their motto was appropriated and modified from the Pathways heart-change curricula: "When you improve yourself, you are indeed improving the entire world. Therefore there is no need waiting on the world to change. Simply improve yourself and your world would change." Beginning as a Bible study group for five women, the Women's Village now includes close to two hundred members.

Their organization is built on the shared values of respect for themselves and others, honesty, compassion, diversity, and self-empowerment. Their mantra is that "as women are empowered to change, the environment will change, as well."[20] Sanctioned and to a degree supported by the prison administration, the Village assists with orientation when a woman enters the prison, counsels prisoners in segregation and those who are taking violence-reduction classes, performs mental health assessments and referrals, works on family reunification, organizes antiviolence campaigns, spearheads sustainability projects, and offers general educational development (also known as the GED) tutoring. Inspired by the Village, women have initiated similar collectives in other prisons as a result of transfers from one institution to another. Members of the Village write that they desire "freedom to be me, to realize and experience my full potential as a person and understand and embrace that discipline is freedom."

The Village relies then on the individualist language of the reformed self, but its aims are collective; members seek to foster a "sense of empathy and communal purpose." Its existence can be said to make the governance of the prison smoother for the administration—except when its members are publicly criticizing the appalling lack of mental health or GED resources in the prison. But their communal sense of heart change does not merely replicate or facilitate the disciplinary dimensions of the penal system; in fact, by counseling and educating they are also helping each other to maintain their sense of humanity and citizenship in a space of violence and coercion. In doing so, they do not simply act as the prison's handmaidens but counter its atomizing and dehumanizing forces. Their networks extend beyond the prison to community and social justice organizations, which then participate in programs—like a recent antiviolence forum—"inside." Commingling a "conservative" belief in personal responsibility and the importance of individual spiritual change with a "progressive" commitment to community, women's empowerment, and the importance of speaking truth to power, such heart-change groups blur the boundaries between the religious and the therapeutic and confound both right- and left-wing criticisms of the latter.

Christian blogger Justin Taylor recently posted the question of whether it is possible to talk about heart change when the Bible teaches that the heart is unknowable to anyone but God.[21] He argues that no therapeutic technique will change hearts and no one but God perceives a person's heart. Like Jim Liske and some Pathways ministers, Taylor emphatically implies that only knowing God can enable the most profound transformation of one's heart and selfhood. But while he believes Jesus is the only worthy ruler of the heart, he also argues we have a duty to craft the narrative of "what rules the heart" in order to liberate it. How mere mortals can "know a heart" that only God is supposed to understand and control is the conundrum of heart-change programs—a conundrum they resolve by an uneasy (and uneven) embrace of therapeutic culture.

CHAPTER 13

Privacy

Elizabeth Spelman

Critics of therapeutic culture typically are not opposed to therapy. But among their concerns is what they take to be the widespread failure to understand the appropriate place of therapeutic language and practices in our lives. Efforts to keep the therapeutic in its place depend upon designation of the place in which it is to be kept. Drawing upon a distinction between private and personal concerns and those that are public and political, many critics worry that private and personal matters are bound to contaminate, colonize, or efface public and political affairs if the distinction is not honored. According to Philip Rieff, when people bewitched by "the gospel of self-fulfillment"[1] are not just allowed but encouraged to be self-absorbed, they become uninterested in and unfit for the responsibilities of citizenship. The impersonal demands of vibrant public life among strangers, Richard Sennett insists, cease to be of importance to those for whom intimacy and authenticity are regnant values.[2]

There are reasons to be concerned about the contributions of therapeutic culture to the erosion of conditions necessary for a healthy democracy. But critics have tended to ignore well-entrenched forms of therapeutic assistance to corporations—what for want of a more felicitous term might be called a culture of corporatherapy. Such nourishment has helped turned favored businesses into institutional versions of the narcissistic, civically impaired individuals whom Rieff, Sennett, and others regard as so threatening to democracy. These corporations are able to shield both their actions and the various forms of government support they receive by counting on protections of privacy that the Fourth Amendment to the US Constitution is broadly understood to have made the prerogative of individual citizens. Even more perversely, while corporations relish and reap the benefits of this privacy, they foster a social climate in which individuals willingly, even eagerly, make public their every thought and activity.

ON THE CARE AND FEEDING OF CORPORATIONS

Although classic critics no doubt recognized that sapping of civic energy could not be laid entirely at the feet of therapeutic culture, their focus on what they saw as the cultural saturation of the therapeutic kept them from attending to the extent to which the democracy they cherished was beginning to take its cues more and more from big corporations. It is not as if the crusaders were not concerned about the power of the corporate world, especially in connection with the commodification of psychological health and healing. But on the whole, their focus was on therapeutic culture as the most immediate and serious culprit, its succoring of individuals estranging them from democratic engagement.

In some ways this inattention is not surprising if we remember the status of US corporations as private entities quite content to keep their internal affairs out of the public eye and thus eager to preserve a distinction between the private and the public. Private corporations are private in the sense that they are not owned by the state. Their status as private is underscored in their being described as part of the "private sector," and "privatization" is the commonly invoked term to refer to the process by which the work of governmental institutions comes to be taken up by private corporations. Prominent examples in recent decades include the privatization of schools and prisons (e.g., the Corrections Corporation of America), transportation (e.g., the UK railway system), and attempts to privatize government programs such as Social Security and the postal service in the United States.

But even if those alarmed about therapeutic culture did not pause to think about the status of corporations as private entities, the terms of their critique invite us to notice that corporations embody many of the features they found so disturbing in therapy-besotted individuals. Recall a central complaint about therapeutic culture: it encourages people to be self-absorbed, indeed narcissistically devoted to self-improvement, thereby rendering them uninterested in and unfit for the responsibilities of citizenship. This description of those chastised by the critics of therapeutic culture closely resembles the picture of the ideal attributes of the legally created "persons" known as private corporations.

For such corporations are supposed to serve the interests of the shareholders who own them, not the needs of society. Their openly professed goal, in fact their legally recognized fiduciary obligation, is to benefit the financial well-being of their owners, not (except incidentally) the good of the larger public. They flourish as corporations precisely to the extent that they keep their focus on their own financial bottom-line success. Insofar as there is an individual person whom such corporations as "persons" call to mind, it is someone who is unabashedly and obsessively self-absorbed, devoutly determined to be as greedy as he or she can get away with, and studiously indifferent to the needs of others.

Do these corporations, like the devotees of therapeutic culture, pose a threat to healthy democracy? Late capitalist democracies such as the United States do not seem to think so. In fact the corporatherapy that polities generously provide is designed to ensure that corporations flourish. This does not mean that corporations cannot or do not fail: of course they can, of course they do. But the corporate sector is understood to play an absolutely crucial role in the overall economy and thus in need of some TLC from the larger community.

In what is called a free-market economic system, corporations are supposed to compete with one another independently of state support and be subject to minimal state regulation. But although corporations would like to keep it on the QT, countries such as the United States provide substantial aid to the corporate sector in the form of mechanisms such as guaranteed loans, tax exemptions, flaccid regulation and oversight, bankruptcy protection, and financial bailouts. Local and state governments go out of their way to attract or keep businesses in their communities not only by using public dollars to build and maintain roads, bridges, sewer systems, and other crucial features of the infrastructure but also by taxing the businesses at a low rate or not at all.[3] This support is thought to be justified on the grounds that corporations play a significant role in the economy and to that extent the well-being of the citizenry. But they can play this role, both corporate executives and lawmakers seem to believe, only if their privacy is protected. Thus many legislative and judicial bodies in the United States work to ensure that their internal affairs are subject to minimal levels of public scrutiny.

Corporations have a very keen appreciation of the value of keeping the major details of their activities private. They count on a version of therapeutic culture that will understand and properly attend to their "personal" corporate needs, especially if they have established themselves as "too big to fail." And therapy of a significant sort they do indeed receive—a level of care and support far beyond what more familiar terms such as "corporate welfare" connote. In a splendid exhibit of the intertwining among the private, personal, public, and political, the massive public aid they receive is inseparable from their treatment as private entities that provide a crucial public service and from their ability to mold political decisions not carried out in public or otherwise made visible. That is, their privacy is thought to be crucial to the public good they deliver even as their privacy shields the ways in which they influence public policy.

Corporations and their supporters are pleased to spread the news about the benefits they offer: they provide the goods and services and jobs crucial to the economic health and growth of the country and the well-being and satisfaction of its people. Without them, we are constantly told, we would not enjoy the cornucopia of, for example, foodstuffs, vehicles, insurance, financing, drugs, communication equipment, and Internet providers to which we have become accustomed. At the same time, corporations would like to keep information about the governmental benefits they receive away from public scrutiny. Corporatherapy helps them in this shell game: unlike benefits going to recipients of individual or family "welfare" or "entitlement" programs such as Medicare and Social Security, publicly funded subsidies and tax breaks for corporations are not readily visible in state and federal budgets.

Corporatherapy also helps obscure the powerful political role corporations play. Groups such as opensecrets.org can search public records to compile information on how much registered corporate lobbyists spend trying to shape legislation. But it takes extraordinary investigative efforts to uncover the influential activities of groups such as the American Legislative Exchange Council (ALEC), an allegedly nongovernmental, nonpartisan body made up of corporate representatives and state legislators (almost exclusively Republican) who jointly create legislation highly favorable to companies such as RJ Reynolds, United Healthcare, and the Corrections Corporation of America.[4] Moreover, the recent Supreme Court ruling in *Citizens United v. Federal Election Commission* makes it next to impossible to trace the extent of corporate donations to political campaigns. Corporatherapy damages democracy not by luring people away from political engagement, as therapeutic culture is charged with doing, but by using the nooks and crannies of political processes to ensure that corporate self-development and growth will be carefully attended to.

THE PRIVATE, THE PUBLIC, THE PERSONAL, THE POLITICAL

Concern about corporate power was not entirely absent in the critics' analyses of therapeutic culture: after all, they worried that too much attention to personal health and happiness, to self-empowerment, allowed capacities for and interest in robust citizenship to atrophy and thus made room for corporations, among others, to lay waste to democracy, in part by feeding, and feeding off, a desire for discovery and improvement of the dear self. But in their confident deployment of the concepts of the private, the personal, the public, and the political, most critics perhaps did not notice what gets obscured when *private* is treated as more or less interchangeable with *personal*, *public* with *political*. While *private* and *personal* often occur in tandem—indeed have appeared that way so far here—they are not synonymous. Similarly, *public* and *political* seem to share close semantic quarters, but they are not synonymous either. The distinction between the private and the public typically but not exclusively has to do with how much access there is or ought to be to people or institutions or to information about them. The distinction between the personal and the political typically but not exclusively has to do with who is or ought to be in a position to deliberate and reach decisions. Not everything that is personal is private (e.g., a published autobiography); not everything that is private is personal (e.g., corporations); not everything that is public is political (e.g., the complaint against therapeutic culture that it conflates the public sharing of information with political engagement in civic affairs); not everything that is political is public (e.g., bargains struck in the halls of Congress that do not show up in the Congressional Record, deals hammered out at meetings of ALEC whose provenance does not appear in the actual legislation produced).[5] The ability of corporations to suck an enormous amount of the resources of the society owes not a little to their being entities that are political without being public. Moreover, they benefit from privacy while engaging in business that could, in no sense, be called personal.

These multiple distinctions help highlight something critics such as Christopher Lasch failed to appreciate: that efforts to prevent the personal from contaminating the political sphere often end up interfering with the right of the individual to decide what should count as private and what should count as public, thereby undermining the power and authority to control the exposure of information about oneself. As legal scholar Reva Siegel has reported, until well into the nineteenth century husbands enjoyed the common law right to "chastise" their wives, children, and household servants.[6] This meant among other things that the husband could physically assault his wife with impunity, as long as in the judgment of the court he did not overdo it. The practice gradually fell into disrepute as a result of heavy and sustained criticism from the temperance movement, growing opposition to corporal punishment, and searing denunciations from women's rights groups. However, the reaction of legislatures and courts to these new attitudes was not, as one might expect, to allow women to press legal charges against their husbands. For to do so, the official bodies feared, would permit, even invite, the public airing of domestic disharmony. Such a prospect appalled most judges, many of whom reasoned that, however evil wife beating or other harmful chastisements might be, a worse evil would attend revelations about the details of family life. Again and again, nineteenth-century courts expressed alarm at the possibility that details of domestic life might be made public.

Women who wanted their experience in the family to be public and subject to adjudication—to move it out of the private sphere and into the public sphere—simply failed to see, according to the courts, that their concerns had to do with affairs of the heart and were matters for private resolution governed by proper appreciation of the relative duties of husband and wife. To cast them as matters for public consumption and subject to legal contestation would be disastrous for the family and for the larger polity in which the family plays such an important role.

Siegel's detailed history lesson vividly depicts some of the stakes involved in being able to establish what counts as private or public, as personal or political. It underscores that people at the margin typically have not had access to the means by which their concerns might be known (which is not the same as having their alleged failures, foibles, and vices be broadcast: having avenues for speaking up is quite different from there being venues in which you are spoken about). Indeed that is part of what it means to be at the margin.

It is clear from Siegel's exploration that while the interests of abused women were not served by declarations that family matters are private, the interests of the men who abused them, and the society that wished to mute evidence of family disharmony, were being catered to. In other situations, however, women's interests would have been in fact advanced by their ability to keep certain matters private. For example, as John Gilliom among others has pointed out, some poor women on welfare work hard to struggle against the "compulsory visibility" demanded by the state in its never-ending effort to "force the poor into the open."[7]

If it had been up to their own personal decisions, not left to judges or legislators or bureaucrats, the women in Siegel's account would have made public what they were required to keep private, and the women interviewed by Gilliom would have kept private what was being made public. But they all lacked the power and authority to decide how much is to be known about them and by whom. While the two situations appear to involve antithetical desires, in neither case do the women enjoy the right to privacy: that is, they are not recognized as having the right to control access to and information about themselves. This is indicative of their relative lack of social, political, and economic standing. At the same time corporations' state-sanctioned control over information about themselves is indicative of their social, political, and economic clout. The right to privacy, in other words, has become a prerogative of power, and almost nobody is as powerful within the current social order as the corporation. Such matters surely ought to be of concern to those who describe themselves as worried about the erosion of democracy.

RETHINKING PRIVACY

To enjoy privacy, rather than having it imposed upon you, is to have control over access to your person and to information about your interests and activities. Such control mattered enough to caretakers of the US Constitution that in 1791 they passed the Fourth Amendment. Although it does not include the word "privacy," that amendment has been at the core of attempts to prevent unwarranted governmental invasions or searches and seizures of "persons, houses, papers, and effects"; related forms of laws and statutes are relied upon to ward off intrusions by nongovernmental snoops such as neighbors or ex-lovers.

But much of twenty-first-century life, certainly in places such as the United States and the United Kingdom, converges to make privacy both less protected and apparently less desirable. It is not an exaggeration to say that we live in a surveillance society. The popular press offers examples every day. Thanks to the Patriot Act, even our library activity can be examined and the library is forbidden from telling us whether inquiries have been made. Mothers who fail to keep their children in seat belts can be arrested and strip-searched. Information that telecommunications companies have about you just as likely as not is shared with the government, as Edward Snowden's recent revelations about the US National Security Agency's (NSA's) strategy of data gathering have confirmed. If you wish to use a day pass at a Disney park, be prepared to have digital copies made of your fingerprints. You may be observed as you try on all those bras in the dressing room. As any decent information technology officer will tell you, do not assume that the contents of your email will not be widely shared or that if they are shared you will learn about it.

The same technological developments that allow for and invite widespread and continuous surveillance also offer hard-to-resist temptations to use modes of communication and expression that are so convenient and attractive that they seem worth the risk of making one's life an open book. We allow Google to keep everything we've ever used it to do—search the web, e-mail, chat, phone, keep a calendar, develop a contact list, store photos. It is under no legal obligation to tell us what it does with that information, but we know it cannot make a profit without the information we so giddily turn over. Our love affair with Facebook is the stuff of the nightmares of therapeutic culture's critics and the dreams of corporatherapists. It does not simply allow but in effect obliges its users to tell and show all. Its founder, Mark Zuckerberg, is committed (at least in public) to the view that no one wants or needs privacy anymore, that everyone wants and needs to know what everyone else is doing, and that all this sharing is at the heart of democratic life. In Facebook's application to the Securities and Exchange Commission to become a publicly traded corporation (but nonetheless still a private one in the sense of not being government owned), Zuckerberg trumpeted Facebook's positive contribution to the well-being of people everywhere: "There is a huge need and a huge opportunity to get everyone in the world connected, to give everyone a voice and to help transform society for the future."[8] There is no gainsaying Facebook's contribution to the Arab Spring uprisings in 2011 (although the extent of that contribution probably has been overstated)[9] or its facilitation of the various Occupy Wall Street actions in 2011 and 2012. But like critics of therapeutic culture, we might balk at the idea that all the "sharing" that goes on via Facebook constitutes vibrant political activity. And we surely ought to question just how committed Facebook is to transparency when, like Google, it refuses to reveal how the enormous amount of information it collects and stores is used—and, especially in light of the Snowden revelations, by whom and for what purposes.[10] Unlike a number of European countries, the United States so far has refused to adopt laws giving users of Internet services more control over their personal information. Moreover, the NSA has not hesitated to procure the information routinely gathered by Google and Facebook, as well as Verizon and other telecommunications companies (the extent to which all these corporations have been able or willing to resist such governmental importing continues to be under discussion).

CONCLUSION

However their filaments came to be intertwined, the lasting effects of therapeutic culture and the embeddedness of corporatherapy come together to create a situation in which individuals swoon at the opportunity to get their story out in public even as corporations relish their right to keep out of the public eye what they do with all that information—including handing it over to governmental agencies. If therapeutic culture primes us to want to tell our stories, corporatherapy handsomely supports those who invite us to do that. And if corporate welfare creates a culture of corporate dependency in the so-called free market, our thoroughgoing devotion to Google and Facebook have made us dependent upon them: it is now unimaginable that Google and Facebook, those huge players in financial life, could be "occupied." It is very difficult, as the saying goes, to shake up the master's house with the master's tools.

Of course none of this may seem cause for concern unless privacy is or should be important to us. As the history lesson from Reva Siegel reminds us, invocations of privacy certainly can amount to polite versions of "shut up already," hardly a welcome response when you desperately need to have information about your life made public in order to protect yourself from harm. But it has become common to dismiss concerns about privacy by insisting that "I have nothing to hide"—as if the only reason to protect privacy is to keep something unsavory about yourself from view. This is a myopic notion of privacy. When privacy is important to us, it is because for a variety of reasons we value keeping others in a state of ignorance about our thoughts and activities. Loss of privacy can mean loss of dignity and respect: after all, loss of privacy is among the first consequences for individuals of government assistance, incarceration, or institutionalization. Whether or not such loss is deserved or ultimately beneficial in any particular case, it functions to remind people of their lowered status. And it hardly amounts to a denial of the necessity for acculturation in the creation of fully realized human beings to point out that in the absence of privacy, of time and space away from the eyes of others, we may become especially vulnerable to the effects of people's designs upon us.

Not being interested in keeping certain kinds of information private is quite different from being willing to give up the right to privacy. Privacy sometimes will be judged to be dangerous or unwanted or unnecessary, sometimes will be fervently desired. But one's wishes in either direction are irrelevant if one hasn't the right to decide what and how much to reveal.

Rethinking therapeutic culture would lose much of its point if the verdict were not still out about the extent to which therapeutic culture has enriched or has depleted the value of democracy and the goods and opportunities it promises to deliver. An important consideration for the jury will be whether the information sharing that therapeutic culture encourages, and on which many corporations, and governments, so handsomely feast, ultimately leads to our dismissing our Fourth Amendment rights as a concern only for wrongdoers and fuddy-duddies.

CHAPTER 14

Pain

Suzanne Bost

. . . to heal
there must be wounds
to repair there must be damage

GLORIA ANZALDÚA, "Healing Wounds"[1]

In "let us be the healing of the wound," the last essay completed before she died, acclaimed Chicana feminist poet and essayist Gloria Anzaldúa explored what forms healing might take after the events of September 11, 2001 heightened Americans' consciousness of their own (corporeal and national) vulnerability.[2] For adjusting to the changed New York City skyline, and more importantly to our changed relationship to global geography, she proposed what she called the Coyolxauhqui imperative, which she theorized based on the model of the Aztec moon goddess.[3] Coyolxauhqui—daughter of the goddess of creation and destruction, Coatlicue—was chopped to pieces and thrown into the heavens by her brother, the war god Huitzilopochtli, when she threatened his power. Coyolxauhqui's amputated body parts were reconstituted in sacred-metaphorical terms as the moon, waxing and waning; these parts were also reconstituted in literal terms in the round stone that bears the image of her detached torso, feet, arms, and legs found in the ruins of Tenochtitlán, in what is now Mexico City. This challenging image confronts us with the painful outcome of war and asks us to rethink what counts as a viable body. In the wake of September 11, Anzaldúa argued that the nation and its people needed to reassemble their broken parts not in the same shape they were in before, which would erase the violence of the attacks, but in a new form that continually remembers dismemberment.

Cherríe Moraga, another of the most famous Chicana feminist writers and a former collaborator of Anzaldúa's, also came to embrace Coyolxauhqui as a model in her 2001 play *The Hungry Woman*. Moraga wrote this play after having spent more than three months with her prematurely born son in the neonatal intensive care unit, a period in which she learned to mother a baby who was hooked up to ventilators and needles, who lost pieces of his body in two separate surgeries, and who, even in his survival, embodied the continued possibilities of sickness and disability. During her baby's extended stay in the hospital, this self-proclaimed Chicana butch dyke, who has explicitly rejected Anglo-American patriarchal culture, found her sense of motherhood and family ultimately intertwined with white surgeons, nurses, and medical instruments—an uncomfortable sort of family making to be sure.[4] Moraga's turn to Coyolxauhqui reflects her need to represent both this discomfort and the difficulty of accepting embodiments that previously seemed unacceptable. Coyolxauhqui presents more than an alternative to Western images of health; she teaches us how to live with mortal pain.

My book *Encarnación: Illness and Body Politics in Chicana Feminist Literature* analyzes instances like these of wounded corporeality in the writings of Chicana feminists. While working on this book ten years ago, I came to value pain as an incarnation of our bodies' encounters with limitations and a source of revolutionary inspiration. In the permeable bodies of Aztec gods and goddesses, as well as in the mass ecstasy of public sacrifice rituals, pain is a sacred part of communal definition. The premodern indigenous cultures that Anzaldúa and Moraga invoke, as well as feminist disability theory, helped me to think beyond contemporary normative body wisdom, and I came to respect the suffering that accompanies vulnerable embodiment in both traditions. As disabilities studies activists and authors have suggested, it is problematic to assume that only robust and pain-free bodies are ones worth being in.[5] This assumption excludes not only many people with disabilities but also the very young, the elderly, and women, whose bodies are typically weaker than men's and whose sex-specific health revolves around pain and corporeal fluctuation.[6] These vulnerable bodies—really, all bodies—constantly experience barriers to mobility, pleasure, and independence in the world as it is currently situated. Highlighting the ways in which environments limit (indeed, disable) bodies fleshes out calls for social and structural change.

In opposition to the pain I found represented in Chicana feminist literature and disability studies loomed a presumed goliath. I began work on *Encarna-*

cion with a view of modern institutionalized medicine as a patriarchal force determined to anesthetize, and thereby to silence, all discomfort and to oversee the regularization of bodies as the living tissues of the capitalist health machine. I needed such a theoretical goliath against which to oppose my own resistant invitation to feel the problems of the world as they intersect with our bodies. Since establishing this opposition, however, I have assumed a more ambivalent relationship to medicine, including an appreciation for the fluid boundaries between "traditional" medicines and "modern" or institutionalized medicine. (After all, binaries are awfully constraining, forcing the complexity of the world into unrealistic poles.) Part of this ambivalence comes from the complexity of health and healing themselves and from the ways in which they are inevitably intertwined with illness and suffering. Seeing that has moved me from being "against health"[7] to being a cautious consumer of a variety of therapeutic practices, one who explores what it means to derive good feeling from institutions that, at some level, exploit and manipulate consumers. In particular, I have found a powerful convergence of pain and communal pleasure in my practice of yoga, a "therapy" that has shaped my own Coyolxauhqui imperative.

To uncover this alternate approach to pain, I'm borrowing a literary genre that Anzaldúa developed throughout her career: "*autohistoria-teoría* . . . a personal essay that theorizes."[8] The data on which this genre rests is individual experience, embodied rather than abstract. Instead of a general history of yoga or of therapeutic approaches to pain (which the historians and anthropologists I cite in my endnotes have already written), I begin with the particular details of my own engagements with pain and therapeutic culture. These specific encounters lay the foundation for a theory of how yoga, as an embodied communal experience, incorporates pain within processes of communal healing.

I have been skeptical of "therapeutic culture," especially when it is represented as a monoculture or a unified worldview, not because I'm a stoic, but because I resist many of the operations that seem to underlie it: the vilification of pain as a problematic response to the world, the individualizing effect of much therapeutic treatment (reducing pain and healing to individual, rather than environmental or communal, concerns), and the capitalist orchestration of people's most intimate feelings (creating new pains and desires while pathologizing others in order to stimulate consumption of "health" commodities). I include both physical and psychological treatments within therapeutic culture since I see the two as inextricably linked. These therapies, even those with non-Western origins like acupuncture and yoga, form part of the larger complex of capitalist medicine in the contemporary United States—all linked through the commodification of health, fears of medical malpractice lawsuits, and the bureaucracy of health insurance. To some extent, all medicine—including "alternative" medicines—forces our unique bodies and feelings into a standard framework of treatments and uniform definitions of health.

For decades, I have taken very seriously the work of one of feminist theory's intellectual gods/demons, Michel Foucault, and his claim that medicine—like schools, prisons, and other institutions—dictates a "normative posture" as it heals. In *The Birth of the Clinic*, Foucault wrote that modern medicine created "a definition of the *model man*" as it outlined "knowledge of *healthy man*."[9] This theoretical stance has informed my strong resistance to sexual and cultural norms (which lead to homophobia, ethnocentrism, and sometimes imperialism), and it also led me to a counterintuitive embrace of pain and illness, which I have valued for their opposition to the normalizing functions associated with therapeutic culture. The obsession with "wellness" and happiness, it seems fairly clear, leads to a quasi-militaristic rejection of pain and vulnerability. Therefore I have resisted any sort of healing that participates in a logic of self-defense, isolating the individual from the world around her (stigmatized as a source of potential injury or infection) just like modern nations shore up their borders against demonized others (terrorists, illegal aliens, and the like).

These theoretical investments have a prehistory in my family. I was raised, in part, by my grandmother, a physically disabled devout Catholic who believed in miracles and who offered up her own pain for social causes, praying for the suffering of others around the world as she got into or out of her wheelchair as if the erosion of her joints could help stop a war. She believed that her pain was productive, that it linked her body to others in pain. Although I never really believed her, I longed for that kind of faith that could shake up the logic of the modern status quo, a faith that eschews individual well-being in order to feel one's place in a turbulent world. From this perspective, pain is not something one passively accepts without choice but, rather, an active process of sacrifice for, and identification with, the world we live in.

In its aims to eliminate pain and to neutralize illness, therapeutic culture would seem to oppose such faith and feeling. Imagine my surprise to discover that conservative critiques of therapeutic culture see the opposite at work, often viewing healing therapies as a dangerous erosion of boundaries. Take Christina Sommers and Sally Satel's *One Nation under Therapy*, for instance. They open with a supposedly damning critique of "therapism" for its valorization of "openness" and the "sharing of feelings." Most dangerous, for Sommers and Satel, is that therapeutic culture assumes that "vulnerability, rather than strength, characterizes the American psyche."[10] *One Nation Under Therapy* "rejects the presumption of fragility" and blames therapy for pointing it out.[11] If therapy highlights permeability, perhaps it could be my political and intellectual ally, after all.

Indeed, it is through my recent engagement with processes that fall under the heading of "therapeutic culture" that I have become most intimate with my own fragility and social/material embeddedness. While writing *Encarnación*, I happened to meet up with a number of painful situations myself, including neck injury, childbirth, and disabling tendonosis in my hands. I tried to practice my pain as a sensation of emplacement in the world. I reread, over and over, Gloria Anzaldúa's late claims that illness is a way to "shift consciousness," to expand our perspective and our feelings of relatedness to others. I tried, following Anzaldúa, to use my "wounds as openings to become vulnerable and available (present) to others."[12] I discussed my faith in pain with my acupuncturist, my midwife, and my physical therapist, but I did become a consumer of therapy.[13] And in the process, I came to realize that, rather than monolithic norms, health and healing are states of permeability: dialogues among bodies, environments, caregivers, commodities, and communities.[14]

Taking antidepressants, for example, is an act of tremendous faith. Here is a pill produced by a corporation designed to maximize its own profits. Our dependence on the pill contributes to the company's profits. Most of us have no knowledge about the neuroscience or chemical science that led to the particular fusion of ingredients in the pills we take, but we trust that the scientists, our doctors, and the pharmacists who make these pills available do have this knowledge. We make ourselves vulnerable to them. We are subject to their understandings of health; they are subject to the faith of people like us. We feel embarrassed for them if the pills don't make us feel better. And what if their definition of "better" is different from ours?

Towards the "non-Western" or premodern end of the therapeutic spectrum, this sense of permeability is more overt with acupuncture, although an underlying profit network remains, as does the potential for conflicting understandings of health. One allows one's body to be penetrated by dozens of needles in key acupuncture points to open the pathways through which energy flows through the body. I came to acupuncture out of desperation. As much as I tried to remind myself that my pain was simply a matter of reaction and interpretation, one of many ways of experiencing injury, my neck injury was making it impossible for me to read, write, or drive a car. Prescription painkillers dulled the pain, but they also made it difficult to perform those same (for me, vital) activities since they clouded my head. I wanted a way to alleviate, or at least to transform my experience of, the pain without altering my brain chemistry (a ridiculous hope given that pain and emotions are both equally matters of brain chemistry). Acupuncture did not obviously alter my thinking or cause chemical dependency. Yet lying almost naked on a table before a practitioner whose language I could hardly understand, allowing him to puncture my body over and over again, at first seemed like madness. I was exposed—to a man I'd never met before and a culture I knew embarrassingly little about—and afraid to move for fear of causing even greater pain to myself. What if a needle broke and the tip got stuck in my skin? What if I rolled on top of one and pushed it in too far? What if the sheet got caught on the needle flapping out of the tip of my ear? It was a fundamentally interesting experience: witnessing my own response to pain and measuring my fear and anxiety against my theoretical speculations. Acupuncture did make me acutely aware of my corporeal and emotional vulnerability. It brought me into contact with new sensations and new cultural experiences. And it made me feel quite a bit better, either because it alleviated my pain or because it gave me the sense of being in the process of healing.

I should confess that I injured my neck while practicing yoga, so in a way therapy begat therapy. Both therapies drew attention to the costs of my own ignorance about the anatomic logic underlying yoga postures, the chemical processes of pharmaceutical "pain management," and the location of acupuncture points and energy channels within my own body. I put my body in the hands of others, quite literally, and therapy did to me exactly what Sommers and Satel fear: it focused my attention on my own fragility and made me vulnerable to therapeutic professionals. Conservative critics like Sommers and Satel argue that therapeutic culture deprives individuals of agency, and they long for a lost culture of self-control. The subject that emerges from therapeutic culture is, for them, dependent and weakened by uncensored attachment to feelings. This subject is poorly individuated and ill suited for competition—a matter of real concern for Sommers and Satel but helpful for those like me who would rather imagine a sociality based on an acknowledgment of our shared responsibilities to a world lined with networks of damage. Therapeutic culture might dangerously lock subjects into self-undermining consumption patterns, like addictions to pharmaceuticals and dependence upon therapists to dictate one's life, but, at the same time, these patterns might also undermine competitive, self-possessed individuality—a contradiction at the heart of capitalism, perhaps.

What does identity look like without self-possession or integrity? One of my favorite statements by Gloria Anzaldúa embraces fragility as an identity: "*I'm not invincible, I tell you. My skin's fragile as a baby's I'm brittle bones and human, I tell you. I'm a broken arm.*"[15] Although the "I" asserts itself five times in this quote, what it asserts itself as is something defined by (potential and actual) damage. I love fragile things. They remind us of impermanence; they invite us to tread with care. They make us aware of the power of our own movements and the ways in which we affect the world around us. What facilitates our understanding of this fragility? How do we live with the truth that we are "not invincible"?

I have learned that opposing health is not a necessary part of the answer. Illness and the pain that often accompanies it are one with healing: fevers burn out infections, diabetes involves finding balance in blood sugar, amnesia helps a body to deal with trauma. Physical and mental health involve constant engagement with external influences; transformations in perception and sensation; the growth of new muscles, neural pathways, and cell formations; the sloughing off of old cells as our bodies scrape against the furniture of our world; the incorporation of cells from the other bodies we touch; the constant forgetting of old memories and old feelings. Health is fluid and permeable.

Probably few health practitioners present their patients with such an inclusive view of health, but their ministrations inevitably produce or highlight vulnerability and pain. Medicine does not work to the extent of eliminating its own reasons for being, and this is not just because medical professionals are capitalists who must extend our illnesses to ensure that we keep coming back. Healing itself is an ongoing encounter with vulnerability; physical and psychological therapies force us continually to reexamine the wounds around which healing processes revolve. I embrace the ways in which therapeutic culture, whether it means to or not, seems to undermine the false idea of a static or coherent subject. Healing reminds us that we are subject to forces around us, embedded; it demands that we rethink liberal notions of agency, individuation, and repression.

In the last five years, I have turned away from pharmaceuticals and acupuncture to focus on yoga exclusively as a more "natural" emotional and physical stimulant. Of course yoga is natural only in the sense that it does not require the intervention of artificial chemicals or tools (although some practitioners of Iyengar yoga insist on the need for props). There is nothing natural about moving bodies into scripted poses. And certainly the yoga "industry" makes profits from me.[16] Indeed, since my medical insurance has limited tolerance for therapies that are not conventionally (Westernly? modernly?) scientific, I pay more money out of pocket to my yoga studio than I ever did for antidepressants or visits to my primary care physician. But I ultimately prefer yoga because it involves movements larger than swallowing a pill and receiving a needle, processes I can actively participate in. There is greater intimacy in yoga than in pharmaceutical prescription. Most importantly, yoga embraces sensation rather than numbing it. (In the spirit of *autohistoria-teoría*, I am speaking here of my personal experience with yoga, since yoga is too heterogeneous to generalize about. Indeed, it would probably be more correct to say "yogas" since the discipline is characterized by such variety—in its contemporary incarnations as well as in its long history in India.[17] What we call yoga in the United States today includes an extremely broad range of practices, all hybridized in some way, but using the plural "yogas" seems too distracting. When I say "yoga," I imply this heterogeneity within it.)

Although most forms of yoga rely to some extent on standard scripts, yoga is not about the production of an ideal or the elimination of problems. It does nothing to protect me. Rather, yoga is more like an exploration of the limits of my strength; the pain that accompanies certain movements is the voice with which my body reminds me of its limits (as when I tore muscles in my neck by pushing my plow pose too far). In yoga, one is meant to notice sensation in a nonjudgmental way, which undermines the hierarchical relationship between pleasure and pain. Indeed, it would be impossible to sit still for hours in yogic meditation without experiencing some pain as part of the transcendent process.

Few yoga studios today embrace pain in their self-marketing; if they do mention pain, it is often in the context of how yoga, unlike other sports, helps us to prevent injury. *New York Times* journalist William Broad's best-selling 2012 book, *The Science of Yoga*, taps into the profit network growing around yoga with scare tactics, accusing yoga of causing permanent corporeal damage when it is practiced incorrectly. Broad is a skeptic who critiques false claims that underlie what he calls "the yoga industrial complex," but he also explains how yoga, when practiced "scientifically," can turn our bodies into "customized pharmaceutical plants," reducing the millions spent on health care by using so-called natural and low-cost methods to lower stress and increase happiness. Broad's definition of "science" is, in my view, too narrow and too exclusively secular.[18] Moreover, his focus on the potential cost-effectiveness of yoga as a method of healing obscures the deeper value of the discipline in order to sell it to mainstream readers.

Yet his ambivalent response to yoga highlights (perhaps unwittingly) a crucial ambivalence at the heart of yoga—and at the heart of pain. He writes that "yoga can kill and maim—or save your life and make you feel like a god." He points out that the yoga we now associate with health and fitness evolved from mysticism and eroticism in ancient India. And he notes that Hatha yoga, the form initially developed in thirteenth-century India and later formalized into the series of postures that began to circulate globally in the nineteenth century, is founded on a sort of violence ("hatha means violence or force"), using physical rigor "to promote the quick attainment of enlightenment through ecstasy."[19] Although *The Science of Yoga* is most interested in promoting a conventional definition of health (following modern Western science), demystifying the magic of yoga, and warning potential practitioners about common causes of injury, points like these demonstrate the intertwinement of pain with enlightenment. Much like the ecstasy of early saints and mystics, the enlightenment and healing that yoga brings are often triggered by sensations of pain. While Broad would not go so far as to admit that pain and injury are themselves enlightening experiences, he describes the "thresholds of pain" to which yoga brings its practitioners and suggests that the physical flexibility produced by yoga's challenging postures can also lead to mental and emotional flexibility. Most importantly, the "mindfulness" of yoga (which follows from proprioception, "inner knowledge of limb position") increases physical and psychological attention.[20] Broad does not unravel the implications of this mindfulness, but the surprises and sensory upheavals that accompany some yoga postures might shock us into new awareness, stretching our attentiveness in new directions, opening up new possibilities for thought and feeling.

My Marxist friends reject yoga as the worst form of bourgeois individualism and critique its practitioners for seeking individual pleasure and peace at a remove from the world. But I think there is a powerful sociality to yoga. Ideally, one practices in a community, and it's a community defined by its heterogeneity, by the different ways that we all move. All postures are part of a process of reaching towards something but getting there to different degrees, in different shapes. I will probably never be able to bend my arms so that my hands can reach prayer position behind my back, but I push them back there again and again, reaching towards a threshold of pain with a goal of increasing my flexibility. The other bodies in the room are struggling with the same pose at the same time. There is a shared understanding that we are *in* something together but that we are in it differently. The conventional closing statement of a yoga practice, "*Namaste*," which roughly translates to "the divine in me bows to the divine in you," reflects a critical humility as well as affinity and exchange between different people.

Yoga creates public intimacy, sharing not just whatever we think our inner "divine" is but also our sweat, our pain, sometimes even our bodily gases. Indeed, since we have just shared a practice together, our bodies share the same tissue adjustments, stretched, tested, and strengthened in the same places. In a recent class, the instructor asked us each, in the beginning, to contribute a posture or a body part to work on. We also did partner poses, in which each body's ability to stand or to stretch relied on the support of another. At the end of our collage-like practice, the instructor pointed out that we had literally incarnated each other's choices, our bodies reshaped through communal effort. Surely all sports offer some sort of corporeal exchange—and shared encounters with pain—but the shared vulnerability, trust, and acceptance engrained within this sort of yoga practice present the kind of sociality I am calling for here.

I am sure it is not a coincidence that the therapeutic professions I have embraced—like acupuncture and yoga—represent premodern and non-Western cultures, and that has to do with my resistance to the anesthetizing consumption, ego-centered competition, and ethnocentric bullying promoted by the dominant capitalist culture around me. There is friction between the sacred origins of "Eastern" healing practices and the modern manifestations of those practices in the Western health and lifestyle industry, and this friction is of deep intellectual and political interest for me as I practice my resistance. Many contemporary yoga therapists secularize their practices to avoid turning away clients reluctant to embrace the spiritual dimensions of these traditions.[21] Often these therapists emphasize physical fitness and happiness over the tortuous emotional and corporeal journey I associate with yoga. "Power Yoga" replaces Ashtanga and "Restorative Yoga" replaces Hatha. This adaptation and decontextualization of practices associated with formerly colonized cultures, to some extent, replicates earlier colonial appropriations.[22]

For me, the friction between cultures, between the secular and the sacred, is central to the experience of these therapies. I approach yoga as tentatively as I approached acupuncture. I try to take seriously the intellectual and epistemological challenges brought on by experiencing sensations that originate in ancient Indian or Chinese traditions. I have modeled my engagement with yoga on my research practices in Chicana/o studies, in which I learn as deeply as I can about the Aztec and Mayan traditions Chicana/o writers often invoke in their resistance to European and Euro-American cultural imperialism. Inevitably, though, practicing yoga, like receiving acupuncture or analyzing Aztec gods and goddesses, is, for me, an encounter with incommensurability and ignorance, acknowledging the chasm that separates my body from the origins of the postures it adopts. I regard my ignorance as part of the therapeutic process: it teaches humility and weakens the ego as it connects me to unfamiliar sources of meaning and sensation.

Again, Gloria Anzaldúa has been my guide in helping me to understand the value of sources of knowledge that seem radically "other." In "Let us be the healing of the wound," her turn to Aztec goddesses presents both a problematic idealization of "lost" native cultures and a radical challenge to what we usually think of as therapeutic. She embraced the amputated goddess, Coyolxauhqui, because she sought "a healing image, one that re-connects [her] to others."[23] Isn't it ironic to describe a dismembered body as a healing image? Coyolxauhqui represents that which we fear most, an utter loss of physical integrity, a permanently painful and incapacitated embodiment:

> Coyolxauhqui is my symbol for the necessary process of dismemberment and fragmentation, of seeing that self or the situations you're embroiled in differently. It is also my symbol for reconstruction and reframing, one that allows for putting the pieces together in a new way. The Coyolxauhqui imperative is an ongoing process of making and unmaking. There is never any resolution, just the process of healing.[24]

This claim that healing is a process without resolution echoes my argument about therapeutic culture. Healing focuses our attention on what ails us, each pain making us aware of another, perhaps even causing another, and we will never find an end to pain. To be a body in the world is to experience decay and friction, to suffer damage.

We never see images of Coyolxauhqui not dismembered, never as a "normal" female body. Indeed, she would not be recognizable to us that way. But the stone that most famously bears her image, the Coyolxauhqui stone at the Templo Mayor in Mexico City, creates a different kind of wholeness. Her head, arms, and feet are arranged in a circle around the amputated torso, reconstituted in a disarming fashion that forces us to rethink everything we've ever thought about the female form. Anzaldúa wrote that "we must use creativity to jolt us into awareness of our spiritual/political problems and other major global tragedies so we can repair *el daño* [the damage],"[25] and the image of Coyolxauhqui certainly presents a jolt and a symbol of the ways in which the world—not just global militarism but most obviously that—wounds us. This is radical therapy: "These healing narratives serve not just self-nurturing 'therapy,' but actually change reality. We revise reality by altering out consensual agreements about what is real, about what is just and fair. We can transshape reality by changing our perspectives and perceptions."[26] Coyolxauhqui does not make us feel more comfortable; she does not care for the self in a nurturing way. Embracing her story means altering the ways in which we have been explaining reality, favoring the image of a rebellious daughter dismembered rather than that of a virgin mother placid. If we have preferred purity, sealed boundaries, and anesthesia as corporeal standards, we have done so in defiance of nature and biology, which are dirty, germy, and constantly undergoing fluctuation and upheaval. Acknowledging this messy body would alter our "consensual agreements" about ourselves and, according to Anzaldúa, "trans-shape" the world.[27]

In making wounds the standard of embodiment, Coyolxauhqui links us all through our shared vulnerability: "We are all wounded, but we can connect through the wound that's alienated us from others. When the wound forms a cicatriz, the scar can become a bridge linking people who have been split apart."[28] I'd like to think that going to my yoga studio (even after having charged $19 per class to my Mastercard) and sharing the pain and pleasure of my practice with a group of relative strangers builds the kind of bridge that Anzaldúa proposes for communal healing. (Once, a cut on my foot started to bleed, and the woman next to me quickly rolled up her mat and moved across the room. I guess she didn't want to heal that intimately with me.)

In fact, it was September 11 that first brought me to yoga, believing I would never find a peaceful way to move through a world now boiling with anger and militarism if I couldn't find that clichéd ideal of inner peace. I cannot claim to have found inner peace, but I do think I've found a new way to belong in a group, a context in which, since we're moving rather than talking, personal and political differences are mere background to a shared project of exploring corporeal possibility and sensation. This is not to say that good communities are silent communities but that there are different forms and shared projects around which we can organize our communities. Finding new ways in which one's body can move, limbs circling around torso in uncomfortable and disorienting twists like the Coyolxauhqui stone, is not just a metaphor for healing; it enacts healing. As even a skeptical science reporter like Broad concedes, yoga loosens the grip of the ego, stimulates emotions, and liberates buried feelings. Not only do I sometimes publicly bleed; sometimes I cry, hum, smile, and sigh. And so do others around me.

CHAPTER 15

Blogging

Michael Sayeau

It has been a running joke of literary culture for decades that, as the popularity of MFA programs in creative writing attest, there are likely more people actively writing novels than there are people actually reading novels. But blogs and their descendents—from MySpace to Facebook to Twitter to Tumblr—make it clear that the problem is far more widespread than even these jokes suggest. In a not very hyperbolic sense, everyone today is writing and not only writing but publishing.

This situation is sociologically relevant, another step in the general direction of mass literacy, technological advancement, and their generally wonderful but sometimes strange consequences. But it also, if relatively silently, is significant in other contexts of consideration. In particular, these new electronic forms of writing—writing with a sense that, in a way that for ages was reserved only for the authors of properly published works, one's work will be read by any number of unseen readers—force a rethinking of our basic assumptions of what it means both within aesthetic and politco-aesthetic frames to write something for others to read. More specifically, if from Aristotle's analysis of tragedy forward we have understood expressive and artistic writing to have a therapeutic dimension, the emergence of these new outlets for the publication of personal writing urges us to reconsider the relationship between writing as a complicated sort of self-help and writing as an act of communication, whether of informational content or beauty. While the therapeutic aims of writing have generally been rendered as surreptitious (in the psychotherapeutic parlance, "repressed") and complex, the advent of the mass writing and publishing as engendered by social networking media forces the issue to the fore.

In short, blogs and other virtual technologies, whose capacity to address the psychological needs of their users would seem to require an expanded sense of what counts as properly therapeutic, actually shed a new kind of light on more traditional forms of therapy. Above all else, as I will argue, blogging and related forms expose a fundamental sociality at the base of therapeutic behavior and practices, one that stands as a corrective rebuttal of the classic critiques of therapeutic culture as purely narcissistic that were advanced by Philip Rieff, Richard Sennett, Wendy Kaminer, and others. These new modes of therapy provide another way of looking at one of the central conundrums addressed in the introduction to this collection, namely, what to make of a practice or mind-set that seems at once intensely focused on the cultivation, improvement, or repair of the individual as such but that despite this atomistic focus is clearly a collective endeavor, a culture. And further, as I will show, it is not so much that the blogger needs to have a sophisticated awareness of the therapeutic nature of her practice, any more than the analysand needs to have brushed up on the works of Freud to benefit from his time in therapy. Rather, beyond or perhaps below everything else, it is the very form, indeed the social form, of such practices that first endows them with their efficacy and significance as well as their ability to reveal certain wider truths about the therapeutic in general. Rather than the content of what is said or written in blogs and other social media, it is the ways that such entries are written, and the structure of their address, that are constitutive of our therapeutic social space.

While of course it is a stretch to think of blogging and the like as properly aesthetic forms, it is useful to consider them in the light of the history of aesthetic theory. It did not take Freud and the advent of psychoanalysis to start us thinking about the therapeutic aspects of art, representation, or writing in general. Aristotle's description of tragedy, a good choice for an originary moment of aesthetic theory, climaxes in a description of the psychological benefit that is provided by watching, for instance, a play in which Oedipus suffers for his hubristic sins. (Aristotle defines tragedy as that form that effects "through pity and fear the purification [catharsis] of such emotions."[1])

Directly confessional works from later in the classical period, such as Augustine's *Confessions*, still put the emphasis on the salutary effect that reading them would have upon their audience rather than the effects that producing them might have on the writer. But even before the advent of psychoanalysis proper, the conception of the redemptive or restorative effects of watching plays (or reading texts, viewing paintings, and so on) began to turn toward the therapeutic effect of creation upon the creator herself or himself. Romanticism urged new attention to the author's own experience of making the work—

and it is thus very difficult not to detect intimations of expressive relief in, for instance, Wordsworth's definition of poetry as the "spontaneous overflow of powerful feelings."

But of course in the aftermath of Freud and his fellow developers of modern psychology came a pervasive sense that many nonartistic forms, including dreams, slips of the tongue, or the speech of the analysand on the therapist's couch are also means to the indirect evasion of repression and thus modes of psychological release. It would seem that the noninstrumentality of these forms, the fact that they are not directly harnessed to the end of purposeful communication, allows them to sidestep the interdictions of the individual's psychology. To dignify these para-aesthetic modes with the same powers as traditional aesthetic forms—that is, to understand seemingly quotidian, undirected, or meaningless discourse as staged or framed expression, like a work of art—is very much at the center of Freud's project. All are legible as indirectly expressive, both symptomatic and therapeutic at once. Further, this sense inaugurates a fundamental change in the dynamics of the ways that we analyse both forms. As the practices of everyday communication and representation become open to aesthetic interpretation, works of art come at the same time to be more definitively seen as autotherapeutic acts. As Freud has it in *Civilization and Its Discontents*,

> Another technique for fending off suffering is the employment of the displacements of libido which our mental apparatus permits of and through which its function gains so much in flexibility. The task here is that of shifting the instinctual aims in such a way that they cannot come up against frustration from the external world. . . . One gains the most if one can sufficiently heighten the yield of pleasure from the sources of psychical and intellectual work. When that is so, fate can do little against one. A satisfaction of this kind, such as an artist's joy in creating, in giving his phantasies body . . . has a special quality which we shall certainly one day be able to characterize in metapsychological terms.[2]

Even beyond sophisticated and self-consciously psychoanalytical analyses of art, it is safe to say that we today reflexively tend to think of aesthetic works as in some sense or another manifestations of psychological tensions and instances of their indirect, halting relief through exposure. Whether it is our sense of Shakespeare's sonnets as efforts to grapple with his own ambiguous sexuality or of Vincent Van Gogh's paintings as releases of chaotic psychological energies, we believe that creation is bound up with psychological trauma and the quest, often errant, for relief. Never in a straightforward way, the work of art, like the dream, releases buried preoccupations and energies, and in so doing provides the artist (or speaker or writer) with an opportunity to make repressed contents manifest.[3] And despite episodes of feigned "impersonality" during the modernist period, literary artists in particular have never strayed far from a postromantic model of expression as confession and, implicitly, as a form of autotherapy.

In this Freudian model, it would seem to be the distancing effect of self-presentation to an audience (even if the audience in question is as proximate as the dreamer to his dream) that allows both aesthetic and para-aesthetic forms to route unconscious contents around the fence works of repression. Of course, blogging and related forms would seem to be a matter quite distant from the intricate dance of the therapeutic and the aesthetic that we find in canonical masterworks. But it is important to note from the start how our ways of talking and thinking about these new modes of writing intersect with or parallel the age-old discussions of the aesthetic that I have telegraphically described above. While there has been plenty of ink spilled (and html coded) discussing the therapeutic nature or potential of blogging and related Internet forms, both in academic and journalistic forums, it is worth noting that there is an even more directly symptomatic way that culture registers these developments, surreptitiously and in advance of any theorization. Even our popular mythologies of the origin of these forms cast them as essentially therapeutic in their very development. *The Social Network* (2010) narrativizes the invention of Facebook as an act of ultimately unsuccessful cathartic revenge on the part of Mark Zuckerberg against an old girlfriend who has left him for being an "asshole." Even Twitter, more baroquely, finds part of the story of its origins in an episode of trauma (albeit of the physical rather than the psychological variety) and therapeutic recovery. Jack Dorsey, the brains behind the operation, apparently suffered a repetitive stress injury to the wrist, entered into massage therapy, and was so fascinated by the art that he trained to be licensed as a therapist himself, an event that in the long run led to his founding of Twitter.[4]

These stories speak vividly, if only indirectly, to the fact that we as a culture perceive these forms therapeutically. Rather than simply the productions of technological innovation or outlets driven by the profit motive, there appears to be a compulsion in us to understand these media as somehow founded out of deep, personal psychological trauma and efforts at recovery. Significantly, in most milieus that are not rampantly high-tech, telling coworkers, friends, or family members that one writes a blog has long brought looks of concern, suspicion, or a bit of both—as if writing in this way is a sign of some mixture of narcissism, self-delusion, an affective disorder, or just generalized strangeness. But when we step beyond moralizing or condescending suspicion, we find that blogging has an important message for us about therapeutic self-expression, whether properly aesthetic or not, and how it relates to our current social and cultural atmosphere.

THERAPEUTIC BLOGGING

The relationship between self-expression and mental health has of course been a preoccupation of the psychological sciences from their very beginning. But in recent years, this issue has become a central concern of research into the mind and its operations. While it might be clear that simply "getting something out on paper" would at least bring a degree of relief through disinhibition and externalization, neurological studies have sharpened our insight into the specific changes in the nervous system that accompany writing.[5] The findings range from ratifications of what is commonsense obvious to elaborately provocative discoveries, but what is perhaps missing is an approach to such acts, especially in terms of their therapeutic usefulness, from an aesthetic perspective.

There have been countless articles, many fittingly written in a first-person, confessional mode, that extol the therapeutic benefits of blogging and other forms of social media. Phrases such as "cyber-catharsis" have long been deployed. The following paragraphs, taken from a 2005 piece in the *Washington Post*, are typical in the advantages that they highlight:

> Pamela Hilger, for example, considers herself a member of a very tightknit community of dozens of people who read each others' online journals—even though, after more than two years, most know her only by her first name.
>
> "My father used to say, 'You don't air your dirty laundry in public,'" she said. But now Hilger, who lives in Los Gatos, Calif., said she shares nearly everything online, including photos of scars from the surgery she had after her lung cancer was diagnosed in June. "After I was diagnosed, the first people I turned to are my friends and journaling buddies," said Hilger, who reads about 50 other blogs. "They're never failing with support and encouragement."[6]

Many of the articles that appeared in the popular press during the early years of blogging advanced similar claims about the value of blogging, casting it as a means towards the discovery of ad hoc support groups. Rather than offer a grand tour of these, most of which say basically the same thing, I want to focus in closely on one that seems at once appropriately emblematic and inadvertently revelatory about the strange dynamics of blogging's therapeutic value.

In a January 2009 article for the UK *Daily Mail*, the author Jane Alexander recounts in fairly representative terms the healing value that this form of writing had for her as she battled with depression.[7]

> A few months ago, I hit one of my lowest ebbs: I barely had the energy to type one word after another. Yet blogging about how awful I felt helped and, with some new-found energy, I went to make a cup of coffee.
>
> When I came back to my computer, there were already five comments offering comfort, support, some sage advice. Then the phone rang—one of my fellow bloggers (from France) was worried and wanted to check I was OK.

As she recounts, the most direct benefit of blogging is that it operates as an always-on, just-in-time outlet for group therapy:

> With a worldwide membership, I knew the site could always provide fellow bloggers in different time zones, who were awake and happy to "talk" even if a crisis hit in the middle of the night.
>
> When you have a support group that numbers around 50 regulars, you get a lot of expertise and life experience on tap. I have been overwhelmed by the care, support and comfort my online friends have given me.

None of this, of course, is surprising. We are all familiar with the Internet's oft-announced power to enable us to overcome the anonymity of contemporary experience through its virtual fora and immaterial relationships. Whether one is looking for work or company, arranging sex or babysitting, selling collectables or finding a freecycled bookshelf, the Internet is famously useful for reestablishing a sense of collectivity and even intimacy amidst the general disconnection of our lives.

But despite these obvious benefits, there does remain one complication that is a little bit harder to understand. It is this aspect of therapeutic blogging that enables us to reopen one of the perennial questions about the nexus of self-revelation, self-healing, and writing that long predates the emergence of Blogger or Wordpress. Alexander, late in her *Daily Mail* piece, evokes this issue without taking note of its strangeness:

> As our house-selling fiasco became a nightmare (it took over two years to sell), blogging became a lifeline. You can't moan endlessly to your "real life" friends; but you can pour your heart out online knowing that people can choose to read and comment or not.
>
> I can't count the times I have sobbed over my keyboard in genuine catharsis. I wasn't the only one to be taken by surprise at how powerful blog-therapy can be.

This might seem to be just banal prose about a banal situation, but I would argue that these two paragraphs are structured around a revealing logical gap. Given that Alexander has just listed at length all of the occasions in which the intervention of her blog's readers made a difference to her in the course of dealing with her problems, what do we make of the non sequitur, both in terms of the overall argument of the piece and within the individual sentence itself, that occurs in "You can't moan endlessly to your 'real life' friends; but you can pour your heart out online knowing that people can choose to read and comment or not"?

Forgive me for pushing so hard on what is, to all appearances, some hastily generated mass-market copy. It is easy to understand the usefulness of those people who comment on the blog to someone who is upset, disturbed, or depressed. But what is less easy to grasp is the value of those who do not comment—who might never actually make their presence as readers felt beyond appearing as raw "clicks" on the blog's statistics page. In the absence of return commentary, does the blog then become a surrogate for the infamously old-school Freudian analyst, silently scribbling notes while the patient endlessly unrolls the talking that will ostensibly bring the cure?

In an age of deracination and ambient anonymity, in which busy work lives, incessant media distraction, and geographic dispersion all conspire to tip what would seem to be increasing individual autonomy over into loneliness and the silent panic that comes of it, the form of communication that Internet self-publishing represents plays a role that at once resists and, just as significantly, mirrors the very social dynamics in response to which it arose and became popular. Beyond the journalistic metaphors, which deploy "therapeutic" as a stand-in for "anything that makes you feel better"—it is worth thinking more specifically about the formal dynamics of these online genres, their affinities with older modes of therapeutic practice, and the ramifications that these dynamics in turn have upon broader social and aesthetic issues. Perhaps, above all else, these forms have something important to tell us about the aesthetic as a category and the therapeutic powers that we sometimes attribute to it.

PRESENCE OF THE LURKER/SILENCE OF THE THERAPIST

It is, then, the figure of what is called in the blog community "the lurker" that invites the most interesting questions about the therapeutic aspects of blogging. This, more than any other aspect of blogging, accounts for the formal specificity of the genre, as the other aspects are present in other forms and media. Shadowy presences who read without commenting, lurkers can be counted (blogs generally have stat counters that permit the writer to know how many are visiting the site, which posts they are reading, and the like) but not known by name or even by a pseudonym. While there are no statistics available on the number of readers an average personal blog attracts, it is worth betting that the majority or even vast majority of most blogs' readers are in fact lurkers. The fact is that so long as a blog is publicly available to read, the writer inevitably writes for this generally anonymous public, and, per Jane Alexander's description above, writes with this fact in mind.

Probably the closest corollary to a blog's audience, at least as it virtually presents itself to the blog writer at the moment of composition or publishing, is in fact the psychotherapist, especially in his or her classical guise. The unknown, only ever potential readers, in their silence at the nearly simultaneous moments of writing and publishing, play the part of the speechless analyst whose mute presence somehow sanctions and renders meaningful the speech of the analysand. Sigmund Freud, in a note entitled "Recommendations to Physicians: The Psycho-analytic Mode of Treatment," urges practitioners to maintain "in regard to all that one hears the same measure of quiet attentiveness—of evenly hovering attention . . . evenly distributed attention is the necessary corollary to the demand on the patient to communicate everything that occurs to him without criticism or selection."[8] For the most part silently listening, sometimes egging the patient on with neutral encouragement, the traditional psychotherapist is the person whose quiet presence and attentiveness without much in the way of intervention nonetheless spurs the revelatory operation of analysis. This sort of anonymous listening is structurally implicit in blogging, just as it has always been in writing for publication, as it is tacitly anticipated in the very act of typing a post and clicking the "publish" button.

But for all the similarities between blogging and previous forms of therapy, there are also obvious and meaningful differences. First, rather than the individual therapist, blogging summons an audience seemingly maladapted to a therapeutic purpose. We have all heard that the Internet is inducing in us a soft epidemic of ADHD, characterized by the fleeting "attention only in distraction" that famously comes of habitually interacting with it. Second, relatedly, our notions of therapy have generally (although not exclusively) privileged the relationship between individuals, whereas blogging might be said to rely upon crowd-sourced, search engine–driven attention, small aggregated instances of reading rather than the prolonged preoccupation of the single individual. As I will show, these two differences point toward a significant change in both our situations as writers and our relation to the society in which we write.

THE THERAPEUTIC AESTHETIC REDEFINED

Blogging and similar forms permit us to rethink writing and similar aesthetic practices, but this time starting not from the masterworks of canonical geniuses or even the cynically developed products of mass culture but through the vulgar masses of typers and clickers, incessantly sharing their words with the world, however many or few may care to read them. And likewise, owing to blogging's similarity to but also essential difference from other forms of personal, confessional, but unpublished writing, this rethinking is one that has to be informed by the role that the audience plays in the psychological drama of composition. Finally, these shifts in turn index other emergent but fundamental changes in the relationship between the individual and her or his social environments—changes that have been in process for a long time but that may be tipping into new arrangement.

We are long accustomed to adopting a sort of vulgar Freudianism when it comes to self-expression, whether artistic or not. Writing in this model is generally posited as a strange form of therapy, not unlike the talking cure of psychoanalysis itself, in the course of which what is latent becomes manifest to the cathartic if always incomplete relief of the artist. But what these theories have great difficulty accounting for is what role the act of making the art public—selling the painting for display, bringing the book or the poem into print—and what the nature of the public in question have to do with the therapeutic process that is allegedly at play. This, to bring things to bear upon the example that I cited above, is what it is mysterious about Jane Alexander's claim that she "sobbed over [her] keyboard in genuine catharsis," especially given her admission that sometimes her readers respond and sometimes they do not. Does this catharsis come of the anticipation of an empathetic response? Or is it simply the act of utterance—but utterance in this case in public, available for anyone who comes along to read—enough to endow the act of writing with the affective energy that it possesses?

When considered from this angle, blogging becomes a mass, unplanned experiment, one that sheds a new light on the relationships between the public and the private, the writer and the reader, and the revelation and self-healing that structure the act of writing and publishing. Perhaps it is because of its uncertain status and relative lack of prestige—because its vulgarity opens it to angles of investigation we would avoid with "real literature"—that blogging legibly exemplifies something that is implicit in all publishing but that we have not been able to see before. This is a case where the very existence of a form, and the fact of the form's tremendous popularity, are in themselves revelatory beyond any content that we might glean from close attention to the contents divulged. It is one thing to keep a journal, but it is something very different to publish personal reflections for anyone—known or unknown—to read. And it is still another thing to derive therapeutic benefit from the diffuse, often silent, generally distracted attention of an aggregate mass of mostly unknown readers.

Like psychotherapy before it, blogging emerges out of and as a compensation for a world in which deep interpersonal relationships are or at least seem to be harder to come by. But the solution it provides is not purely a restoration of what has ostensibly been lost. Rather than simply providing a means to regain the intimacy that seems so often missing from the modern world, it harnesses the faceless anonymity and contingency of interaction in service of a different model of human contact. That is, rather than affording a retreat from or a solution to alienated anonymity, it is alienated anonymity itself that both enables and defines the contact in the first place. Just as with traditional psychotherapy, what would seem to be an alienating aspect of the process—that the therapist is not your lover, mother, or friend but rather a total stranger—is exactly what permits the process (so the idea goes) to work, and so it is with blogging, only on a mass scale and on a purely voluntary basis. As such, blogging urges a reconsideration of the therapeutic nature of other more definitively aesthetic forms of writing, suggesting that the structural situation of writing for an unknown audience, not any specific content, is what bears the healing potential of the practice.

The therapeutic value of blogging, then, the catharsis that arrives, comes in large part from the complex social situation in which it occurs. In the Freudian and post-Freudian theories of transference, the therapist functions as a surrogate for those who are responsible for or at least bound up with the trauma that initiates the psychological problem at hand. Rather than simply talking to him- or herself, or addressing those who are entangled in his or her problem, the patient addresses the therapist, who stands in for the problematic parent or lover. Significantly, it is the fact that the therapist is like and is not like the person in question that enables therapy to function.

Blogging thus takes what it has inherited from previous forms and intensifies it to a point such that it tips over into something very new. Psychoanalysis—as well as the forms of art that echo its preoccupation with the turbulent human interiority—emerged in response to the changing pressures of modernizing society at the turn of the previous century. The destabilization of hierarchies both inside and outside of the home, a developing awareness of the links between physiology and the psyche, and the shattering effects of rampant urbanization and financialization all conspired to culture new neuroses and therapeutic practices that respond to them. But while none of these factors have disappeared, blogging shows us something that perhaps we all already know, if not particularly vividly. Our problems now—as well as the solutions to them that we seek—derive less and less from the close claustrophobia of the bourgeois family home per the Freudian model and more from the lonely socialization that takes place in bustling, mostly anonymous avenues of cyberspace and even a physical environment that increasingly takes on the features of it.

Thus we begin to turn to the aggregate mass of distracted readers rather than the paid therapist. Our needs are exacerbations of the old dilemmas of modern life, but at the same time we seem to have come to terms with what was always implicit in therapeutic models of psychology.[9] Through blogging, one addresses himself or herself exactly to that ever-present but never fully proximate crowd that is, ultimately, both the cause of the problem as well as its potential solution. Of course, this is a situation that, like therapy itself, is as dangerous as it is therapeutic. As with other earlier pre-Internet forms of therapy, there remains a fundamental ambiguity as to whether this "cure" is itself as symptomatic as the symptoms it would seem bent on alleviating.

And yet, as symptomatic a solution as blogging may be, it still significantly differs from the situation that gives rise to it. It makes—or attempts to make—of the crowd an audience, although one as transient as those that fill a theater from night to night. An audience is not a family or a group of friends but rather a crowd that listens, a crowd that by its very act of freely showing up attests to at least some degree of sympathy and interest in one's feelings, observations, and preoccupations. The importance of the negotiation between the liberatory randomness of the Internet and the desire to enclose a community within it is visible even in the development of social media forms that have emerged out of blogging. Facebook, for instance, could be seen as a retrenchment against the contingency and anonymity of blogging, given its privacy features that allow writers more control over their readerships than blogs do.

In all of this, blogging points us towards a conception of communicative, "vulgar" aesthetics whose therapeutic nature has as much to do with the relation to a countable but not knowable readership as it does with the personal "working through" of a psychological problem. We might even say that the very existence and popularity of blogging urge us to move from the age of the "death of the author" to the age of the "birth of the lurker," as they bring into focus the strange and complex sociality involved every time we type into the windows on our screens, every time we click "send" or "post." In doing so, it not only reminds us of the self-entanglement and correspondent interminability of all of our efforts to develop modern solutions to the problem generated by modernity itself but also compels us to think again about some of our reflexive notions of expressive or aesthetic writing. On the one hand, there has, in recent decades, been a turn toward the social analysis of works of art—the consideration of them in terms of the influence of the world around the artist, in its economic, political, or ideological guises, upon his or her work. On the other hand, psychologically minded theorizations of art have long urged us to consider the formal attributes of the work as the evidence of a personal negotiation on the part of the artist with her or his internal psychology. But the dynamics of blogging and their therapeutic aesthetic, which I have delineated here, suggest that we might also begin to see these psychological aspects, the aspects that would be considered most private and internal, in terms of their essential and formative sociality.

CHAPTER 16

Practice

Philip Cushman

In this chapter[1] I discuss what it is like for a therapist who is aware of the critiques of therapeutic culture to continue working as a therapist and an educator of future therapists. I continue working not in spite of the critique but because of it—not to disprove it, but to honor it and carry it on. I know this might sound contradictory—sometimes it does to me—but it is also the truth. I do my best in what follows to understand this and explain why it is true.

AN EARLY STORY

Sometime in the mid-1980s I was driving on Highway 80 up the east side of San Francisco Bay in order to attend a weekly peer consultation group. As I was driving along, I happened to glance up at the Berkeley Hills. I thought of the baby boom therapists who were once lefty political activists in the '60s and '70s and how expensive their houses now were. How settled they were, how sure they seemed of their practices, how central they were to forensic work such as divorce settlements, child custody disputes, and conservatorship determinations. I thought about how influential they had become by using theories that often reduced suffering to individual, subjective, and intrapsychic causes and about how pervasive their therapeutic worldview had become—pervasive and integral to the affluent '70s, '80s, and '90s of urban California living and the consumerism that it so comfortably fit and so perfectly exemplified. And the thought occurred to me that my cohort was still culturally and politically influential but now mostly unaware of the kind of politics we were reproducing. I remember looking up into the hills and saying out loud in my car, "*What* are we *doing?* What are we *really doing*?"

In the early 1970s, like many wanting to contribute, I went into teaching (college history), but history department budgets had been severely cut. In desperation, I returned to an earlier interest, psychology. I discovered that under the influence of the times, psychotherapy had become less rigid and doctrinaire. I entered and graduated from a family therapy program, began practicing, and then later completed a doctoral psychology program, hoping that I had found a way to do good and along the way also do pretty well. For many years, I did what most therapists do: I searched for the best therapeutic modality by reading, enrolling in trainings and workshops, and attending my own therapy. And for a while this stance was sufficient.

For the politically inclined in my left-leaning cohort, a crucial element of a career in psychotherapy was being able to justify middle-class affluence—not a particularly easy task for those still strongly committed to social justice. Our strategy for accomplishing this generally consisted of two activities: entering individual therapy to explore and hopefully resolve the personal meanings of one's discomfort with making a decent amount of money and coming to believe that one's billing rates were justified because one had found the one true—or at least the most effective—way of practicing.

The convenient relationship between activity one and activity two was sometimes apparent to us, but usually the persuasiveness of activity two muffled our conflicts about activity one. Also, for at least some of us, the escalating economic pressures of advancing age—the high cost of family living in urban settings such as the Bay Area, the burden of graduate school loans, and the ongoing costs associated with membership in the professional middle class—forced us out of community agencies and necessitated the repeated raising of private practice fees. We found ourselves charging more just to stay afloat.

The paradox of charging more and working more undoubtedly made us, at least unconsciously, more insecure and self-critical, if not straight out guilty. And there are few things as effective as guilt to push one into true believership. Encouraging that tendency, of course, was the increasing pressure to justify psychotherapy according to the scientized rules of the powerful health insurance companies that were beginning to control health care. By the late twentieth century, as moral traditions and communal life became ever-more eroded, Americans increasingly seemed to admire the speed and accuracy of electronic computing machines and trust more in quantitative measures and procedural rules than in the intelligence and moral integrity of their fellow humans. The enormous increase in proceduralism in everyday social life affected psychotherapy; cost containment was not the only factor driving a mistrust in if not outright fear of unregulated human interaction. Combine this with the general alienation, confusion, and insecurity that characterized American life in the last quarter of the twentieth century, and you have got a pretty strong motivation for believing that *this* theory of personality or *that* model of family dynamics was the silver bullet your practice needed.

I do not mean to suggest that we were all trapped in some simple-minded hypnotic trance, nor are we now. Most psychotherapists are well educated and well intentioned; we take our responsibilities seriously and work conscientiously. But it is extremely difficult to work under the pressures mentioned above, confront hour after hour the suffering of those you are committed to serve, and at the same time regularly place into question and interrogate your most cherished explanatory models and practices. The pressures on therapists tended to push us into a relationship with our theories of choice that made it difficult to fully avail ourselves of the intellectual movements that were developing some nuanced—and challenging—critiques of the field as a whole.

I was certainly not immune to these cultural forces and their economic and psychological pressures. Initially, I too practiced without a strong critical perspective. But over time, I was changing. Under the influence of the post–World War II critiques of therapeutic culture I encountered, I had begun to question much of what I had initially assumed (or hoped) about the political goodness of psychotherapy. Fortunately, unlike some of my peers, early on I had been introduced to a very different philosophical/spiritual tradition in my first graduate program, a rabbinic seminary, and then later to the critical, historical perspective of what has been called the Interpretive Turn.[2]

A NEW FRAMEWORK

Much of academic psychology has been dedicated to the modern-era project of propagating the Cartesian split: distinguishing mind from body, rationality from emotions, masculine from feminine, biochemical from psychological. From its inception, psychology has attempted to claim a scientific warrant for its practices, and by extension for psychotherapy, which tries to ride psychology's coattails. Therapy's positivist, scientistic bent has become increasingly pronounced in recent years as large insurance corporations gained control of managing mental health care and insisted on compliance with cognitive-behavioral models. Such a stance reinforces concepts such as self-contained individualism and the utility of a psychological cost-benefit analysis in personal life, presumes the universality of the empty self and more recently of the multiple self, and naturalizes current configurations of gender, race, and sexual orientation. This uncritical reliance on scientism and technicism results in a similarly uncritical and strongly normative vision of proper behavior and meaningful human life. The therapist's narrow functionalist striving after the truest theory and the most effective modalities flows logically from this banal positivism.

In the postwar era, a vigorous critique of therapy's romantic-era influences and then modern-era scientism began to percolate, most influentially in the humanities and social science disciplines that have historically informed psychology's assumptions. With the Interpretive Turn, scholars such as Martin Heidegger, Hans-Georg Gadamer, and more recently Charles Taylor in philosophy, Michel Foucault in history, and Jacques Derrida in literary and social criticism challenged epistemological and moral assumptions in ways that repositioned the very meaning and function of psychotherapy.[3]

Although some late nineteenth-century philosophers such as Nietzsche, Dilthey, and Husserl contributed to the Western intellectual tradition that began the Turn, it was Heidegger in 1927 who really instantiated it. In his first book, *Being and Time*, he directly challenged the Cartesian split between matter and spirit, mind and body, and by doing so set out a new way of understanding human being. Humans, Heidegger argued, are historical beings. We do not have a universal essence separate from and unaffected by our social surround. The two are so entangled that any presumption of their radical separation must be considered wrongheaded.

However, the last four hundred years of Western society have been built on exactly that split. Central to that framework is the certain belief that the only way to determine the truth is to bracket off all "prejudgments" (in other words, the social realm) in order to develop a putatively objective view of nature as it is. This is the scientism that has fed some of the worst impulses in academic psychology.

But philosophers who have followed Heidegger, such as Gadamer and Taylor, have argued that when it comes to what matters in life, to what philosophers call "the good," it is not possible to bracket off prejudgments. Without prejudgments there would be no language, no culture, no traditions or social life of any kind. We learn about the world, about human limitations and potentialities, and about how we should comport ourselves by performing social practices, which over time come to constitute us. Without such practices, humans could not be human. We live through them and use them as tools long before we understand them. Social understandings are carried forward by historical traditions, and these traditions, as Taylor has explained, are always, "inescapably," moral.[4]

They are also traditions of power, and the better-known strain of thought within the Interpretive Turn, postmodernism, has focused on identifying the subtlest workings of domination and influence. Deconstruction, for instance, searches texts and practices for their rhetorical strategies and disguised power relations. Social constructionism emphasizes how intellectual theories and practices are cultural artifacts and examines how artifacts often serve disguised sociopolitical agendas. At times these insights have informed the practice of therapy. For instance, feminist psychologists like Muriel Dimen, Virginia Goldner, Adrienne Harris, and Rachel Hare-Mustin and Jeanne Maracek have critiqued psychotherapy theories that take for granted and thus perpetuate oppressive understandings and arrangements of gender.[5] Kimberlyn Leary and Derald Wing Sue and David Sue have uncovered a similar dynamic regarding race and ethnicity,[6] and Steve Botticelli and Stephen Hartman have done the same for socioeconomic class and sexual orientation.[7]

The insights of the hermeneutic tradition within the Turn have received less attention, but their impact on the practice of psychotherapy in time could be more far-reaching. This is because of the emphasis hermeneutics places on history, culture, and dialogue, broadly defined. Hermeneuticists do not think of traditions as homogeneous and monolithic, but as composed instead of various streams of influence. Each person is thought to be a point of intersecting moral traditions. In Gadamer's concept of what he called "dialogue" or "genuine conversation," an encounter with difference can open up opportunities to learn something new about the social world that brings the other to light and by doing so also makes available a new perspective about the social world that brings oneself to light. Everyday social life, then, takes on a particular form: we are, in Gadamer's view, involved in a continuing process of sifting through the embodied moral understandings we encounter in others and in ourselves (usually without being aware of it), testing one with the other, trying to determine which prejudgments are fitting and which are not, trying to determine how to live the right kind of life.[8] Of course, we do that imperfectly and with defensiveness and self-deceit. But at least sometimes it is possible to break through our guardedness and allow others and their traditions to influence us. When we do, we come to stand in a slightly different place than before, and as a result we are able to see our world and thus ourselves in a slightly different light. Such dialogue is an important element of moral discourse—it makes it possible to conceive of how people can be historical and yet also be capable of change.

Both deconstruction and hermeneutics present critiques of the epistemologies, political arrangements, and cultural ways of being that, following Descartes, brought first academic psychology and then psychotherapy into existence. They demonstrate therapy's fit with the cultural terrain and thus its complicity with the political status quo. That individual therapists within their practices unwittingly reinforce that status quo should come as no surprise.

One way of understanding the critique of therapeutic culture is to recognize two of its most prominent traditions. In one, writers such as Foucault and Derrida, Nicholas Rose, Robert Fancher, and Thomas Szasz have probed the many ways psychotherapy practices reinforced self-contained individualism, self-centeredness, and instrumentalism; colluded with Big Pharma; and in general fit with and reproduced the political arrangements of Western society.[9] These studies critique the ideology of therapeutic theories and examine the political and economic effects of therapeutic practices, for instance, the ways those practices reinforced racism, misogyny, and classism; the panopticism of modern-era living; and the institutions and everyday relations of the capitalist marketplace. In the second tradition, writers such as Robert Bellah et al., Anthony Giddens, Jerome Frank, Ian Hacking, Philip Rieff, and Louis Sass examined larger questions about the culture that brings psychotherapy to light.[10] These authors focus on therapeutic practice not only as a cause but also especially as an effect of the larger social terrain.

Although sometimes it might be helpful to distinguish between the two forms of the critique, given the nature of social life it is often difficult to do so. The concept of the hermeneutic circle—the relationship of part and whole, the interactive process of a particular culture and its artifacts—suggests that therapy is both cause and effect. That means it is also possible that therapy can play a role not only in reinforcing but also in resisting oppressive aspects of the status quo. It can do so by intentionally emphasizing and living out good, worthy values and commitments in the culture—ones that oppose its more oppressive features. However, that is a hard-won achievement, developed only through a complex process of psychological reflection, political study, and moral discourse. In the same way that Freud's concept of free association and Marx's concept of class warfare were at once both an embodiment of and a resistance to the Victorian era, so too is contemporary psychotherapy capable of being both cause and effect, revealer and revealed, proponent and opponent.

Most political critiques of therapeutic culture do not fully encompass the meanings and motivations—the moral dimensions—of therapy, because they do not fully recognize the moral dimensions of the social. Political academic critique does not usually directly experience the suffering of the other, grapple up close with one's moral responsibility to the other, carry out what therapists such as Donna Orange and Donnel Stern have called "witnessing."[11] There are times, as Emmanuel Levinas said, when the face of the other calls out to us.[12] This is why the hermeneutic focus on the primacy of the moral is so helpful in understanding the possibilities that inhere in the therapeutic encounter. In other words, trenchant political and philosophical critiques, important as they are, leave something to be desired. It is one thing to carry on a life dedicated to textual and social critique at a remove. It is quite another to sit with and be expected to attenuate immediate and acute suffering.

As I grappled with this fact and with the insights of the Interpretive Turn during the 1980s, I felt myself changing. My ability to think critically about therapeutic practices increased; yet sometimes, when sitting with patients, even with the critique fresh in mind, I would still believe that something valuable was happening in our engagement together. So I tried to conceive of a worthwhile therapy that consists of maintaining the kind of posture toward and relationship with patients that I valued while integrating it with a more overt hermeneutic and active moral and political perspective. I wanted a practice that recognized human beings as historical and human knowledge as built on interpretative processes that produce necessarily uncertain and incomplete ideas, that saw social life as framed by moral understandings, and that thus treated psychotherapy as a type of moral discourse with political consequences. In other words, I wanted to take the foundational concepts used in the hermeneutic critique of psychotherapy and develop a more hermeneutic way of doing psychotherapy.

PRACTICE AND THE SOCIAL TERRAIN

At the center of this vision of practice was the hermeneutic understanding of the mysterious, impossibly complex relationships among the culture and institutions of a society and (1) the characteristic ways of being that get developed within that culture (what cultural anthropologists sometimes call "the self"), (2) the strengths and ills that are manifested by those particular selves, (3) those who take on the responsibility for healing those ills, and (4) the healing practices that are applied to those ills.[13] Grasping the profound interweaving of culture with selves, ills, healers, and healing practices requires rejecting the notion that there is one universal understanding of human being, one complete theory of human psychology, one certain or effective means of cure.

In order to resist being blinded to the ways practices reinforce the status quo, I realized I could apply to the life of my patients the same approach I used to understand a historical era or a text.[14] I reminded myself that humans are contextual beings in the broad and radical sense hermeneutics provides and that human theories and practices, such as those used by psychotherapy, are equally contextual—they are historical and cultural artifacts. For these reasons, as a therapist I needed to think about how a theoretical idea or a practice functions morally and politically in the larger society. I began to put these ideas into practice by imagining that surrounding my patients was the social terrain they were implicitly describing to me. I began to pay attention to the details of that terrain: where my patients and their families and friends and enemies were located, what was possible and not possible and visible and unknowable within that world, what was considered good and bad. I began to think about the patients' experiences as reflective of the moral understandings and political forces of their social world. And I began trying to help my patients put all that into words.

The first time I used the image of the terrain in a session, I was listening to a troubled patient, one who was certain that no one wanted to know how he really felt, that everyone hated him and rejected him for what he thought, and that no one would allow him what he needed. What he described to me was the world that he lived in when he was in this particular state of mind. I saw it spread out before him on all sides, peopled with certain characters and voices from the past, from a time when the horizon was originally formed, like those pop-up books made for children.

I described this idea to him and suggested that in this world the people of his young life lived and interacted, all according to the rules that he had described to me or enacted with me. Those rules created positions within which they had to live, and these positions determined their destinies, because we unconsciously bring these understandings, arrangements, and rules to life each day. I described some of these rules as I had come to understand them.

"Well," he said, "that's life. That's all there is." Then he paused, puzzled. "What do you mean—that there's some other world?" Then he laughed, in a relaxed and pleasant way I had rarely heard from him.[15]

I believe this moment had an effect on my patient first of all because for some time he had already been experiencing a somewhat different world with me in the clinical hour. It was a world partly composed of the moral understandings of the traditions that constituted me, some moral commitments from his traditions, and the collaborative mix or synthesis of worlds that we developed over time together. I listened, cared about him, tried to understand him, sometimes disagreed with him, respectfully challenged him, made mistakes and was able to admit them, was openly affected by him—things "relational" therapists often do.[16] He was able to understand the concept of a different world because to some degree we had been living it together during our sessions.

Of course, seeing one's life from a slightly different perspective marks the beginning, not the end, of therapeutic change. But something happened in that moment that we could build on. Conceiving of a patient's life in a contextual, topographical manner helps me think hermeneutically about my patients. Instead of relying on theories that claim to reveal the universal, interior truths about human being (and thereby in various ways unknowingly reproducing the status quo), I now seek to practice in ways that recognize the importance of the patient's sociopolitical context; emphasize the interpretive, critical aspect of the therapeutic encounter; and be aware of the good and bad consequences of the practices I utilize, thus aiming for an integration of the personal, the moral, and the political.[17]

Attention to the patient's social terrain also requires that I become more aware of how much my feelings, opinions, and actions—both overt and covert, obvious and hidden—affect my patients, how much theirs affect me, and how much our mutual dynamics affect us both. The insights of the Interpretive Turn challenge the therapist's absolute authority, the validity of the therapist's unproblematic access to reality, the viability of the belief that the therapist is the healthy one and the patient the sick one, and the assumption that intrapsychic forces are the major source of psychopathology. With these caveats in mind, therapy became more an interpersonal and collaborative process and less unilateral. Relational psychoanalysis calls this the shift from a one-person to a two-person psychology; shifting to a more truly hermeneutic stance might mean a shift from a two-person to a three-person psychology.[18] Emphasizing hermeneutic dialogue helped me get better at noticing and admitting my mistakes and over time being able to understand better why they happen. In fact, it helped me be more honest and responsive to my patients throughout a session, not just when we noticed a mistake. I came to realize all of this is an expression of my moral responsibility to them and to myself, as the kind of therapist and person I aspire to be. I learned to encourage my patients to talk more honestly about me and the pattern of our interactions. In turn, encounters with difference have become more obvious, and thus it has become easier to talk about our different—and sometimes conflicting—understandings about the good.

I find that all of this makes it easier for patients to do the hard work of therapy: to tell the truth about themselves, to complain about me, to talk about how the larger forces of our social world affect them. It is easier for me to ask them about how they are feeling about the political events of our time, both large and small, and that is important. Therapists have been trained to ignore or dismiss the political responses of their patients because they are thought to be nonpsychological responses, defensive and avoidant. But, as Lane Gerber has demonstrated, those responses are an integral part of everyday life, rich with meaning and profoundly entangled with the ground of our being.[19] They are an opening to some of the most important concerns, wishes, hopes—and suffering—that patients experience. It seems ridiculous—in fact, self-defeating—to try to exclude it from the therapeutic hour.

I have found that avoiding overt political issues in the everyday lives of my patients contributes significantly to the insecurity, disappointment, fear, disillusionment, helplessness, and hopelessness from which they suffer, even though mainstream psychotherapy usually attributes these reactions to intrapsychic processes. When combined with a complementary avoidance by the therapist, these issues become mystified, lost from sight, and thus increasingly powerful (and thus untreatable) influences on behavior. If I can take their political struggles seriously, it becomes easier to wonder with them about what they are avoiding in their life outside of my office that they might benefit from actively addressing or becoming engaged in.

While doing that, of course, I am simply doing what therapists from Freud onward have often done, which is to look for what patients are not noticing, what the therapist is not talking about, or what both are avoiding together. The insights of the Interpretive Turn illuminate the moral and political dimensions of that inattention. By presenting a vision of human being that is uncompromisingly contextual and paradoxical, practitioners influenced by the Turn draw our collective focus to the limited ways that any healing practice addresses the suffering occasioned by a society. No healing practice could survive if it were not saturated with the cultural language of the people it was setting out to heal, if it could not describe, explain, and provide understandable—and politically less threatening—solutions to the various sufferings characteristic of its time and place. Therein lie the paradox and the danger of "the therapeutic."

The fit between the cultural terrain and the understandings, theories, practices, and institutions of the era are shockingly—sometimes bizarrely—complementary. It is ultimately a profoundly mysterious collaboration, one that works on an embodied, unconscious level, the genius of which is rarely perceived by those of us who live it out in daily life. The "rightness" of individualism; the felt sense of the accuracy of the "empty self" description of the post-WWII era; the taken-for-granted truth of the computer metaphor for the human brain; the astounding way anorexia is both a rebellion against and yet a disguised compliance with consumer society and its gendered and racialized power relations; and, most recently, the shift from seeing the self as hungry consumer to seeing it as minor celebrity, multiple, external, exhibitionistic—these are all examples of the mysterious fit between the self and its society. And thus, inevitably, they are examples of the fit between psychotherapy practices and the political terrain. Because they seek to ease our dis-ease, ultimately, healing practices—to varying degrees—unintentionally and yet inevitably reproduce the political status quo.

But awareness of this does not mean we should jettison the practice of therapy; quite the contrary, in the face of suffering, healers have a moral and political imperative to critique the prevailing institutions of their society and address the links between those institutions and the suffering they treat. If they do not, their work supports, even furthers, the sociopolitical arrangements of their world, and thus the suffering those arrangements produce. We see this complicity in theories that, for example, use consumer metaphors like the empty self to explain human development and psychotherapy cure, use computer metaphors to explain human mentation, embrace the ideology of self-contained individualism, and adopt a physical science epistemology and a medical model of practice.[20] While adopting such metaphors, therapists unknowingly often efface the fact that we are all imperfect beings whose understandings are always uncertain and incomplete. Our job is not to try to be perfect, or objective, or disengaged. Our job is to engage, to face what emerges between us and our patients, to know and honor where we stand, and yet to notice difference and take up the challenge of questioning our prejudgments and help our patients do the same.

Mountains of technical psychotherapy theory have been devoted to how people change. But hermeneuticists suggest that human mentation, emotion, and social communication form one immense, fearsome, beautiful mystery—a mystery far beyond our ability to understand it. Human life is a miracle, and our ideas about how it operates depend on profoundly culture-bound metaphors about complex processes far beyond what the latest theory du jour or neuroscientific study can capture. All we accomplish by claiming a certain objective knowledge about the mind, cross-cultural emotions, the development of the universal self, or the processes of psychological cure is to unknowingly disguise a set of moral understandings, uncritically support the political status quo, and further our own professional and financial ambitions in the capitalist marketplace.

I don't know how to fully understand, let alone explain, how people change, and I haven't really found anyone who could. Theory and practice that address moral traditions, dialogue, and the moveable horizon are about as explicit as you can get about clinical technique from a hermeneutic point of view. It is an uncertain and incomplete vision, but it is all we've got. And mercifully, it is enough. Living with therapeutic uncertainty has not been easy, but I feel much gratitude. Drawing from the Interpretive Turn's critique of therapeutic culture has brought much richness and meaning to my work and my life. I'd do it all again in a heartbeat. Really.

Afterword

Jackson Lears

Forty years on, the therapeutic culture of the 1970s seems benign and unthreatening, if sometimes self-parodic. Consider the list of panaceas embraced by ex-student radical Jerry Rubin and quoted by Christopher Lasch in *The Culture of Narcissism*: "EST, gestalt therapy, bioenergetics, rolfing, massage, jogging, health foods, tai chi, Esalen, hypnotism, modern dance, meditation, Silva Mind Control, Arica, acupuncture, sex therapy, Reichian therapy, and More House—a smorgasbord course in New Consciousness."[1] The cultural critics of the time brooded over this muddle, believing it symptomatic of broader public pathologies. They were right to brood, and many of their insights (especially Lasch's) have survived to this day. But as these fine essays remind us, the critics missed a lot, even at the time.

Perhaps the therapeutic culture critics' greatest shortcoming was their apparent inability to sympathize (at least in print) with psychotherapeutic patients. Public maladies, however worthy of critique, conceal private suffering that deserves more than mere dismissal. Behind therapeutic fads and slogans there is always a wealth of human misery. Therapeutic culture, before it is anything else, is an effort to relieve pain. To the extent that its critics have forgotten that fundamental fact, their critiques have lost persuasive power.

The further problem with the older criticism was that much of it was foreshortened historically. The turn to therapy for relief from pain was rooted in particular historical circumstances among the Anglo-American bourgeoisie in the late nineteenth century—what Donald Meyer, in his pioneering history of therapeutic culture, called "Pastors and Doctors Who Didn't Help."[2] Orthodox Christianity was failing its flock; established medicine was disappointing its patients. Spiritual religion and materialist medicine were trapped on different sides of the same dualism; neither could address their constituencies' emotional needs, which arose from the interactions of body and mind. Therapeutic solutions filled the void. No conscientious historian could blame desperate people for embracing them.

The key to capturing the full complexity of therapeutic culture is discriminating between sympathy and conceptual flexibility. Even as we recognize the deep connections between the personal and the political, the distinction between those two realms remains crucial to creating a coherent, humane critique of therapeutic culture. In my own work, I have tried to cultivate sympathy for people's longings for deliverance from pain even as I also tried to trace the impact of the idiom used to address those longings. (Lasch tried to do this as well, more successfully in *The Minimal Self* than in *The Culture of Narcissism.*) One can sympathize with people's need to relieve their own suffering through therapy while at the same time criticizing the larger culture therapists and their patients (not to mention journalists, politicians, intellectuals, and celebrities) have unwittingly helped to create. Therapeutic culture, in my view, has at most a remote and circuitous relationship to the actual treatment of mental or emotional disorders; it is an unintended public consequence of efforts to promote private well-being.

Since the 1970s, the chief unintended public consequence of therapeutic culture has been the rise of identity politics. There was a kind of tragic necessity about this development—tragic because it meant the eclipse of an older progressive politics dedicated to social justice, necessary because it was rooted in legitimate dissatisfaction with the rationalist universalism that animated the Old Left. As Lasch acknowledged, "The left has too often served as a refuge from the terrors of the inner life."[3] In rejecting that refuge, identity politics reinforced a drift from social justice to self-esteem as the main goal of political action. On the left, therapeutic ideals began to inform policy debate, with good reason—at least at first. No one can deny the urgency of the need felt by feminists, black power advocates, and gay activists to demand equality on their own terms—to reject the assumption that full participation in society required acceptance of the norms set by straight white males. The critique of those norms and the creation of a broader, more capacious culture has been one of the great accomplishments of the last several decades.

Yet the tragic—and unintended—accompaniment to that achievement has been the fragmentation of the left into multiplying interest groups and the loss of a common commitment to equality for all. In the academy, the fate of the "race, class, gender" mantra epitomizes this process: the category of "class" nearly always drops out. As Adolph Reed has observed, the Obama presidency embodies the culminating triumph of identity politics. "He is a triumph of image and identity over content; indeed, he is the triumph of identity *as* content." He embodies race as "an abstraction, a feel-good evocation severed from history and social relations." And few on the left want to spoil those good feelings by raising the sharp critique Obama deserves. Instead we have, in Reed's words, "a desiccated leftism" preoccupied with "making up 'Just So' stories about dispossession and exploitation recast in the evocative but politically sterile language of disparity and diversity."[4] Identity politics, in other words, has hollowed out political language and left us no solid alternative to the neoliberal discourse of efficiency, productivity, and innovation. The vision of social democracy that inspired progressive politics from the New Deal through the Great Society has become dimmer and dimmer until it has now nearly disappeared.

It would be the silliest sort of reification to say that therapeutic culture had in some way caused this state of affairs. What has happened is far subtler. The "expressive individualism" that Robert Bellah and his colleagues found at the core of the therapeutic ethos became, under Reaganism and after, a counterpart to the economic individualism promoted by the Republican right. (Daniel Rodgers has told this story well in *Age of Fracture*.)[5] What was lost was any sense of commonweal, or public good, that transcended the needs of individual interest groups. Democratic party platforms became a laundry list of identity group concerns coupled with a commitment to neoliberal economics that was virtually indistinguishable from the free-market blatherings of the Republicans.

Much of therapeutic culture continues to embody individualist assumptions. I can testify from personal experience that some therapists, at least, remain committed to a familial version of the "harmony of interests" theory promoted by Bernard Mandeville: if every individual in a family pursues his or her own self-interest, somehow the family will prosper. This is not simply a matter of therapists playing the hand they are dealt—of recognizing that people have to survive and with any luck flourish within the current social universe, for all its faults. It is, rather, a simple-minded celebration of the mythic, autonomous self. This kind of therapy is clearly implicated in the creation of the neoliberal consensus.

Yet not all therapists are indifferent to political concerns, as Philip Cushman's essay in this volume makes clear. Significant tensions have arisen between the therapeutic and neoliberal worldviews—especially when the therapeutic outlook participates, however indirectly, in the psychoanalytic tradition.

That is the big reason to rethink therapeutic culture: it looks far more genuinely countercultural now than it did forty years ago—less because the therapeutic outlook has changed than because the dominant culture has been subsumed by the utilitarian demands of market discipline. Under these circumstances, the helping professions look less like citadels of sanctioned power and more like redoubts of humane wisdom. As public discourse has descended into technodeterminism and entrepreneurial fantasy, therapeutic culture has become part of the humanities, the only part of our public idiom that acknowledges an inner life, that takes emotions seriously, and that treats subjective experience as a source of knowledge.

The extraordinary revival of mechanistic positivism, seen in everything from pop-evolutionary thought to the New Atheism and the cult of neuroscience, has made it clear that scientism is the appropriate ideology for our neoliberal moment. Scientism is not, to be sure, an outlook actually based on scientific method—the patient weighing of experimental results, the reframing of questions in response to contrary evidence, the willingness to live with uncertainty. Quite the contrary. Scientism is a revival of the nineteenth-century positivist faith that a reified science has discovered (or is about to discover) all the important truths about human life. Precise measurement and rigorous calculation, from this view, are the basis for finally settling all the old metaphysical and moral controversies—explaining consciousness and choice, replacing ambiguity with certainty. The most problematic applications of scientism have usually arisen in the behavioral sciences, where the varieties and perversities of experience have often been reduced to quantitative data that are alleged to reveal an enduring "human nature."

Certain varieties of therapeutic culture have embraced the scientistic outlook. It is especially evident in the vogue of positive psychology and the cottage industry of self-help books telling people how to be happy. The scientism on display in the happiness manuals is a strikingly vacuous worldview, devoid of history, culture, or political economy. Its chief method is self-reported survey research; its twin conceptual pillars are pop-evolutionary psychology, based on parables about what life was like on the savannah a hundred thousand years ago, and pop-neuroscience, based on sweeping, unsubstantiated claims about brain function from fragments of contemporary research.

Like older, more humane forms of therapeutic culture, the happiness industry allows structural constraints to disappear into the black box of personal choice. The difference is that the happiness industry has (paradoxically) almost nothing to say about conflicted emotions or the complexities of the inner life. In keeping with the contemporary cult of neuroscience, the happiness industry reduces the mind to the brain and the brain to a computer. Nothing could be more easily assimilated to the market utilitarianism that pervades the neoliberal consensus.

We are, in other words, back in the Dickensian world of Uriah Heep and Thomas Gradgrind—only now they run an Institute for Cognitive Science with research grants from the National Institutes of Health. So once again, perhaps more successfully than in the 1970s, therapeutic culture could help create a necessary counterpoint to dominant political (maybe even ontological) assumptions—particularly if its devotees connect public and private, acknowledging that psychic pain can be traceable to the demands of a punishing political economy. To get to that point, we need to revive an intellectual tradition that refuses reductionist fashion, that treats all experiences—including hallucination and despair—as potential sources of insight, and that delights in the contrarieties of consciousness rather than attempting to explain them away. It is the tradition of Freud and William James, and its area of inquiry is what James called the great "Unclassified Residuum"[6]—the mysterious bonds of body and soul that remain at the core of therapeutic culture.

NOTES

INTRODUCTION

1. On early international therapeutic culture among professionals, see, for example, Jan Goldstein, *Console and Classify: The French Psychiatric Profession in the Nineteenth Century* (Chicago: University of Chicago Press, 1986); Janet Oppenheim, *Shattered Nerves: Doctors, Patients, and Depression in Victorian England* (Oxford: Oxford University Press, 1991); Christopher Goetz, "Poor Beard! Charcot's Internationalization of Neurasthenia, the 'American Disease,'" *Neurology* 57 (2001): 510–14; Andrew Scull, *Hysteria: The Disturbing History* (Oxford: Oxford University Press, 2012). The development of vernacular therapeutic culture in Europe and its migration to the United States are discussed in Peter Washington, *Madame Blavatsky's Baboon: A History of the Mystics, Mediums, and Misfits Who Brought Spiritualism to America* (New York: Shocken, 1995). Scholarship on contemporary transnational therapeutic norms examines their circulation through informal channels (for example, Ethan Watters, *Crazy Like Us: The Globalization of the American Psyche* [New York: Free Press, 2010]), the practices of mental health professionals (for example, Michael J. Stevens and Uwe Gielen, eds., *Toward a Global Psychology: Theory, Research, Intervention, and Pedagogy* [Oxford: Psychology Press, 2006]; Arthur Kleinman, "Global Mental Health: A Failure of Humanity," *Lancet* 374 (2009): 603–4), and the international security state (for example, Vannessa Pupavac, "Human Security and the Rise of Global Therapeutic Governance," *Conflict, Security and Development* 5 [2005]: 161–81; Sharon Abramowitz, *Searching for Normal in the Wake of the Liberian War* [Philadelphia: University of Pennsylvania Press, 2014]).

2. Benjamin Franklin, *Autobiography* (1817; reprint, New York: DC Heath, 1908). On Franklin's influence, see John Cawelti, *Apostles of the Self-Made Man* (Chicago: University of Chicago Press, 1965). "Oprah Winfrey Show Suffers Ratings Slump," *Telegraph*, February 9, 2011. http://www.telegraph.co.uk/news/newstopics/celebritynews/2037083/Oprah-Winfrey-Show-suffers-ratings-slump.html, accessed March 17, 2014.

3. Ronald W. Dworkin, "The Rise of the Caring Industry," *Policy Review* June/July (2010): 45–46; Eva S. Moskowitz, *In Therapy We Trust: America's Obsession with Self-Fulfillment* (Baltimore: Johns Hopkins University Press, 2001), 5–6.

4. David Beito, *From Mutual Aid to the Welfare State: Fraternal Societies and Social Services, 1890–1967* (Chapel Hill: University of North Carolina Press, 2000). On AA membership, see *AA Fact File* (New York: AA World Services Organization, n.d.). http://www.aa.org/lang/en/catalog.cfm?origpage=282&product=92, accessed March 17, 2014.

5. See Jacobellis v. Ohio, U.S. 184, 197 (Stewart, concurring).

6. Some of the most influential accounts of the therapeutic worldview include Philip Rieff, *The Triumph of the Therapeutic: Uses of Faith after Freud* (New York: Harper, 1966); Christopher Lasch, *The Culture of Narcissism: American Life in the Age of Diminishing Expectations* (New York: Norton, 1978); Richard Sennett *The Fall of Public Man* (New York: Knopf, 1977); T.J. Jackson Lears, *No Place of Grace: Antimodernism and the Transformation of American Culture, 1880–1920* (New York: Pantheon, 1981); Robert Bellah et al., *Habits of the Heart: Individualism and Commitment in American Life* (Berkeley: University of California Press, 1985); and Wendy Kaminer, *I'm Dysfunctional, You're Dysfunctional: The Recovery Movement and Other Self-Help Fashions* (New York: Vintage, 1993). Adumbrations of this canonical critique appear in Elizabeth Lasch-Quinn, *Race Experts: How Racial Etiquette, Sensitivity Training, and New Age Therapy Hijacked the Civil Rights Revolution* (New York: Rowman and Littlefield, 2001); Frank Furedi, *Therapy Culture: Cultivating Vulnerability in an Uncertain Age* (New York: Routledge, 2003); and Jonathan Imber, ed. *Therapeutic Culture: Triumph and Defeat* (New Brunswick, N.J.: Transaction Publishers, 2004). A more considered treatment of the phenomenon appears in Eva Illouz, *Saving the Modern Soul: Therapy, the Emotions, and the Culture of Self-Help* (Berkeley: University of California Press, 2008).

7. John Stuart Mill may be the preeminent liberal philosopher to directly address the pursuit of happiness; see R.S. Downie's "Mill on Pleasure and Self-Development," *Philosophical Quarterly* 16 (1966): 69–71. More generally, see Darrin M. McMahon, *Happiness: A History* (New York: Atlantic Monthly Press, 2006). The idea of the First Amendment as a guarantee of "individual self-realization" is discussed by Martin Redish in "The Value of Free Speech," *University of Pennsylvania Law Review* 130 (1982): 591–645.

8. Karen Halttunen, *Confidence Men and Painted Women: A Study of Middle-Class Culture in America, 1830–1870* (New Haven: Yale University Press, 1982); Ann Fabian, *The Unvarnished Truth: Personal Narratives in Nineteenth Century America* (Berkeley: University of California Press, 2000); Henry David Thoreau, *Walden* (1854; reprint, New York: Empire Books, 2012), 85; Harriet Beecher Stowe, *Uncle Tom's Cabin* (1852; reprint, New York: Signet Classics, 1998), 480.

9. Joyce Appleby, "The Heroic Model of Science," in *Telling the Truth about History*, written by Joyce Appleby, Lynn Hunt, and Margaret Jacob (New York: Norton, 1995), 15–51.

10. John Corrigan, *Business of the Heart: Religion and Emotion in the Nineteenth Century* (Berkeley: University of California Press, 2002); Colin Campbell, *The Romantic Ethic and the Spirit of Modern Consumerism* (Oxford: Basil Blackwell, 1987); John Tosh, *A Man's Place: Masculinity and the Middle-Class Home in Victorian England* (New Haven: Yale University Press, 1999); Rosalind Williams, *Dream Worlds: Mass Consumption in Late Nineteenth Century France* (Berkeley: University of California Press, 1991). See also Joel Pfister, "On Conceptualizing the Cultural History of Emotional and Psychological Life in America," in *Inventing the Psychological: Toward a Cultural History of Emotional Life in America*, ed. Joel Pfister and Nancy Schnog (New Haven: Yale University Press, 1997).

11. Charles Filmore, *Prosperity* (1936; reprint, New York: Tarcher/Penguin, 2008); Ralph Waldo Trine, *In Tune with the Infinite or Fullness of Peace, Power, and Plenty* (New York: Dodge, 1897).

12. For discussion of the cross-fertilization between mainline religions and their esoteric counterparts, see Leigh Eric Schmidt, *Restless Souls: The Making of American Spirituality* (New York: HarperOne, 2005). William James, *The Varieties of Religious Experience* (1902; reprint, New York: Oxford World Classics, 2012).

13. For a description of these developments in the United States, see Edward Shorter, *A History of Psychiatry: From the Era of the Asylum to the Age of Prozac* (New York: Wiley, 1997), and Eric Caplan, *Mind Games: American Culture and the Birth of Psychotherapy* (Berkeley: University of California Press, 1998). In Europe, see Oppenheim, *Shattered Nerves*, and George Drinka: *The Birth of Neurosis: Myth, Malady, and the Victorians* (New York: Simon and Schuster, 1984).

14. See Washington, *Madame Blavatsky's Baboon*; Olva Hammer, *Claiming Knowledge: Strategies of Epistemology from Theosophy to the New Age* (Leiden: Brill Academic Publishing, 2004); Cathy Jrade, *Rubén Darío and the Romantic Search for Unity: The Modernist Recourse to Esoteric Tradition* (Austin: University of Texas Press, 1983). Caplan, Mind Games, 151.

15. Barbara Sicherman, *The Quest for Mental Health in America, 1880–1917* (New York: Arno Press, 1967).

16. Hendrik Ruitenbeek, *Freud and America* (New York: Macmillan, 1964); Nathan G. Hale, *Freud and the Americans: The Beginnings of Psychoanalysis in the United States, 1876–1917* (New York: Oxford University Press, 1971).

17. Ellen Herman, in *The Romance of American Psychology: Political Culture in the Age of Experts* (Berkeley: University of California Press, 1995), and Eva Moskowitz, in *In Therapy We Trust*, both comment on the way World War II altered popular perceptions of therapy. See also Engel, *American Therapy: The Rise of Psychotherapy in the United States* (New York: Gotham Books, 2008), chapter 2.

18. For statistical evidence of the growth of psychotherapy in America during this period, see Joseph Veroff, Richard Kulka, and Elizabeth Douvan, *Mental Health in America: 1957 to 1976* (New York: Basic, 1981).

19. Lears, *No Place of Grace*, 47 and passim.

20. Noah Worcester, *The Atoning Sacrifice: A Display of Love, Not Wrath* (1824; reprint, Whitefish, Montana: 2009); Ann Douglas, *The Feminization of American Culture* (New York: Knopf, 1977), especially chapter 4; Laura Curtis, *Faith in the Great Physician: Suffering and Divine Healing in American Culture, 1860–1900* (Baltimore: Johns Hopkins University Press, 2007); Peale, *The Power of Positive Thinking* (New York: Prentice-Ha11, 1952). On criticisms of Peale, see Reinhold Niebuhr, "Varieties of Religious Revival," *New Republic*, June 6, 1955, 13–16; Elmer George Homrighausen, "Receipt for the Full Life," *Princeton University Seminary Bulletin* 51 (1957): 11–15; Paul Hutchinson, "Have We a 'New' Religion?" *Life*, April 11, 1955, 138–58.

21. James Morone, *Hellfire Nation: The Politics of Sin in American History* (New Haven: Yale University Press, 2003).

22. R.D. Laing, *The Divided Self: A Study of Sanity and Madness* (Chicago: Quadrangle Books, 1960); Thomas Szasz, *The Myth of Mental Illness: Foundations of a Theory of Personal Conduct* (New York: Harper, 1961); Michel Foucault, *Madness and Civilization*, trans. Richard

Howard (New York: Pantheon, 1965). An overview of the antipsychiatry movement appears in Nick Crossley, "R.D. Laing and the British Anti-Psychiatry Movement: a Socio-Historical Analysis," *Social Science and Medicine*, 47 (1997): 877–89.

23. See Betty Friedan, *The Feminine Mystique* (New York: Norton,1963); Kate Millet, *Sexual Politics* (Garden City: Doubleday, 1970). The most fulsome analysis in this vein appears in Phyllis Chesler, *Women and Madness* (New York: Doubleday, 1972).

24. Nikolas Rose, *Governing the Soul: The Shaping of the Private Self* (New York: Routledge, 1990) and *Inventing Ourselves: Psychology, Power, and Personhood* (Cambridge: Cambridge University Press, 1996); Wendy Brown, *States of Injury: Power and Freedom in Late Modernity* (Princeton: Princeton University Press, 1995). See also Barbara Cruikshank, *The Will to Empower: Democratic Citizens and Other Subjects* (Ithaca: Cornell University Press, 1999).

25. The *Partisan Review* published the most influential discussion of mass society among midcentury intellectuals. See Phillips, William and Philip Rahv, eds. "Our Country and Our Culture: A Symposium, i-111," *Partisan Review* 19 (1952): 282–326; 420–50; 562–97. See also Bernard Rosenberg and David Manning White, eds. *Mass Culture: The Popular Arts in America* (Glencoe, IL.: Free Press, 1957).

26. John Kenneth Galbraith, *The Affluent Society* (Boston: Houghton Mifflin, 1958). Lears, *No Place of Grace*, 32 and passim.

27. Charles Sykes, *A Nation of Victims: The Decay of the American Character* (New York: St. Martin's Press, 1992). See also David Rieff, "Victims All: Recovery, Co-Dependency, and the Art of Blaming Somebody Else," *Harper's*, October 1991, 49–56. More recent examples of the socially conservative version of this critique can be found in Christina Hoff Summers and Sally Satel, *One Nation under Therapy: How the Helping Culture Is Eroding Self-Reliance* (New York: St. Martin's Griffin, 2006), and Alan Petigny, *The Permissive Society* (New York: Cambridge University Press, 2009).

28. Elayne Rapping, *The Culture of Recovery* (New York: Beacon, 1996); Dana Cloud, *Control and Consolation in American Culture and Politics: Rhetorics of Therapy* (New York: Sage, 1997); Jerry Lembcke, *The Spitting Image: Myth, Memory, and the Legacy of Vietnam* (New York: New York University Press, 1998).

29. On "liberation psychotherapy," see John Steadman Rice, *A Disease of One's Own: Psychotherapy, Addiction, and the Emergence of Co-dependency* (New Brunswick, NJ: Transaction, 1995).

30. These attachments to a traditional moral order are probably most pronounced in Rieff, *Triumph of the Therapeutic*, and Alasdair MacIntyre, *After Virtue: A Study in Moral Theory* (Notre Dame: University of Notre Dame Press, 1981).

31. Mariana Valverde, *Diseases of the Will: Alcohol and the Dilemmas of Freedom* (New York: Cambridge University Press, 1998).

32. This trajectory is best discerned in the works of Lauren Berlant, beginning with *The Queen of America Goes to Washington City: Essays on Sex and Citizenship* (Durham, NC: Duke University Press, 1997) and, most recently, *Cruel Optimism* (Durham, NC: Duke University Press, 2011). The more general lineaments of this strain of thought are evident in Eve Sedgwick, *Touching Feeling: Affect, Performativity, Pedagogy* (Durham, NC: Duke University Press,

2003); Patricia Ticiento Clough and Jean Halley, eds. *The Affective Turn: Theorizing the Social* (Durham, NC: Duke University Press, 2007); Sara Ahmed, *The Promise of Happiness* (Durham, NC: Duke University Press, 2010); and Ann Cvetkovich, *Depression: A Public Feeling* (Durham, NC: Duke University Press, 2012). For a critical overview of this intellectual trajectory in recent affect theory, see Ruth Leys, "The Turn to Affect: A Critique," *Critical Inquiry* 37 (2011): 434–72.

33. Sheldon Stryker, Timothy J. Owens, and Robert W. White, eds. *Self, Identity, and Social Movements* (Minneapolis: University of Minnesota Press, 2000).

34. Betty Friedan, *The Feminine Mystique*, 429.

CHAPTER ONE

1. Elaine Forman Crane, Sarah Blan Dine, Alison Duncan Hirsch, Arthur Scherr, and Anita J. Rapone, eds. *The Diary of Elizabeth Drinker*, 3 vols. (Boston: Northeastern University Press, 1991); Drinker, *Diary*, vol. 1, xxi–xxxii; Drinker, *Diary*, October 22, 1798.

2. Drinker, *Diary*, September 4, 1794; April 6, 1795.

3. Drinker, *Diary*, September 7, 1803; Elaine Forman Crane, "'I Have Suffer'd Much Today': The Defining Force of Pain in Early America," in *Through a Glass Darkly: Reflections on Personal Identity in Early America*, ed. Ronald Hoffman, Mechal Sobel, and Fredrika J. Teute (Chapel Hill: University of North Carolina Press, 1997), 370–403.

4. Amanda Porterfield, *Conceived in Doubt: Religion and Politics in the New American Nation* (Chicago: University of Chicago Press, 2012).

5. Drinker, *Diary*, January 30, 1796.

6. On the growth of sympathy in the antebellum United States, see Margaret Abruzzo, *Polemical Pain: Slavery, Cruelty, and the Rise of Humanitarianism* (Baltimore: Johns Hopkins University Press, 2011); James C. Turner, *Reckoning with the Beast: Animals, Pain, and Humanity in the Victorian Mind* (Baltimore: Johns Hopkins University Press, 2000); Elizabeth B. Clark, "'Sacred Rights of the Weak': Pain, Sympathy, and the Culture of Individual Rights in Antebellum America," *Journal of American History* 82 (1995): 463–93; Karen Halttunen, "Humanitarianism and the Pornography of Pain in Anglo-American Culture," *American Historical Review* 100, no. 2 (1995): 303–34.

7. Abruzzo, *Polemical Pain*, 58.

8. "To Pain," *New York Weekly Museum*, April 9, 1814, 196.

9. Frederick Douglass, *Narrative of the Life of Frederick Douglass, An American Slave* (London: H.G. Collins, 1851), 60.

10. Charles W. Burr, "The Causes of Hysteria," *International Clinics* (1897): 144. On narrative and suffering following the Civil War, see Joseph M. Gabriel, "Restricting the Sale of 'Deadly Poisons': Pharmacists, Drug Regulation, and Narratives of Suffering in the Gilded Age," *Journal of the Gilded Age and Progressive Era* 9 (2010): 145–69.

11. Eva Illouz, *Saving the Modern Soul: Therapy, Emotions, and the Culture of Self-Help* (Berkeley: University of California Press, 2008), 7.

12. Thomas Szasz, *The Therapeutic State: Psychiatry in the Mirror of Current Events* (Buffalo: Prometheus Books, 1984).

CHAPTER TWO

1. Rachel Wharton, "Back of the House: Murray's Cheese," *Edible Manhattan*, March 5, 2012. http://www.ediblemanhattan.com/magazine/murrays-cheese/, accessed March 31, 2014.

2. Amanda Gore, *The Gospel of Joy* (Dallas: Head2Heart Pty Ltd, 2010).

3. On antipsychiatry in the twentieth century, see David Cooper, *Psychiatry and Anti-Psychiatry* (New York: Tavistock Press, 1967); Zbigniew Kotowicz, *R.D. Laing and the Paths of Anti-Psychiatry* (London: Routledge, 1997); Matthew Thomson, *Psychological Subjects: Identity, Culture and Health in Twentieth-Century Britain* (Oxford: Oxford University Press, 2006).

4. Eva S. Moskowitz, *In Therapy We Trust: America's Obsession with Self-Fulfillment* (Baltimore: Johns Hopkins University Press, 2001), 1.

5. Bruce Metzger, *The Canon of the New Testament: Its Origin, Development, and Significance* (New York: Oxford University Press, 1997).

6. Adela Yarbro Collins, *Mark: A Commentary* (Minneapolis, MN: Fortress Press, 2007), 20.

7. Elizabeth A. Clark, *Founding the Fathers: Early Church History and Protestant Professors in Nineteenth-Century America* (Philadelphia: University of Pennsylvania Press, 2011).

8. Laurie Maffly-Kipp, ed., *American Scriptures* (New York: Penguin Books, 2010).

9. Judith Snodgrass, *Presenting Japanese Buddhism to the West: Orientalism, Occidentalism, and the Columbian Exposition* (Chapel Hill: University of North Carolina Press, 2003), 222–44.

10. Paul Carus, *The Gospel of Buddha*, 5th ed. (Chicago: Open Court Publishing Co.: 1897), vi.

11. My understanding of biography is assisted by Catherine N. Parke, "Biography: An Overview of the Genre," *Biography: Writing Lives* (New York: Routledge, 2002), 1–34; and Rob Wilson, "Producing American Selves: The Form of American Biography," *Boundary* 2 18 (1991): 104–29.

12. Christopher G. White, *Unsettled Minds: Psychology and the American Search for Spiritual Assurance, 1830–1940* (Berkeley: University of California Press, 2009).

13. Marsha G. Witten, *All Is Forgiven: The Secular Message in American Protestantism* (Princeton: Princeton University Press, 1993).

14. Susan E. Myers-Shirk, *Helping the Good Shepherd: Pastoral Counselors in a Psychotherapeutic Culture, 1925–1975* (Baltimore: Johns Hopkins University Press, 2009).

15. Krista L. Phair, "The Gospel According to: A Theory of Transformative Discursive Allegory," *Communication Studies* 61 (2010): 112, 111. For a complete listing of titles, see the Westminster John Knox Press series site, http://www.wjkbooks.com/Products/CategoryCenter/BRC!GATO/Gospel_according_to.aspx, accessed March 31, 2014.

16. Watt, *A Transforming Faith: Explorations of Twentieth-Century American Evangelicalism* (New Brunswick: Rutgers University Press, 1991), 138.

17. Watt, *A Transforming Faith*, 139.

18. "Boundless Webzine—About Us," Boundless.org, http://www.boundless.org/about/overview, accessed March 31, 2014.

19. "About Focus on the Family," FocusontheFamily.com, http://www.focusonthefamily

.com/about_us.aspx, accessed June 16, 2011. For more on gender prescriptions of Focus on the Family, see Ludger H. Viefhues-Bailey, *Between a Man and a Woman? Why Conservative Christian Oppose Same-Sex Marriage* (New York: Columbia University Press, 2010).

20. David Powlison, "The Therapeutic Gospel: Part 1," Boundless.org, http://www.boundless.org/faith/2008/the-therapeutic-gospel-part-1, accessed March 31, 2014.

21. Powlison, "The Therapeutic Gospel: Part 1," italics in original.

CHAPTER THREE

1. For example, Winnifred Fallers Sullivan, "We are All Religious Now. Again," *Social Research* 76 (2009): 1–18; William Connolly, *A World of Becoming* (Durham, NC: Duke University Press, 2011).

2. Modern writes "marks of spirituality . . . are not simply phenomena within religion but discursive effects of secularism (bound up, for example, with ideologies of the market, the triumph of the therapeutic, sentimental individualism, and the progressive telos that accompanies each)" (John Modern, *Secularism in Antebellum America* [Chicago: University of Chicago Press, 2011], 120–1). In other words, spirituality is not an extension of religion or its secularized shadow but rather a product of secularism and a language through which to indicate and enchant its effects.

3. For some recent work in religious studies and history that helps us to rethink the concept of spirituality, see Catherine Albanese, *A Republic of Mind and Spirit* (New Haven: Yale University Press, 2006); Leigh Eric Schmidt, *Restless Souls* (San Francisco: Harper San Francisco, 2005). See also Courtney Bender, *The New Metaphysicals: Spirituality and the American Religious Imagination* (Chicago: University of Chicago Press 2010); John Modern, *Secularism in Antebellum America*; Kathryn Lofton, *Oprah: Gospel of an Icon* (Berkeley: University of California Press, 2011); Courtney Bender and Ann Taves, eds. *What Matters?: Ethnographies of Value in a Not So Secular Age* (New York: Columbia University Press, 2012) for alternative presentations.

4. Max Weber, "The Protestant Ethic and the Spirit of Capitalism" (New York: Routledge Classics, 2002), 124. Hereafter PESC.

5. The semiotic, legal, and scholarly play of "possession" and "possessed" is discussed fruitfully in Paul C. Johnson, "An Atlantic Genealogy of 'Spirit Possession,'" *Comparative Studies in Society and History* 53 (2011): 393–425.

6. Weber, PESC, 18.

7. Weber, PESC, 31. On this issue see, in particular, Philip Gorski, *The Disciplinary Revolution: Calvinism and the Rise of the State in Early Modern Europe* (Chicago: University of Chicago Press, 2003).

8. Max Weber, PESC, 115.

9. Max Weber, *Economy and Society*, volume 2 (Berkeley: University of California Press, 1978), 1186.

10. Fosdick, "Concerning Prayer," pp. 75–90 in *Adventures in Religion* (New York: Harper and Brothers, 1926); Ralph Waldo Trine, *In Tune with the Infinite, Or, Fullness of Peace, Power and Plenty* (New York: T.Y. Crowell, 1897).

11. Donald Meyer, *The Positive Thinkers: Religion as Pop Psychology from Mary Baker Eddy*

to Oral Roberts (New York: Pantheon Books, 1980), 207; Barbara Ehrenreich, *Bright-Sided: How the Relentless Promotion of Positive Thinking Has Undermined America* (New York: Henry Holt, 2009), 203. Adorno's classic "Theses against Occultism" equates positive thinking and fascism, in *Adorno: The Stars Down to Earth and Other Essays on the Irrational in Culture* (New York: Routledge, 1994), 128–33.

12. A more charitable reading might argue that they reject rather than ignore this central aspect of Weber's argument. However, none of those who directly deal with the PESC note that they are rejecting or supplying an alternative reading. Insofar as most Americans actually come to understand Weber through these secondary glosses, it is likely no wonder that Weber's name is problematically attached to the "Protestant work ethic."

13. Wendy Kaminer, *Sleeping with Extra-Terrestrials: The Rise of Irrationalism and the Perils of Piety* (New York: Pantheon, 1999). 249; Ehrenreich, *Bright Sided*, 204–5, italics added.

14. William James, *A Pluralistic Universe* (Cambridge: Harvard University Press, 1977), pp. 145–7.

15. Courtney Bender, *The New Metaphysicals* (Chicago: University of Chicago Press, 2010).

16. Bender, *New Metaphysicals*, chapter 5.

17. In other words, their books did not make their worlds for them. Which should caution us of course against using other people's books to make our worlds about them.

18. Emma Sutton makes an argument to this effect in "Interpreting 'Mind-Cure': William James and the 'Chief Task . . . of the Science of Human Nature'" *Journal of the History of the Behavioral Sciences* 48 (2012): 115–33.

19. William James, *Pragmatism* (Indianapolis: Hackett Publishing, 1981), 92.

CHAPTER FOUR

1. Keneth Kinnamon and Michel Fabre, eds. *Conversations with Richard Wright* (Jackson: University Press of Mississippi, 1993), 230–31.

2. Jonathan M. Metzl, *The Protest Psychosis: How Schizophrenia Became a Black Disease* (Boston: Beacon Press, 2009), xi.

3. St. Philip's Church, *Newsletter*, 11, no. 7, March 15, 1946, pp. 2–3, box 3, folder 1, Lafargue Clinic Records, Schomburg Center for Research in Black Culture, New York Public Library (hereafter LCR). From June 1947 to June 1952, the Veterans Administration maintained a contract with Lafargue to provide treatment to veterans in New York, box 1, folder 1, LCR.

4. Fredric Wertham, "The Social Basis of Psychotherapy." Lecture Presented at Columbia University, November 13, 1947. Papers of Fredric Wertham. Library of Congress. Washington, DC.

5. See Walter Jackson, *Gunnar Myrdal and America's Conscience: Social Engineering & Racial Liberalism, 1938–1987* (Chapel Hill: University of North Carolina Press, 1990), 272–93, and Ellen Herman, *The Romance of American Psychology: Political Culture in the Age of Experts* (Berkeley: University of California Press, 1995), 174–207.

6. The most prominent exponent of the theory of frustration and aggression in race relations was social psychologist John Dollard; see his "Hostility and Fear in Social Life," *Social Forces* 17 (1938): 15–26.

7. Jay Garcia, *Psychology Comes to Harlem: Rethinking the Race Question in Twentieth-Century America* (Baltimore: Johns Hopkins University Press, 2012). Regarding psychiatrists and the military, see the US Army Medical Department, *Neuropsychiatry in World War II*, 2 vols. (Washington, DC: Government Printing Office, 1966–1973); and Ellen Herman, *The Romance of American Psychology*.

8. Lorraine Maynard (in Collaboration with Laurence Miscall, MD), *Bellevue* (New York: Julian Messner, 1940), 61, 139–40, italics in original; see also Cheryl Lynn Greenberg *"Or Does it Explode": Black Harlem in the Great Depression* (New York: Oxford University Press, 1991), 86–91.

9. Gerald N. Grob, *From Asylum to Community: Mental Health Policy in Modern America* (Princeton: Princeton University Press, 1991); Grob, *The Mad Among Us: A History of the Care of America's Mentally Ill* (New York: The Free Press, 1994).

10. Robert Bendiner, "Psychiatry for the Needy," *Tomorrow*, May 1946, 24.

11. See Steven F. Lawson, ed., *To Secure These Rights: The Report of Harry S. Truman's Committee on Civil Rights* (Boston: Bedford/St. Martin's, 2004 [1947]).

12. Richard Wright Journal, March 26, 1945, box 117, folder 1860, Wright Papers, Beinecke Library, Yale University; Fredric Wertham, *Episodes: From the Life of a Psychiatrist*. Unpublished Manuscript, n.d., Wertham Papers.

13. It helps to consider Wertham's emphasis on the social basis of mental functioning in conversation with Frantz Fanon's use of the concept of sociogenesis as an analytical tool in grasping the social origins of the mental lives of racialized and colonized peoples, in his case "the black." See Fanon's *Black Skin, White Masks*. Translated by Charles Lam Markmann (New York: Grove Press, 1967 [1952]), 11.

14. "The Story of the City-Wide Citizens' Committee on Harlem," May 23, 1943, box 338, folder 5, Viola W. Bernard Papers, Columbia University.

15. See Wertham's *The Show of Violence* (Garden City, NY: Doubleday, 1949) and *A Sign for Cain: An Exploration of Human Violence* (New York: Macmillan, 1966).

16. Wertham, "What Is Social Psychiatry," December 5, 1946, p. 8, box 51, folder 10, Wertham Papers.

17. "The Head Fixers," *Monthly Review*, November, 1958, 282.

18. Handwritten notes on Wertham, "What Is Social Psychiatry."

19. "Psychotherapy at the Clinic," May 6, 1947, box 51, folder 11, Wertham Papers.

20. See Helen Swick Perry's introduction to Harry Stack Sullivan's *The Fusion of Psychiatry and Social Science* (New York: Norton, 1964); and Nathan G. Hale, *The Rise and Crisis of Psychoanalysis* (Oxford: Oxford University Press, 1995)

21. See Mari Jo Buhle, *Feminism and Its Discontents: A Century of Struggle with Psychoanalysis* (Cambridge: Harvard University Press, 1998), chapter 3, esp. pp. 111–124; Hale, *The Rise and Crisis of Psychoanalysis*, chapter 8.

22. "Lafargue Clinic Organization," September 1, 1952, box 1, folder 1, LCR.

23. Ibid.

24. "Mrs. Zucker's Suggestion for first examination," n.d., box 1, folder 1, LCR.

25. Sidney M. Katz, "Jim Crow Is Barred from Wertham's Clinic," *Magazine Digest*, September 1946, box 3, folder 1, LCR.

26. James L. Tuck, "Here's Hope for Harlem," *This Week Magazine, New York Herald Tribune*, January 26, 1947, box 3, folder 1, LCR.

27. "Lafargue Clinic Statistics," March 6, 1956, box 1, folder 9, LCR.

28. Grob, *From Asylum to Community*, 171–73. "Memorandum Re: Contracts with the NYC Community Mental Health Board," September 16, 1955, box 1, folder 1, LCR.

29. Fredric Wertham, "Society and Problem Personalities: Praetorian Psychiatry," *American Journal of Psychotherapy* 17 (1963): 404–16.

30. Dr. Hilde L. Mosse to Dr. Paul H. Hoch, August 20, 1955, box 1, folder 1, LCR.

31. One exception to this is Bendiner, "Psychiatry for the Needy."

32. Richard Wright, "Psychiatry Comes to Harlem," *Free World*, September 1946, 45–51; Ralph Ellison, "Harlem is Nowhere," in *Shadow and Act* (New York: Random House, 1964).

33. The American Psychiatric Association, "Cultural Competencies for the Clinical Interaction" cited in Metzl, *The Protest Psychosis*, 200.

34. Kenneth Spencer, "Sans Funds, LaFarge [sic] Clinic Lives," *The People's Voice*, July 13, 1946, box 3, folder 1, LCR.

CHAPTER FIVE

1. Kate Millet, *Sexual Politics* (New York: Doubleday Press, 1970), 178.

2. Ellen Herman, *The Romance of American Psychology: Political Culture in the Age of Experts* (Berkeley: University of California Press, 1995), chapter 6; and Eva S. Moskowitz, *In Therapy We Trust: America's Obsession with Self-Fulfillment* (Baltimore: Johns Hopkins University Press, 2001), chapter 4.

3. Rebecca Jo Plant, *Mom: The Transformation of Motherhood in Modern America* (Chicago: University of Chicago Press, 2010).

4. Jennifer Terry, "'Momism' and the Making of Treasonous Homosexuals," in *"Bad" Mothers: The Politics of Blame in Twentieth-Century America*, ed. Molly Ladd-Taylor and Lauri Umansky (New York: New York University Press, 1998), 169–90; Laura Ellen Schreibman, *The Science and Fiction of Autism* (Cambridge: Harvard University Press, 2005), chapter 4; and Carol Eadie Hartwell, "The Schizophrenogenic Mother Concept in American Psychiatry," *Psychiatry* 59 (1996): 274–97.

5. Insightful discussions of advice literature for mothers include Rima D. Apple, *Perfect Motherhood: Science and Childrearing in America* (New Brunswick: Rutgers University Press, 2006); Julia Grant, *Raising Baby by the Book: The Education of American Mothers* (New Haven: Yale University Press, 1998); and Jay Mechling, "Advice to Historians on Advice to Mothers," *Journal of Social History* 9 (1975): 44–63.

6. Ruth H. Bloch, "American Feminine Ideals in Transition: The Rise of the Moral Mother, 1790–1815," *Feminist Studies* 4 (1978): 100–26; Jan Lewis, "Mother's Love: The Construction of an Emotion in Nineteenth-Century America," in *Social History and Issues in Human Consciousness: Some Interdisciplinary Connections,* ed. Andrew E. Barnes and Peter N. Stearns, (New York: New York University Press, 1989), 209–29; Mary P. Ryan, *Cradle of the Middle Class: The Family in Oneida County, New York, 1790–1865* (Cambridge: Cambridge University Press, 1981); and *The Empire of the Mother: American Writing about Domesticity* (New York: Harrington Park Press, 1982).

7. Ryan, *Empire of the Mother*, 57–8, 45–6.

8. Hazel Felleman, "Like Mother, Like Son," in *Best Loved Poems of the American People* (Garden City, NY: Doubleday, 1959), 370.

9. Peter N. Stearns, *American Cool: Constructing a Twentieth-Century Emotional Style* (New York: New York University Press, 1994), 34–8, 79–80, 164–71; and John C. Spurlock and Cynthia A. Magistro, *New and Improved: The Transformation of American Women's Emotional Culture* (New York: New York University Press, 1998), chapter 5

10. Sidney Fine, *Frank Murphy: The Detroit Years* (Ann Arbor: University of Michigan Press, 1975), 6–7.

11. "The Army's Poets," *Stars and Stripes,* May 10, 1918, 3.

12. "A Mother's Love," *Godey's Lady's Book*, January 1867, 39.

13. Plant, *Mom*, chapter 4.

14. Ann Douglas discusses the cultural assault on the "late-Victorian matriarch" in *Terrible Honesty: Mongrel Manhattan in the 1920s* (New York: Farrar, Straus, and Giroux, 1995).

15. Kathleen W. Jones, *Taming the Troublesome Child: American Families, Child Guidance, and the Limits of Psychiatric Authority* (Cambridge: Harvard University Press, 1999), 175.

16. Julia Grant, "A 'Real Boy' and Not a Sissy: Gender, Childhood and Masculinity, 1890–1940," *Journal of Social History* 37 (2004): 829–41.

17. John B. Watson, *Psychological Care of Infant and Child* (New York: Norton, 1928), 81–82.

18. Quoted in Henry Jenkins, "The Sensuous Child: Benjamin Spock and the Sexual Revolution," in *The Children's Culture Reader* (New York: New York University Press, 1998), 213–14.

19. Quoted in Christopher Lasch, *Haven in a Heartless World: The Family Besieged* (New York: Basic Books, 1975), 209.

20. Michael Paul Rogin, "Kiss Me Deadly: Communism, Motherhood, and Cold War Movies," *Representations* 6 (1984): 1–36.

21. Elizabeth Cook, "Taking off the Halo," *American Magazine*, February 1935, 39.

22. "The 'Gush' of Mothers' Day," *Literary Digest*, May 21, 1932, 20.

23. Philip Wylie, *Generation of Vipers* (New York: Farrar and Rinehart, 1942), 196.

24. Mari Jo Buhle, *Feminism and Its Discontents: A Century of Struggle with Psychoanalysis* (Cambridge: Harvard University Press, 1998), 129. See also Ruth Feldstein, *Motherhood in Black and White: Race and Sex in American Liberalism, 1930–1965* (Ithaca: Cornell University Press, 2000); and Jennifer Terry, "'Momism' and the Making of Treasonous Homosexuals," 169–90.

25. Anna Freud and Dorothy Burlingham, *Infants without Families* (New York: International Universities Press, 1944); John Bowlby, *Maternal Care and Mental Health* (Geneva: World Health Organization Monograph Series, no. 2, 1951). For an astute analysis of these developments, see Marga Vicedo, *The Nature and Nurture of Love: From Imprinting to Attachment* (Chicago: University of Chicago Press, 2013).

26. For a particularly vehement attack on behaviorism, see Leo Kanner, "Child-Rearing by the Book," *American Mercury*, January 1945, 23–28.

27. Margaret Ribble, *The Rights of Infants: Early Psychological Needs and Their Satisfaction* (New York: Columbia University Press, 1943), 14.

28. Nancy Pottisham Weiss, "Mother, the Invention of Necessity: Dr. Benjamin Spock's Baby and Child Care," *American Quarterly* (1977): 519–46.

29. Ferdinand Lundberg and Marynia F. Farnham, *Modern Woman: The Lost Sex* (New York: Harper Brothers, 1947), 320.

30. Anna W. Wolf, *The Parent's Manual: A Guide to the Emotional Development of Young Children* (New York: Simon and Schuster, 1941), 285.

31. "Tobe's Topics," program no. 70, box 22, folder 6, David M. Levy Papers, Oskar Diethelm Library, Institute for the History of Psychiatry, Department of Psychiatry, Weill Medical College of Cornell University, New York, NY.

32. Maurice Zolotow, *American Weekly*, September 2, 1956, 10.

33. Betty Friedan, *The Feminine Mystique* (New York: W. W. Norton, 1963), 104.

34. Betty Friedan, *Life So Far: A Memoir* (New York: Simon and Schuster, 2006), 121–22.

35. Friedan, *Life So Far*, 121–22.

36. Friedan, *The Feminine Mystique,* 344.

37. bell hooks, *Feminist Theory: From Margin to Center* (Boston: South End Press, 1984), 1–3.

38. [Richmond, VA], November 22, 1963, box 19, folder 681, Betty Friedan Papers, Schlesinger Library, Harvard University, Cambridge, Massachusetts [hereafter BFP].

39. [N.p.], n.d., box 19, folder, 687; and [Palo Alto, CA], February 22, 1963, box 19, folder 684, BFP.

40. [Liberal, KS], March 1, 1963, box 21, folder 745; and [N.p.], February 2, 1963, box 21, folder 741, BFP.

41. [Nacogdoches, TX], April 3, 1963, box 21, folder 751, BFP.

CHAPTER SIX

1. Joel Pfister, "Glamourizing the Psychological: The Politics of Performance of Modern Psychological Identities," in *Inventing the Psychological: Toward a Cultural History of Emotional Life in America*, ed. Joel Pfister and Nancy Schnog (New Haven: Yale University Press, 1997), 172.

2. George Gerbner, "The Social Role of the Confession Magazine," *Social Problems* 6 (1958): 29.

3. Gerbner, "The Social Role," 31.

4. On April 27, 1946, the *New York Amsterdam News* ran the headline "Mental Hospitals Bar Negroes" on its front page. The article claimed that despite the fact that the "taxes of every citizen of New York state" supported the Psychiatric Institute, which was primarily responsible for the mental health services of those residing in New York City, the institute "had been charged with the complete exclusion of Negro patients, both children and adults, from the hospital, and giving inadequate psychotherapy to those few who are treated in the out-patient clinic" (p. 1). This incident typifies a larger pattern of exclusion experienced by African Americans who sought psychological help.

5. Thomas Jefferson, *Notes on the State of Virginia* [1781], ed. William Peden (Chapel Hill: University of North Carolina Press, 1982), 138.

6. Tricia Rose, *Longing to Tell: Black Women Talk about Sexuality and Intimacy* (New York: Picador, 2004), 4.

7. John H. Johnson, "Letter from the Editor," *Tan Confessions*, November 1950, 1.

8. Ibid, 1.

9. "The Press: Purpose without Passion," *Time*, September 22, 1952, 13, http://content.time.com/time/magazine/article/0,9171,822525,00.html, accessed May 19, 2011.

10. Candice M. Jenkins, *Private Lives, Proper Relations: Regulating Black Intimacy* (Minneapolis, University of Minnesota Press, 2007), 10.

11. Roseann Mandziuk, "Confessional Discourse and Modern Desires: Power and Pleasure in *True Story* Magazine," *Critical Studies in Media Communication* 18 (2011): 182.

12. Mandzuik, "Confessional Discourse," 183.

13. Johnson, "Letter" 1.

14. In a 1952 interview with *Time* magazine, John H. Johnson announced his decision to shift the emphasis of *Tan Confessions* from a confessions magazine to a women's lifestyle publication. Explaining his decision to change *Tan Confessions* to simply *Tan*, Johnson remarked, "Our magazines help the Negro to have a greater dignity and pride in his own accomplishments. I found I had to apologize for *Tan Confessions*. I had thought we could dignify even a confessions magazine." "The Press: Purpose without Passion," *Time*, September 22, 1952, 13. If Johnson's original intent was indeed to "dignify" the confessions magazine, his remark concedes his failure to resolve the very dilemma I presented at the outset—to represent black women as both sexual and respectable subjects. Further, Johnson's intent may partially explain the consistently conservative heteronormative resolutions of these narratives. It is doubtful that women originally submitted these stories in such a uniform, paradigmatic form; thus, it was undoubtedly the work of the magazine's editorial staff to fashion them in a way that satisfied Johnson's project to instill within black folks a "greater dignity and pride."

15. Kathy M. Newman, "True Lies: True Story Magazine and Working-Class Consumption in Postwar America," *Minnesota Review: A Journal of Committed Writing* 55–57 (2002): 223–24.

16. Rose, *Longing to Tell*, 3.

17. "Object to Confessions," Letters to the Editor, *Tan Confessions*, November 1950, 52.

18. "Object to Confessions," 52

19. "Sex Stories," Letters to the Editor, *Tan Confessions*, December 1950, 3.

20. *Tan Confessions*, February 1951, 55.

21. "Do Good Husbands Make Unhappy Wives?" *Tan Confessions*, August 1951, 7.

22. "Do Good Husbands Make Unhappy Wives?" 79.

23. "Do Good Husbands Make Unhappy Wives?" 79.

24. Gerbner, "The Social Role," 31.

25. Gerbner, "The Social Role," 31.

26. Fred Sammie, *The Woman that Taxes Made* (New York: True Story Women's Group, n.d.) quoted in Gerbner, "The Social Role," 34.

27. "Do Mail Order Marriages Work?" *Tan Confessions*, December 1951, 66.

28. "Objects to Strange Love," Letters to the Editor, *Tan Confessions*, December 1950, 3.

29. "Strange Love," *Tan Confessions*, November 1950, 63.

30. "Strange Love," 63.

31. "Strange Love," 65.

32. Ibid, 65.

33. W.E.B. DuBois, "On the Damnation of Women," in *Darkwater: Voices from within the Veil.* (New York: Harcourt Brace and Company, 1920). Penn State Electronic Classics Series, Jim Manis, ed. PDF e-book, 110–25, accessed August 4, 2012.

CHAPTER SEVEN

1. The Radical Therapist Collective, "Introduction," in *The Radical Therapist*, ed. Jerome Agel (New York: Ballantine Books, 1971), ix, xi.

2. Michael Glenn, "Manifesto," *Radical Therapist* 1 (1970): 2.

3. Claude Steiner, "Guiding Principles of a Community 'RaP' Center," in *Toward Social Change: A Handbook for Those Who Will*, ed. Robert Buckhout (New York: Harper & Row, 1971), 370.

4. Hogie Wyckoff, "Permission," in *Readings in Radical Psychiatry*, ed. Claude Steiner et al. (New York: Grove Press, 1975), 112.

5. Michael Glenn and Richard Kunnes, *Repression or Revolution? Therapy in the United States Today* (New York: Harper & Row, 1973), 34.

6. Susan Sontag, "Approaching Artaud," *The New Yorker*, May 19, 1973.

7. Joseph Berke quoted in *R. D. Laing and Anti-Psychiatry*, ed. Robert Boyers and Robert Orrill (New York: Harper & Row, 1971), 275.

8. Mary Ellen Hombs and Mitch Synder, *Homelessness in America: A Forced March to Nowhere* (Washington, DC: Center for Creative Non-Violence, 1982), 43.

9. Dennis Jaffe, "Number Nine: Creating a Counter-Institution," in *The Radical Therapist*, 220. Also see Dennis Jaffe and Ted Clark, *Number Nine: Autobiography of an Alternate Counseling Service* (New York: Harper & Row, 1975).

10. James M. Statman, "Community Mental Health as a Pacification Program," in *Toward Social Change*, 372–373. Skepticism towards community psychiatry was not limited to those on the radical left. Also see H. Warren Dunham, "Community Psychiatry," *Archives of General Psychiatry* 12 (1965): 303–13; and Lawrence Kubie, "Pitfalls of Community Psychiatry," *Archives of General Psychiatry* 18 (1968): 257–66. Also note the comments of Judge David Bazelon in 1970: "When poverty, or racism, or crime is labeled a mental health problem, then society can defer to the experts for its solution, and everyone else is free to go on with business as usual." David Bazelon, "Follow the Yellow Brick Road," *American Journal of Orthopsychiatry* 40 (1970): 563.

11. Howard Levy, "Prison Psychiatrist: New Custodian," *Liberated Guardian*, June 3, 1970, 15.

12. Richard Kunnes, "Psychiatry: Instrument of the Ruling Class," *Radical Therapist* 1 (1970), 4.

13. Saul Wasserman, "Does Psychiatry Pacify or Liberate?" *The Free You* 4 (1970): 7.

14. Claude Steiner, "Principles," in *Readings in Radical Psychiatry*, 12. This essay originally appeared in *Radical Therapist* 1 (1970–1971).

15. Claude Steiner, "Radical Psychiatry: Principles," in *The Radical Therapist*, 6.

16. Emma Jones Lapsansky, "'Black Power Is My Mental Health': Accomplishments of the Civil Rights Movement," in *Black America*, ed. John F. Szwed (New York: Basic Books, 1970), 13.

17. See Seymour L. Halleck, *The Politics of Therapy* (New York: Harper & Row, 1971).

18. "Feminist Therapy," *Rough Times*, November 1972, 5.

19. Betty J. Kronsky, "Feminism and Psychotherapy," *Journal of Contemporary Psychotherapy* 3 (1971): 98.

20. Kathie Sarachild, "A Program for Feminist 'Consciousness Raising,'" in *Notes from the Second Year: Women's Liberation—Major Writing of the Radical Feminists*, ed. Shulamith Firestone and Anne Koedt (New York: Radical Feminism, 1970), 78.

21. Their key text was Frederick S. Perls, Paul Goodman, and Ralph Franklin Hefferline, *Gestalt Therapy: Excitement and Growth in the Human Personality* (New York: Delta Books, 1951).

22. Carolyn Zerbe Enns, *Feminist Theories and Feminist Psychotherapies: Origins, Themes, and Variations* (Binghamton, NY: Haworth Press, 1997), 138. Also see the Gestalt-inspired feminism described in Elizabeth Friar Williams, *Notes of a Feminist Therapist* (New York: Dell, 1976).

23. See Carl Rogers, *On Becoming a Person* (Boston: Houghton Mifflin, 1961).

24. Abraham H. Maslow, *Toward a Psychology of Being* (New York: D. Van Nostrand Co., 1962), 168, 4–5.

25. Eric Berne, *Games People Play: The Psychology of Human Relationships* (New York: Grove Press, 1964), 15. Also see Berne, *Transactional Analysis in Psychotherapy: A Systematic Individual and Social Psychiatry* (New York: Grove Press, 1961).

26. Hogie Wyckoff, "Radical Psychiatry in Women's Groups," *Radical Therapist* 1 (1970): 16.

27. Ellen Cantarow, Elizabeth Diggs, Katherine Ellis, Janet Marx, Lillian Robinson, and Muriel Schien, "I Am Furious (Female)," in *Roles Women Play: Readings Toward Women's Liberation,* ed. Michele Hoffnung Garskof (Belmont, CA: Wadsworth Publishing Co., 1971), 186.

28. Nadine Miller, "Letter to Her Psychiatrist," in *The Radical Therapist*, 140, 142.

29. Meredith Tax, *Woman and Her Mind: The Story of Daily Life* (Boston: New England Free Press, 1970), 9–10.

30. Garskof, *Roles Women Play*, 60.

31. Phyllis Chesler, *Women and Madness* (New York: Doubleday & Co., 1972), 18.

32. See Ellen Herman, *The Romance of American Psychology* (Berkeley: University of California Press, 1995), 297–303. Also see Alice Echols, *Daring to Be Bad: Radical Feminism in America: 1967–1975* (Minneapolis: University of Minnesota Press, 1989).

33. Jo Freeman, "The Tyranny of Structurelessness," *Berkeley Journal of Sociology* 17 (1972–73): 151–64.

34. Hogie Wyckoff, "A Résumé of the Criticisms of Radical Psychiatry Made by the New Radical Psychiatry Group (November 1971)," in *Readings in Radical Psychiatry*, 188.

35. Quoted in Claude Steiner, "Radical Psychiatry and Movement Groups Plus a Postscript," *Readings in Radical Psychiatry*, 172–3.

36. Shelley Blue, "Ode to My Therapist," *Rough Times*, September 1974, 6.

37. Tacie Dejanikus and Fran Pollner, "Feminist Counseling: A Catalyst Not a Cure," *Off Our Backs* 3 (1973): 2.

38. Karin Wandrei, "Lesbians in Therapy," *Rough Times*, November 1975, 3–4.

39. Shulamith Firestone, *The Dialectic of Sex: The Case for Feminist Revolution* (New York: Bantam, 1971), 71.

40. Quoted in Herman, *The Romance of American Psychology*, 389.

41. Dorothy Tennov, "Feminism, Psychotherapy and Professionalism," *Journal of Contemporary Psychotherapy* 5 (1973): 110, italics in original.

42. Carol Wolman, "Therapy and Capitalism," *Issues in Radical Therapy* 3 (1975): 4–5.

43. Dejanikus and Pollner, "Feminist Counseling," 2–4.

44. Inge K. Broverman, Donald M. Broverman, Frank E. Clarkson, Paul S. Rosenkrantz, and Susan R. Vogel, "Sex-Role Stereotypes and Clinical Judgments of Mental Health," *Journal of Consulting and Clinical Psychology* 34 (1970): 6.

45. Quoted in Dot Vance, "Offing Piggery in Women's Groups," *Radical Therapist* 1 (1971): 2.

CHAPTER EIGHT

1. Christopher Lasch, *The Culture of Narcissism: American Life in an Age of Diminishing Expectations* (New York: Norton, 1978), xv–xvi, 4; Tom Wolfe, "The Me Decade and the Third Great Awakening" (1976), in *The Purple Decades: A Reader* (New York: Farrar, Straus, Giroux, 1982), 279, 277.

2. Henry Malcolm, *Generation of Narcissus* (Boston: Little, Brown, 1971); Marie Coleman Nelson, ed., *The Narcissistic Condition: A Fact of Our Lives and Times* (New York: Human Sciences Press, 1977); Aaron Stern, *ME: The Narcissistic American* (New York: Ballantine Books, 1979); and Richard M. Restak, *The Self Seekers* (Garden City, New York: Doubleday, 1982). Bruce Mazlish, "American Narcissism," *Psychohistory Review* 10 (1982): 185–202, at 185, makes a point similar to the last here. Among other evidence of and guides to the temper of the times are Ernest van den Haag, *Passion and Social Constraint* (New York: Stein and Day, 1957); Kenneth Keniston, *The Uncommitted: Alienated Youth in American Society* (New York: Harcourt, Brace & World, 1960); Clemens E. Benda, *The Image of Love: Modern Trends in Psychiatric Thinking* (Glencoe, IL: Free Press, 1961); Fred J. Cook, *The Corrupted Land: The Social Morality of Modern America* (New York: Macmillan, 1966); Charles A. Reich, *The Greening of America* (New York: Random House, 1970); Robert Liebert, *Radical and Militant Youth: A Psychoanalytic Inquiry* (New York: Prager, 1971); Richard King, *The Party of Eros: Radical Social Thought and the Realm of Freedom* (Chapel Hill: University of North Carolina Press, 1972); Herbert Hendin, *The Age of Sensation* (New York: Norton, 1975); Daniel Yankelovich, *New Rules: Searching for Self-Fulfillment in a World Turned Upside Down* (New York: Random House, 1981); and Peter Clecak, *America's Quest for the Ideal Self: Dissent and Fulfillment in the 60s and 70s* (New York: Oxford University Press, 1983).

3. Paul Federn, "On the Distinction between Healthy and Pathological Narcissism" (1936), in *Ego Psychology and the Psychoses*, ed. Edoardo Weiss (New York: Basic Books, 1952), 323–64.

4. Federn, "On the Distinction," 333–34.

5. Sigmund Freud, "On Narcissism: An Introduction" (1914), in vol. 14, *Standard Edition of the Complete Psychological Works of Sigmund Freud*, trans. and ed. James Strachey (London: Hogarth Press, 1953–1974), 67–107. Kohut and Kernberg published books as well as papers in the psychoanalytic journal literature. Lasch, *Culture of Narcissism*, 43.

6. David Riesman, in collaboration with Reuel Denney and Nathan Glazer, *The Lonely*

Crowd: A Study of the Changing American Character (New Haven: Yale University Press, 1950); Allen Whellis, *The Quest for Identity* (New York: Norton, 1958).

7. Lasch, *Culture of Narcissism*, 25.

8. Stephanie Engel, "Femininity as Tragedy: Re-examining the 'New Narcissism,'" *Socialist Review* 55 (1980): 77–103.

9. See, for example, Maurice Green, "The Culture of Narcissism," *Journal of the Academy of Psychoanalysis and Dynamic Psychiatry* 9 (1981): 330–31.

10. Jim Miller, "Liberation's Limits," review of Lasch, *The Minimal Self: Psychic Survival in Troubled Times* (1984), *Newsweek*, November 5, 1984.

11. Natasha Zaretsky, *No Direction Home: The American Family and the Fear of National Decline, 1968–1980* (Chapel Hill: University of North Carolina Press, 2007), 210–14.

12. On the speech, see Daniel Horowitz, *Jimmy Carter and the Energy Crisis of the 1970s: The "Crisis of Confidence" Speech of July 15, 1979* (Boston: Bedford/St. Martin's, 2005).

13. "Gratification Now Is the Slogan of the '70s, Laments a Historian," *People Magazine*, July 9, 1979. Gil Troy, *Morning in America: How Ronald Reagan Invented the 1980s* (Princeton: Princeton University Press, 2007), 24–49.

14. Raina Kelley, "Generation Me," *Newsweek*, April 27, 2009.

15. Jean M. Twenge and W. Keith Campbell, *The Narcissism Epidemic: Living in the Age of Entitlement* (New York: Free Press, 2009), 3, 23.

16. Twenge and Campbell, *The Narcissism Epidemic*, 189–94.

17. Malcolm, *Generation of Narcissus*, 201.

18. William Braden, *The Age of Aquarius: Technology and the Cultural Revolution* (Chicago: Quandrangle Books, 1970), 257–58, quoting a conversation with Lasch.

19. Rieff, *Triumph of the Therapeutic*, 26.

20. Lasch, *Culture of Narcissism,* 51.

21. "Now, the California Task Force to Promote Self-Esteem," *New York Times*, October 11, 1986. http://www.nytimes.com/1986/10/11/us/now-the-california-task-force-to-promote-self-esteem.html, accessed October 20, 2013. Beth Ann Krier, "California's Newest Export: Culture: The Self-Esteem Task Force Will Fold this Month," *LA Times*, June 5, 1990. http://articles.latimes.com/1990-06-05/news/vw-433_1_task-force, accessed October 20, 2013.

22. Twenge and Campbell, *The Narcissism Epidemic*, 57 ff.

23. Barbara Cruikshank, *The Will to Empower: Democratic Citizens and Other Subjects* (Ithaca: Cornell University Press, 1999) 87–103; Alfie Kohn, "The Truth about Self-Esteem," *The Phi Delta Kappan*, 1994. http://www.alfiekohn.org/teaching/tase.htm, accessed October 20, 2013.

24. Kernberg, interviewed by Linda Wolfe, "Why Some People Can't Love," *Psychology Today*, June 1978, 55–59, at 55.

25. Daniel Bell, *The Cultural Contradictions of Capitalism* (New York: Basic Books, 1978 [1976]), xvi.

26. Campbell, "Is Narcissism Really So Bad?," *Psychological Inquiry* 12 (2001): 214–6. The NPI can be found on the web (http://psychcentral.com/quizzes/narcissistic.htm) and in Drew Pinsky and S. Mark Young, *The Mirror Effect: How Celebrity Narcissism Is Seducing America* (New York: Harper, 2009), 261–7.

27. Campbell, "Is Narcissism Really So Bad?"; Freud, "Libidinal Types" (1931), in *Standard Edition* 21, 215–20, at 218.

28. Stephanie Rosenbloom, "Generation Me vs. You Revisited," *New York Times*, January 17, 2008.

29. See, for example, the list of books compiled by one therapist under the rubric "voicelessness and emotional survival," the majority of them on dealing with narcissists, http://astore.amazon.com/richardgrossman, accessed October 20, 2013.

30. Yolanda Reid Chassiokos, "Healthy Narcissism Can Help You Succeed," *Huffington Post,* May 20, 2010. http://www.huffingtonpost.com/yolanda-reid-chassiakos/self-esteem-healthy-narci_b_577237.html, accessed October 20, 2013. Linda Hatch, "Sex Addicts Need Healthy Narcissism," http://www.sexaddictionscounseling.com/sex-addicts-and-their-partners-need-healthy-narcissism/, accessed October 20, 2013.

CHAPTER NINE

1. Thanks to Timothy Aubry, Trysh Travis, Timothy W. Baker, and Kirsten Swinth for their critiques of drafts of this essay.

2. All book-length studies of RC are by RC members. For example, see Katie Kauffman and Caroline New, *Co-Counselling: The Theory and Practice of Re-evaluation Counselling* (Hove and New York: Brunner-Routledge, 2004); see Colin Feltham's review in *Counselling & Psychotherapy Journal* 16 (2005): 51. I have drawn on academic articles on RC, published material and internet postings by RC adherents and critics, and personal interviews. Five of my six interviewees requested anonymity.

3. Christopher Lasch, *The Culture of Narcissism* (New York: Norton, 1979), 43.

4. Lasch, *Culture of Narcissism*, 396–7.

5. Lasch, *Culture of Narcissism*, 315.

6. Lasch, *Culture of Narcissism*, 252, 258, 336.

7. Lasch stated that "black studies" created "a reign of universal ignorance." Lasch, *Culture of Narcissism*, 250. Elisabeth Lasch-Quinn attacks black studies in *Race Experts* (New York: Norton, 2001).

8. Beryl Satter, "The Sexual Abuse Paradigm in Historical Perspective: Passivity and Emotion in Mid-Twentieth-Century America," *Journal of the History of Sexuality* 12 (2003): 424–64.

9. Daniel Belgrad, *The Culture of Spontaneity* (Chicago: University of Chicago Press, 1998).

10. Doug Rossinow, *The Politics of Authenticity: Liberalism, Christianity, and the New Left in America* (New York: Columbia University Press, 1998).

11. Ellen Herman, *The Romance of American Psychology* (Berkeley: University of California Press, 1995); Jeffrey Kripal, *Esalen and the American Religion of No Religion* (Chicago: University of Chicago Press, 2007); see Lasch-Quinn, *Race Experts.*

12. Bernard J. Somers, "Re-evaluation Therapy: Theoretical Framework," *Journal of Humanistic Psychology* 12 (1972): 57.

13. R.D. Rosen, *Psychobabble: Fast Talk and Quick Cure in the Era of Feeling* (New York: Atheneum Press, 1977), 73–74; Kauffman and New, *Co-Counselling*, 41–42; Harvey Jackins, *The*

Human Side of Human Beings: The Theory of Re-evaluation Counseling (Seattle: Rational Island Publishers, 1965), 30, 104.

14. Jackins, *Human Side of Human Beings*, 45, 83–84; Thomas J. Scheff, "Revaluation Counseling: Social Implications," *Journal of Humanistic Psychology* 12 (1972): 58–71; Phyllis Bronstein, "Re-Evaluation Counseling: A Self-Help Model for Emotional Distress," *Women & Therapy* 5 (1986): 41–54. For more critical accounts, see Rosen, *Psychobabble*, 70–94; Dennis Tourish and Pauline Irving, "Group Influence and the Psychology of Cultism within Re-evaluation Counselling: A Critique," *Counselling Psychology Quarterly* 8 (1995): 35–50.

15. Documents on Jackins and Scientology are available at http://home.comcast.net/~Re-evaluation-counseling/documents.html, accessed March 16, 2014. Hubbard eventually denounced Jackins to the Federal Bureau of Investigation. Also see http://home.comcast.net/~Re-evaluation-counseling/articles.html, accessed March 16, 2014.

16. On Scientology, see Russell Miller, *Bare-Faced Messiah: The True Story of L. Ron Hubbard* (London: Sphere Books, 1987); see documents on Jackins and Scientology at http://home.comcast.net/~Re-evaluation-counseling/documents.html.

17. Interview with Michelle Murphy, March 13, 2012; interview with Sarah Sanders (pseudonym), January 11, 2012. Late 1980s workshop prices ranged from $75 to $250. Jackins sold "Re-evaluation Counseling Videocassettes" for $25 each on issues ranging from "classist oppression" to "How Parents Can Counsel Their Children." See *Present Time* 66, vol. 18, no. 1 (January 1987), 85–86, 89–92 (in author's possession). This publication iformation comes from the cover of the magazine. It is unclear what "66" refers to. In general, *RC* publications are characterized by irregularities and nonstandard formats.

18. Janice Haaken, *Pillar of Salt: Gender, Memory, and the Perils of Looking Back* (London: Free Association Books, 1998), 63–66, 68, 73–75; Michael Kenny, "The Proof Is in the Passion," in *Believed-In Imaginings: The Narrative Construction of Reality*, ed. Joseph De Rivera and Theodore R. Sabin (Washington, DC: American Psychological Association, 1998), 278–9; Satter, "Sexual Abuse Paradigm," 441–2.

19. "Adultism" referred to adults' tendency to discipline and disparage children.

20. See Murphy interview; Sanders interview; "Report from the Middle-Class Caucus at the 1985 World Conference," and "The Oppression of Science and Scientists," *Present Time* 66, vol. 18, no. 1 (January 1987), 43, 46–47.

21. See *Working for a Living* 6 (1988); *Ruah Hadashah* (1980), in author's possession (both are irregular serials digesting articles from *Present Time*); Murphy interview; Mathew Lyons, "Sex, Lies, and Co-Counseling," available at http://home.comcast.net/~Re-evaluation-counseling/sexlies.htm, accessed March 16, 2014.

22. Rosen, *Psychobabble*, 91.

23. Tourish and Irving, "Group Influence and the Psychology of Cultism"; "A Documentary History of the Career of Harvey Jackins and Re-Evaluation Counseling," http://home.comcast.net/~Re-evaluation-counseling/articles.html, accessed March 16, 2014.

24. See Scheff, "Revaluation Counseling," 60, 69, and Bronstein, "Re-Evaluation Counseling," 44–45, 52–53.

25. See Jackins, *Human Side of Human Beings*, xi.

26. Jackins, *Human Side of Human Beings*, 12. The "inherent, natural human being" that

RC promised to "recover" was elusive. Did this perfect human exist at birth? At one week? Two years? "'Why do you think that underneath it all is some perfect little individual?" a former RC member asked her RC instructor. "Do you have any evidence for believing there is?'" Rosen, *Psychobabble*, 84.

27. Murphy interview.

28. Jackins, *Human Side of Human Beings*, 76–78. RC healed distress that parents created by telling children how "to dress, eat, [and] talk." This implied that parents should allow children to wear sandals in the snow, eat food that would sicken them, and interrupt others, since even reasonable restrictions were forms of "invalidation." See Scheff, "Revaluation Counseling," 67. Also see Bronstein, "Re-Evaluation Counseling," 47.

29. Lasch-Quinn, *Race Experts*, 158, italics in original.

30. Murphy interview; Sanders interview; Tourish and Irving, "Group Influence and the Psychology of Cultism"; Lundy Bancroft, "Excerpt from *The Roots of Authoritarianism*," http://home.comcast.net/~Re-evaluation-counseling/roots.htm, accessed March 14, 2014.

31. Scheff, "Revaluation Counseling," 67–68; see Bronstein, "Re-Evaluation Counseling," 47.

32. Lasch-Quinn takes RC as typical of the New Left. See *Race Experts*, 145–46.

33. Robin Morgan, "Introduction: The Women's Revolution," in *Sisterhood Is Powerful*, ed. Robin Morgan (New York: Vintage Books, 1970), xxvii.

34. Jackins, *Human Side of Human Beings*, 77–78, also see 93.

35. Sanders interview.

36. See Somers, "Re-evaluation Therapy," 57; Lasch-Quinn, *Race Experts*, 150–58; Rosen, *Psychobabble*.

37. Sanders interview.

38. Jackins, *Human Side of Human Beings*, 93, see 77–80.

39. Interview with Martha Laney (pseudonym), March 12, 2012.

40. John D'Emilio, *Sexual Politics, Sexual Communities: The Making of a Homosexual Minority in the United States, 1940–1970* (Chicago: University of Chicago Press), x. D'Emilio led a "Wide World Change" RC workshop in 1987; see "Workshops," *Present Time* 66, vol. 18, no. 1 (January 1987), 85. See "'Aunt Academe' Shares Her Journey to Feminist Psychology," http://www.apadivisions.org/division-35/leadership/great-leaders/bronstein-phyllis.aspx, accessed March 16, 2014; Thomas J. Scheff, "Catharsis and Other Heresies: A Theory of Emotion," http://www.soc.ucsb.edu/faculty/scheff/main.php?id=57.html, accessed March 16, 2014.

41. Murphy describes how RC members were pressured to recall experiences of childhood sexual abuse, real or false; also see Carol Martin (pseudonym) interview, March 9, 2012, and Sanders interview. See "RC and Working on Early Sexual Memories: A Personal Reflection," http://home.comcast.net/~Re-evaluation-counseling/esm.htm, accessed March 16, 2014.

Similar results are produced by therapeutic groups unconnected to the left, from the EST-derived "Landmark Forum" to corporate "motivational seminars." All promise that heightened emotion and artificially induced intimacy will clear "blocks" and enhance personal efficiency. See Barbara Ehrenreich, *Bright-Sided* (New York: Picador, 2010).

42. Lasch-Quinn, *Race Experts*, 164.

43. Interview with Deborah Weinstein (pseudonym), December 10, 2011.

44. Lasch-Quinn, *Race Experts*, 151.

45. Serotta's and Rose's comments appear in Ezra Berkley Nepon, *Justice, Justice Shall You Pursue: A History of the New Jewish Agenda* (Philadelphia: Thread Makes Blanket Press, 2012), available at http://newjewishagenda.net/njas-story/agendas-within-agenda-the-challenge-of-mobilizing-diverse-jewish-communities/, accessed March 16, 2014.

46. Evan Hart, "Building a More Inclusive Women's Health Movement: Byllye Avery and the Development of the National Black Women's Health Project, 1981–1990" (Ph.D. diss., University of Cincinnati, 2012), 74.

47. Martin interview.

48. Martin interview; Murphy interview.

49. Lyons, "Sex, Lies, and Co-Counseling"; Murphy interview; see http://home.comcast.net/~Re-evaluation-counseling/articles.html; Feltham, *Counselling & Psychotherapy Journal*.

50. Weinstein interview; see Tourish and Irving, "Group Influence and the Psychology of Cultism"; Lyons, "Sex, Lies, and Co-Counseling."

51. Weinstein interview.

52. Sanders interview.

53. Nathan Guttman, "J Street Makes a Strategic Acquisition," Forward.com, September 18, 2009.

54. Cherie Brown, "Unhealed Terror," *Tikkun*, Winter 2011; and "Un Numbing from the Holocaust," *Tikkun*, May/June 2008; see Cherie Brown, "Seven Principles about the Israeli-Palestinian Conflict," *Tikkun*, March/April 2009.

55. Interview with Stacey Taylor (pseudonym), March 13, 2012; see Helen Lill, "Wake-Up Call for Co-Counsellors Working in the NHS," *Counselling & Psychotherapy Journal* 16 (2005): 24.

56. Weinstein interview.

CHAPTER TEN

1. Christopher Lane, *Shyness: How Normal Behavior Became a Sickness* (New Haven: Yale University Press, 2007), 8–9.

2. For "new pharmaceutical history" framing, see Liz Watkins's keynote speech at the Modern Medicines conference, held by the American Institute for the History of Pharmacy in Madison, Wisconsin, October 17–18, 2008. For psychiatric meds see David Healy, *The Antidepressant Era* (Cambridge: Harvard University Press, 1999) and *The Creation of Psychopharmacology* (Cambridge: Harvard University Press, 2004); Jonathan Metzl, *Prozac on the Couch: Prescribing Gender in the Era of Wonder Drugs* (Durham, NC: Duke University Press, 2003); Edward Shorter, *Before Prozac: The Troubled History of Mood Disorders in Psychiatry* (Oxford: Oxford University Press, 2008); Nicolas Rasmussen, *On Speed: The Many Lives of Amphetamine* (New York: New York University Press, 2009); Laura Hirshbein, *American Melancholy: Constructions of Depression in the 20th Century* (Piscataway Township, NJ: Rutgers University Press, 2009); Andrea Tone, *The Age of Anxiety: A History of America's Turbulent Affair with Tranquilizers* (New York: Basic Books, 2009); David Herzberg, *Happy Pills in America: From Miltown to Prozac* (Baltimore: Johns Hopkins University Press, 2009); Gary

Greenberg, *Manufacturing Depression: The Secret History of a Modern Disease* (New York: Simon & Schuster, 2010); Robert Whitaker, *Anatomy of an Epidemic: Magic Bullets, Psychiatric Drugs, and the Astonishing Rise of Mental Illness in America* (New York: Crown Publishers, 2010). For modern pharmaceuticals more generally, the literature is too massive to cite fully, but for representative recent literature see Jeremy Greene, *Prescribing by Numbers: Drugs and the Definition of Disease* (Baltimore: Johns Hopkins University Press, 2008); Andrea Tone and Liz Watkins, *Medicating Modern America: Prescription Drugs in History* (New York: New York University Press, 2007); Liz Watkins, *The Estrogen Elixir: A History of Hormone Replacement Therapy* (Baltimore: Johns Hopkins University Press, 2010); Robert Bud, *Penicillin: Triumph and Tragedy* (Oxford: Oxford University Press, 2009); Jeremy Greene and Liz Watkins, *Prescribed: Writing, Filling, Using, and Abusing the Prescription in Modern America* (Baltimore: Johns Hopkins University Press, 2012).

3. Charles Barber, *Comfortably Numb: How Psychiatry Is Medicating a Nation* (New York: Pantheon Books, 2008), 6.

4. Melody Peterson, *Our Daily Meds: How the Pharmaceutical Companies Transformed Themselves into Slick Marketing Machines and Hooked the Nation on Prescription Drugs* (New York: Picador, 2009), 2.

5. This literature is too vast to cite fully, but see, for example, Marcia Angell, *The Truth about the Drug Companies: How They Deceive Us and What to Do about It* (New York: Random House, 2004); David Healy, *Let Them Eat Prozac: The Unhealthy Relationship between the Pharmaceutical Industry and Depression* (New York: New York University Press, 2004) and *Pharmageddon* (Berkeley: University of California Press, 2012); John Abramson, *Overdosed America: The Broken Promise of American Medicine* (New York: HarperCollins, 2004); Ray Moynihan and Alan Cassels, *Selling Sickness: How the World's Biggest Pharmaceutical Companies Are Turning Us All into Patients* (New York: Nation Books, 2005); among others.

6. Peter Kramer, "The Transformation of Personality," *Psychology Today*, July/August 1993, 42–53.

7. Herzberg, *Happy Pills*, chapters 2 and especially 4.

8. Here I am following the lead of Nancy Tomes, who used similar reasoning to pursue a slightly different goal, to wit, understanding efforts to exploit and to protect physicians as "consumers" of pharmaceuticals in the twentieth century. See Tomes, "Merchants of Health: Medicine and Consumer Culture in the United States, 1900–1940," *Journal of American History* 88 (2001): 519–47.

9. This reasoning is borrowed from David Herzberg and Jeremy Greene, "Intermediate Consumers," Organization of American Historians, Houston, Texas, March 17–20, 2011; and Jeremy Greene and David Herzberg, "Hidden in Plain Sight: The Popular Promotion of Prescription Drugs in the 20th Century," *American Journal of Public Health* 100 (2010): 793–803.

10. Enstad "Popular Culture" in *Blackwell Companion to American Cultural History* (Hoboken, NJ: Wiley-Blackwell, 2008), 356–70.

11. See, e.g., Kathy Peiss, *Cheap Amusements: Working Women and Leisure in Turn-of-the-Century New York* (Philadelphia: Temple University Press, 1986); Roy Rosenzweig, *Eight Hours for What We Will: Workers and Leisure in an Industrial City, 1870–1920* (Cambridge: Cambridge University Press, 1985); Nan Enstad, *Ladies of Labor, Girls of Adventure* (New York:

Columbia University Press, 1999); Lizabeth Cohen, *Making a New Deal: Industrial Workers in Chicago, 1919–1939* (Cambridge: Cambridge University Press, 1990); Barbara Dianne Savage, *Broadcasting Freedom: Radio, War, and the Politics of Race, 1938–1948* (Chapel Hill: University of North Carolina Press, 1999); Steven Ross, *Working Class Hollywood: Silent Film and the Shaping of Class in America* (Princeton: Princeton University Press, 1998).

12. See, e.g., Lizabeth Cohen, *A Consumers' Republic: The Politics of Mass Consumption in Postwar America* (New York: Knopf, 2003); Lawrence Glickman, *Buying Power: A History of Consumer Activism in America* (Chicago: University of Chicago Press, 2009); Robert Weems, *Desegregating the Dollar: African American Consumerism in the 20th Century* (New York: New York University Press, 1998).

13. Robin D.G. Kelley, "Riddle of the Zoot: Malcolm Little and Black Cultural Politics During World War II," in *Race Rebels: Culture, Politics, and the Black Working Class* (New York: Free Press, 1996), 161–82.

14. E.g., Herzberg, *Happy Pills*, 122–3; Gerald Klerman, "Psychotropic Hedonism vs. Pharmacological Calvinism," *Hasting Center Reports* 2 (1972), 1–3; see also, e.g., Peter Kramer, *Against Depression* (New York: Viking, 2005).

15. See, e.g., Herzberg, *Happy Pills*, 219 n. 66, and Greene and Herzberg, "Hidden in Plain Sight," nn. 1–4.

16. See, e.g., Greene and Watkins, *Prescribed*; Daniel Carpenter, *Reputation and Power: Organizational Image and Pharmaceutical Regulation at the FDA* (Princeton: Princeton University Press, 2010); Dominique Toebbel, *Pills, Power, and Policy: The Struggle for Drug Reform in Cold War America and Its Consequences* (Berkeley: University of California Press, 2011).

17. Barbara Gordon, *I'm Dancing as Fast as I Can* (New York: Harper & Row, 1979), 37.

18. Herzberg, *Happy Pills*, chapter 4.

19. Gordon, *I'm Dancing*, 8

20. Gordon, *I'm Dancing*, 31. Interestingly, her lover later published his own rebuttal memoir, *Prince Valium*, in which he portrayed Valium use as a pretentious kind of alcoholism identifying an inauthentic woman afraid of true connection to her lover—a pithy, nasty version of arguments like Christopher Lane's. See Anton Holden, *Prince Valium* (New York: Stein and Day, 1982).

21. Patricia Burstein, "TV Producer Barbara Gordon Danced to Valium's Tune—and Landed in a Mental Ward, *People*, June 18, 1979, 98.

22. See, e.g., Rasmussen, *On Speed*.

23. Eric Schneider's *Smack: Heroin and the American City* (Philadelphia: University of Pennsylvania Press, 2008) has an effective takedown of this argument for postwar urban heroin markets; otherwise look to any global history of drugs, e.g., David Courtwright, *Forces of Habit: Drugs and the Making of the Modern World* (Cambridge: Harvard University Press, 2001); Wolfgang Schivelbusch, *Tastes of Paradise: A Social History of Spices, Stimulants, and Intoxicants* (New York: Pantheon Books, 1992); R.P.T. Davenport-Hines, *The Pursuit of Oblivion: A Global History of Narcotics* (New York: Norton, 2002).

24. Caroline Jean Acker, *Creating the American Junkie: Addiction Research in the Classic Era of Narcotic Control* (Baltimore: Johns Hopkins University Press, 2002), 109–10.

25. See, e.g., David Herzberg, "Busted for Blockbusters: 'Scrip Mills' and Prescribing Power in the 1970s," in Greene and Watkins, *Prescribed*, 207–231.

26. These and following quotes from http://www.crazyboards.org/forums/index.php/topic/29131-aplenzin/, last accessed March 25, 2014.

27. One could also go the gullible and venal route, as per Amy Harmon, "Young, Assured and Playing Pharmacist to Friends," *New York Times*, November 16, 2005. http://www.nytimes.com/2005/11/16/health/16patient.html?pagewanted=1&_r=1&ei=5094&en=627559b0d55ad8a6&hp&ex=1132117200&partner=homepage, accessed March 25, 2014.

28. http://www.mindfreedom.org/about-us, accessed May 26, 2011.

CHAPTER ELEVEN

1. Robert Jay Lifton, *Witness to an Extreme Century* (Chapel Hill: University of North Carolina Press, 1991).

2. A.J. Cienfuegos and Cristina Monelli, "The Testimony of Political Repression as a Therapeutic Instrument," *American Journal of Orthopsychiatry* 53 (1983): 43–51; Shoshana Felman, *Testimony: Crisis of Witnessing in Literature, Psychoanalysis, and History* (New York: Routledge, 1992).

3. Michael Jackson, *The Politics of Storytelling: Violence, Transgression, and Intersubjectivity* (Denmark: Museum Tusculanum Press, 2002), 332.

4. Tony Judt with Timothy Snyder, *Thinking the Twentieth Century* (New York: Penguin Press, 2012), 277–79.

5. Stevan Weine, *Testimony after Catastrophe: Narrating the Traumas of Political Violence* (Evanston: Northwestern University Press, 2006).

6. Robert Bellah, Richard Madsen, William M. Sullivan, Ann Swindler, and Steven M. Tipton, *Habits of the Heart: Individualism and Commitment in American Life* (New York: Harper Perennia1,1985); Richard Sennett, *The Fall of Public Man* (New York: Norton, 1974), 338.

7. Leanh Nguyen, "The Ethics of Trauma: Re-traumatization in Society's Approach to the Traumatized Subject," *International Journal of Group Psychotherapy* 61 (2011): 26–47.

8. Cienfuegos and Monelli, "Testimony of Political Repression"; Inger Agger, *The Blue Room: Trauma and Testimony among Refugee Women: A Psycho-social Exploration* (London: Zed Books, 1992): 115.

9. Stephen D. Smith, "Considering the Role of Testimony" *PastForward*, Autumn 2010, 3.

10. Achille Mbembe, "Memory and African Modes of Self-Writing" (paper presented at the International Conference on Memory and History: Remembering, Forgetting and Forgiving in the Life of the Nation and the Community, Cape Town, August 2000).

11. Debra Kaminar, Dan J. Stein, Irene Mbanga, and Nompumelelo Zungu-Dirwayi, "The Truth and Reconciliation Commission in South Africa: Relation to Psychiatric Status and Forgiveness Among Survivors of Human Rights Abuses," *British Journal of Psychiatry* 178 (2001): 373–7.

12. Karen Brouneus, "Truth-Telling as Talking Cure? Insecurity and Retraumatization in the Rwandan Gacaca Courts," *Security Dialogue* 39 (2008): 55–76; Phuong P. Pham, Patrick Vinck, Mychelle Balthazard, Judith Strasser, and Chariya Om, "Victim Participation and the

Trial of Duch at the Extraordinary Chambers in the Courts of Cambodia," *Journal of Human Rights Practice* 3 (2011): 264–87.

13. Brandon Hamber, *Transforming Societies after Political Violence: Truth, Reconciliation, and Mental Health* (Dordecht: Springer, 2009), 71.

14. Weine, *Testimony after Catastrophe*, 64.

15. "Sexual Exploitation Survivor Stories," Manna Freedom, http://www.mannafreedom.com/get-informed-about-human-trafficking/sexual-exploitation-survivor-stories/, accessed September 27, 2013.

16. Sennett, *Fall of Public Man*, 4.

17. Richard Sennett, "Disturbing Memories," in *Memory*, ed. P. Fara and K. Patterson (Cambridge: Cambridge University Press, 2006), 23.

18. Judt, *Twentieth Century*, 273–283; Sennett, "Disturbing Memories," 18–23.

19. "The National Center for Victims of Crime," https://www.ncvc.org/ncvc/Main.aspx, accessed May 1, 2012.

20. Henry Greenspan, *On Listening to Holocaust Survivors: Beyond Testimony* (St. Paul: Paragon House, 2010); "Fortunoff Video Archives for Holocaust Testimony," Yale University Library, last modified December 7, 2009. http://www.library.yale.edu/testimonies/, accessed May 1, 2012.

21. "Yad Vashem." http://www.yadvashem.org/, accessed May 1, 2012.

22. "USC Shoah Foundation Institute for Visual History and Education," USC Dornsife College of Letters, Arts, and Sciences. http://dornsife.usc.edu/vhi/, accessed May 1, 2012.

23. Ian Lovett, "The Shoah Foundation Widens Scope," *New York Times*, November 16, 2011: C1.

24. Fiona Ross, "On Having a Voice and Being Heard: Some After-Effects of Testifying before the South African Truth and Reconciliation Commission," *Anthropological Theory* 3 (2003): 326.

25. Ross, "On Having a Voice," 330.

26. Catherine M. Cole, *Performing South Africa's Truth Commission: Stages of Recognition* (Bloomington: Indiana University Press, 2010), 108.

27. Ross, "On Having a Voice," 338.

28. "Reading of the Testimonies," http://www.readingofthetestimonies.com/06aboutReadingOfTheTestimonies.html, accessed May 1, 2012.

29. Larisa Epatko, "George Clooney on Sudan: 'It Gets in Your Bloodstream," *PBS Newshour*, March 24, 2012.

30. Inger Agger, Victor Igreja, Rachel Kiehle, and Peter Polatin, "Testimony Ceremonies in Asia: Integrating Spirituality in Testimonial Therapy for Torture Survivors in India, Sri Lanka, Cambodia, and the Philippines," *Transcultural Psychiatry* 49 (2012): 568–89.

31. Sennett, *Public Man*, 37–40.

32. Weine, *Testimony after Catastrophe*.

33. Sennett, *Public Man*, 5.

34. Mikhail Bakhtin, *Problems of Dostoevsky's Poetics* (Minneapolis: University of Minnesota Press, 1984), 298.

35. Sennett, "Disturbing Memories," 19.

CHAPTER TWELVE

1. See for example Philip Rieff, *The Triumph of the Therapeutic: The Uses of Faith after Freud* (New York: Harper and Row, 1966); and Robert Bellah et al., *Habits of the Heart: Individualism and Commitment in American Life* (New York: Harper Perennial, 1985), esp. pp. 223–49.

2. Jim Liske, "The Heart of the Matter," *Prison Fellowship Ministries Newsletter*, August 30, 2012.

3. Jonathan Simon, "Beyond the Panopticon: Mass Imprisonment and the Humanities," *Law, Culture and the Humanities* 6 (2010): 327.

4. Angela Davis, *Are Prisons Obsolete?* (New York: Seven Stories Press, 2003), 13. Jennifer Graber, *The Furnace of Affliction: Prisons and Religion in Antebellum America* (Chapel Hill: University of North Carolina Press, 2011), 1. See also http://www.sentencingproject.org/template/page.cfm?id=107, accessed September 23, 2013.

5. See Anne Hendrixson, "Super-predator Meets Teenage Mom: Exploding the Myth of the Out-of-Control Youth," in *Policing the National Body: Race, Gender, and Criminalization*, ed. Jael Silliman and Anannya Bhattacharjee (Boston: South End Press, 2002); Khalil Gibran Muhammad, *The Condemnation of Blackness: Race, Crime, and the Making of Modern Urban America* (Cambridge: Harvard University Press, 2010); Jonathan Simon, *Governing through Crime: How the War on Crime Transformed American Democracy and Created a Culture of Fear* (New York: Oxford University Press, 2009); Bruce Western, *Punishment and Inequality in America* (New York: Russell Sage Foundation, 2007).

6. Robert Perkinson, "Guarded Hope: Lessons from the History of the Prison Boom," *Boston Review*, July 14, 2008.

7. Graber, *The Furnace of Affliction*.

8. Graber, *The Furnace of Affliction*, 12.

9. Heather Thompson, "Why Mass Incarceration Matters: Rethinking Crisis, Decline, and Transformation in Postwar American History," *Journal of American History* 97 (2010): 703–34.

10. Wendy Erisman and Jeanne Bayer Contardo, "Learning to Reduce Recidivism: A 50-State Analysis of Postsecondary Correctional Education Policy," *Institute for Higher Education Policy* (November 2005); Francis Allen, *The Decline of the Rehabilitative Ideal* (New Haven: Yale University Press, 1981).

11. E. Ann Carson and William J. Sabol, "Prisoners in 2011," http://bjs.gov/content/pub/pdf/p11.pdf, accessed March 16, 2014.

12. *Keith Chen* and *Jesse* M. *Shapiro*, "Does Prison Harden Inmates? A Discontinuity-based Approach" (January 2004) Cowles Foundation Discussion Paper No. 1450. Available at SSRN: http://ssrn.com/abstract=470301. See also "Prisoners and Prison Re-Entry," http://www.justice.gov/archive/fbci/progmenu_reentry.html.

13. David Dagan and Steven M. Teles, "The Conservative War on Prisons," *Washington Monthly*, November/December, 2012. See also http://www.rightoncrime.com/.

14. "Faith-Based Programs," OJP Fact Sheet, Office of Justice Programs, November 2011, http://www.ojp.usdoj.gov/newsroom/factsheets/ojpfs_faith-basedprog.html, accessed November 18, 2014. See also Alexander Volokh, "Do Faith-Based Prisons Work?" *Alabama Law Review* 63 (2001): 43–95; US Department of Justice, National Institute of Corrections,

"Residential Faith-Based Programs in State Corrections," September 2005, http://nicic.gov/Library/020820, accessed March 16, 2014; and "Faith-Based and Community Initiatives in Corrections," n.d., http://nicic.gov/FaithBasedInitiatives, accessed March 16, 2014.

15. For a description of how prisoners interact in the many religious groups active in contemporary prisons, see Joshua Dubler's ethnography of Graterford Prison, *Down in the Chapel: Religious Life in an American Prison* (New York: Farrar Strauss and Giroux, 2013).

16. I have also altered the names of the prison ministries discussed in this essay in order to protect confidentiality. The names of all volunteers and inmates participating in the groups have been changed.

17. Robert Walker, L.M.H.C., and Ron Dahlbeck, Psy.D., *2009 Statistics on Screening Admissions*, May 1–July 31, 2009.

18. "Gate money" varies from state to state. In Washington and New York, prisoners receive forty dollars plus transportation costs; in Texas and California, they receive a fixed sum of between one and two hundred dollars. For state-by-state comparisons, see http://americanradioworks.publicradio.org/features/hardtime/gatemoney/, accessed March 16, 2014.

19. Tanya Erzen, "Testimonial Politics: The Christian Right's Faith-Based Approach to Marriage and Imprisonment," *American Quarterly* 59 (2007): 991–1015.

20. "Organizational Charter of 'The Women's Network.'" Washington Corrections Center for Women, September 2010.

21. Justin Taylor, "Why Talk about the Heart When the Bible Says It's Unknowable?" June 2010. http://thegospelcoalition.org/blogs/justintaylor/2010/07/19/why-talk-about-the-heart-when-the-bible-says-its-unknowable/, accessed March 16, 2014.

CHAPTER THIRTEEN

1. Many thanks to editors Tim Aubry and Trysh Travis, and to Monique Roelofs, for helpful comments on earlier drafts. Philip Rieff, *The Triumph of the Therapeutic: Uses of Faith after Freud* (New York: Harper & Row, 1966), 252.

2. Richard Sennett, *The Fall of Public Man: On the Social Psychology of Capitalism* (New York: Knopf, 1977).

3. See, for example, Paulette Olson and Dell Champlain, "Ending Corporate Welfare As We Know It: An Institutional Analysis of the Dual Structure of Welfare," *Journal of Economic Issues* 32 (1998): 762. For a detailed study of the corporate welfare enjoyed by Wal-Mart, go to http://cps-news.com/wp-content/corporate-welfare/Corporate-Subsidies.html, accessed March 24, 2014, and follow the link to "$1 Billion: The amount Wal-Mart has received from taxpayers directly or in the form of Tax Expenditures."

4. http://www.alecexposed.org/wiki/What_is_ALEC%3F, accessed March 24, 2014.

5. This is related to but a quite different point than the rebuttal to critics by feminists and others that "the personal is the political." For the aim here is to bring out not the interdependence of the private/personal on the one hand and the public/political on the other, but rather to highlight the difference between the two terms melded together on each side.

6. Reva Siegel, "'The Rule of Love': Wife Beating as Prerogative and Privacy," *Yale Law Journal* 105 (1996): 2117–207.

7. John Gilliom, "Resisting Surveillance," *Social Text* 23 (2005): 78.

8. Andrew Keen, "Opinion: We Must Avoid Facebook's 'creepy' Cult of Transparency," http://www.cnn.com/2012/02/02/opinion/keen-technology-facebook/keen-technology-facebook/index.html, accessed March 24, 2014.

9. See, for example, Evgeny Morozov, "Facebook and Twitter Are Just Places Revolutionaries Go," http://www.guardian.co.uk/commentisfree/2011/mar/07/facebook-twitter-revolutionaries-cyber-utopians, accessed March 14, 2014.

10. Perhaps believing that no one would note the apparent retreat to a double standard, Zuckerberg recently reported being "confused and frustrated" by Snowden-based revelations of governmental piggybacking on Facebook's stash of information about its users. "The US government should be the champion for the Internet, not a threat. They need to be much more transparent about what they are doing, or otherwise people will believe the worst." Vindu Goel, "Facebook's Zuckerberg Complains to Obama over Government Spying," http://bits.blogs.nytimes.com/2014/03/13/facebooks-zuckerberg-complains-to-obama-over-government-spying/?_php=true&_type=blogs&emc=eta1&_r=0, accessed March 24, 2014.

CHAPTER FOURTEEN

1. Gloria Anzaldúa, "Healing Wounds," in *The Gloria Anzaldúa Reader*, ed. AnaLouise Keating (Durham, NC: Duke University Press, 2009), 249.

2. Gloria Anzaldúa died of complications related to diabetes in 2004. Throughout her life she suffered not just with diabetes but with hormone imbalances, painful menstruation, and depression. I discuss the significance of Anzaldúa's pain and illnesses extensively in *Encarnación.* Suzanne Bost, *Encarnación: Illness and Body Politics in Chicana Feminist Literature* (Bronx: Fordham University Press, 2009).

3. Anzaldúa, "Let us be the healing of the wound," in *One Wound for Another/Una herida por otra: Testmonios de Latin@s in the U.S. through Cyberspace (11 de septiembre de 2001–11 de marzo de 2002)*, ed. Claire Joysmith and Clara Lomas (Mexico City: Universidad Autónoma de México, 2005).

4. Moraga, *Waiting in the Wings: Portrait of a Queer Motherhood* (Ithaca: Firebrand, 1997).

5. See, for instance, David Mitchell and Sharon Snyder, "Exploring Foundations: Languages of Disability, Identity, And Culture," *Disability Studies Quarterly* 17 (1997): 241–47. Margrit Shildrick has explored the implications of permeable embodiment for feminist theory. Margrit Shildrick, *Embodying the Monster: Encounters with the Vulnerable Self* (London: Sage, 2002), and *Leaky Bodies and Boundaries: Feminism, Postmodernism, and (Bio)ethics* (London: Routledge, 1997).

6. This is not to say that men's bodies do not undergo regular pain and fluctuation, or that all women's bodies undergo the same fluctuations. Rather, what is known as "women's health" revolves around reproduction, menstruation, menopause, changes in the breasts, and so on. Cultures have developed stories and icons, like Coyolxauhqui and Eve, to explain women's seemingly special and inevitable relationship to corporeal pain.

7. Jonathan M. Metzl and Anna Kirkland, eds. *Against Health: How Health Became the New Morality* (New York: New York University Press, 2010).

8. Anzaldúa, "now let us shift," in *This Bridge We Call Home: Radical Visions for Transformation*, ed. Gloria Anzaldúa and AnaLouise Keating (New York: Routledge, 2002), 578n.

9. Michel Foucault, *The Birth of the Clinic: An Archeology of Medical Perception* (New York: Vintage, 1997), 34, italics in original.

10. Christina Hoff Sommers and Sally Satel, *One Nation under Therapy: How the Helping Culture Is Eroding Self-Reliance* (New York: St. Martin's, 2005), 5.

11. Sommers and Satel, *One Nation under Therapy*, 9.

12. Anzaldúa, "now let us shift," 571–72.

13. When she was diagnosed with diabetes, Anzaldúa also turned to a variety of different "therapeutic cultures" to find new ways of living with her illness. In the Gloria Evangelina Anzaldúa Papers, held at the Benson Latin American Collection at the University of Texas at Austin, I have found articles from the *American Journal of Medicine* and the American Diabetes Association; food logs and diabetes nutritional "pyramids"; recipe books of all sorts; guides to using vitamins, herbs, gemstones, colored candles, and charm pillows; samples of Bee Pollen, Butcher's Broom, and Nature's Way vitamins; advice from the I Ching; Aztec calendars; chakra lists; sacred Jewish texts; guides to dream analysis; and pamphlets on energy healing and "Self-Realization Fellowship" and one called "Rainbow Medicine," featuring traditional remedies of native women in the Ozark Mountains.

14. I am indebted here to Stacy Alaimo's theory of transcorporeality. Alaimo, "Trans-Corporeal Feminisms and the Ethical Space of Nature," in *Material Feminisms*, ed. Stacy Alaimo and Susan Hekman (Bloomington: Indiana University, 2009).

15. Anzaldúa, "la prieta," in *This Bridge Called My Back: Writings by Radical Women of Color*, 2d ed. ed. Cherríe Moraga and Gloria Anzaldúa (New York: Kitchen Table, 1981), 204, italics in original.

16. Yoga has been a global commodity since Swami Sivananda and the Divine Life Society began circulating pamphlets, records, movies, and conferences transnationally in the 1930s. One might also consider Swami Vivekananda's presentation of yoga at the Parliament of the World's Religions during the 1893 World's Fair in Chicago as the origin of yoga's packaging as a global commodity.

17. Anne-Cécile Hoyez also confronts the difficulty of defining yoga and settles on the term "orthopraxy" to describe the variety of forms yoga has taken since it became "re-placed" in a global therapeutic discourse. Anne-Cécile Hoyez, "The 'World of Yoga': The Production and Reproduction of Therapeutic Landscapes," *Social Science and Medicine* 54 (2007): 112–24. For a history of modern yoga's transnational development, see Sarah Strauss, *Positioning Yoga: Balancing Acts across Cultures* (New York: Berg, 2009). For an overview of recent histories of transnational yoga, see Andrea Jain, "Mystics, Gymnasts, Sexologists, and Other Yogis: Divergence and Collectivity in the History of Modern Yoga," *Religious Studies Reviews* 37 (2011). Also see Mark Singleton and Jean Byrne, eds., *Yoga in the Modern World: Contemporary Perspectives* (New York: Routledge, 2008).

18. William Broad, *The Science of Yoga* (New York: Simon and Schuster, 2012), Nook edition, 34, 232, 239.

19. Broad, *The Science of Yoga*, 43–48.

20. Broad, *The Science of Yoga*, 126, 129, 219.

21. In its long history, yoga was oriented around meditation and spiritual transcendence, but the global rise of yoga practice (as a series of postures, or *asanas*) in the twentieth century hinged on its association with physical health (its "modernization").

22. According to Mark Singleton, yoga has been adaptive and syncretic from the start, especially the transnational evolution of postural yoga in the nineteenth and twentieth centuries. In this light, there is no authentic Yoga that is violated in modern adaptations. Mark Singleton, *Yoga Body: The Origins of Modern Posture Practice* (Oxford: Oxford University Press, 2010).

23. Anzaldúa, "Let us be the healing," 92.

24. Anzaldúa, "Let us be the healing," 100.

25. Anzaldúa, "Let us be the healing," 100.

26. Anzaldúa, "Let us be the healing," 102.

27. I think Anzaldúa writes "transshape" rather than "reshape" to emphasize the process of transformation. She is not proposing that we abandon one reality for another but, instead, insists that we transform the one we are in.

28. Anzaldúa, "Let us be the healing," 102.

CHAPTER FIFTEEN

1. Aristotle, *Poetics*, trans. Malcolm Heath (New York: Penguin, 1996), 10.

2. Sigmund Freud, *Civilization and Its Discontents*, trans. James Strachey (New York: Norton, 1961), 29–30.

3. Freud's *Psychopathology of Everyday Life* makes a strong case for this blurring of the lines between dream and life, art and "normal" speech, when it comes to the psychological processes at play in each. See *Psychopathology of Everyday Life*, trans. A. A. Brill (London: T. Fisher Unwin, 1901).

4. David Fitzpatrick, "Twitter Was Act One," *Vanity Fair*, April 2011, http://www.vanityfair.com/business/features/2011/04/jack-dorsey-201104, accessed September 12, 2012. As Fitzpatrick has the story:

> After the dNet disaster, Dorsey returned to St. Louis and began studying botanical illustration at the Missouri Botanical Garden. As a teenager, he had spent hours in gardens, drawing with a graphite pencil. Suddenly, he considered this hobby a possible career path. He indulged his fascination with the challenge of precisely rendering a flower's intricate details. "I fell in love with flora of all types, especially ferns. Loved the sparse structure and repetition of shape—almost fractal." Illustrating flowers, like programming, was a "perfect intersection of art and science."
>
> But shortly thereafter, deciding that illustration really wasn't for him, his wrist started hurting. He went to a massage therapist for treatment and, in short order, became consumed by the field. After a thousand hours of training he was certified and returned to San Francisco, where he moved into a shed in Kidd's backyard. He quickly learned, to his dismay, that the city had a surfeit of massage therapists. So, while working as a nanny for Kidd's daughter, Dorsey started thinking again about software—and that message he'd sent from Golden Gate Park.

The message in question was one that anticipated the development of Twitter a year earlier: "That evening, he wrote some code that enabled him to have an e-mail re-posted to as many people as he wanted. He entered the e-mail addresses of five friends into the software, and took a walk in Golden Gate Park. In an e-mail's subject line he wrote, 'I'm at the Bison Paddock watching the bison.'"

5. For an example of the two approaches to this issue, the psychological and the neurological, see in the case of the former, James W. Pennebaker, "Writing about Emotional Experiences as a Therapeutic Process," *Psychological Science* 8 (1997): 162–66. In the case of the latter, see Matthew D. Lieberman, Naomi I. Eisenberger, Molly J. Crockett, Sabrina M. Tom, Jennifer H. Pfeifer, and Baldwin M. Way, "Putting Feelings into Words: Affect Labeling Disrupts Amygdala Activity in Response to Affective Stimuli," *Pyschological Science* 18 (2007): 421–28, a study that discovers through neuroimaging that the act of "affect labeling"—that is pressing distinct words upon amorphous feelings—has the effect of "diminish[ing] the response of the amygdala and other limbic regions to negative emotional images." In other words, speaking or writing calms you down.

6. Yuki Noguchi, "Cyber-Catharsis: Bloggers Use Web Sites as Therapy," *Washington Post*, October 12, 2005, http://www.washingtonpost.com/wp-dyn/content/article/2005/10/11/AR2005101101781.html, accessed September 12, 2012.

7. Jane Alexander, "Blog Your Way to Health: Therapy at a Click," *Daily Mail*, January 10, 2009, http://www.dailymail.co.uk/home/you/article-1107962/Blog-way-health-Therapy-click.html, accessed September 12, 2012.

8. Sigmund Freud, "Recommendations to Physicians on the the Psycho-analytic Method of Treatment," *Collected Papers*, vol. 2 (1912): 323–33, as cited in Miriam Elson, "Silence, Its Use and Abuse: A View from Self Psychology," *Clinical Social Work Journal* 29 (2001): 352–53.

9. Even the history of psychoanalysis points in this direction. After all, Jacques Lacan's work takes the matrices that Freud discovers in the family home and generalizes them into universal pattern facing the self as it deals with a murky and amorphous otherness.

CHAPTER SIXTEEN

1. The original title of this chapter was "Living in the Politics of Uncertainty."

2. See, e.g., David R. Hiley, James F. Bohman, and Richard Shusterman, eds., *The Interpretive Turn: Philosophy, Science, Culture* (Ithaca: Cornell University Press, 1991).

3. Martin Heidegger, *Being and Time*, trans. John Macquarrie and Edward Robinson (New York: Harper & Row, 1962); Hans-Georg Gadamer, *Truth and Method*, trans. Joel Weinsheimer and Donald G. Marshall (New York: Continuum, 1989); Charles Taylor, *Sources of the Self: The Making of the Modern Identity* (Cambridge: Harvard University Press, 1989); Michel Foucault, *Discipline and Punish: The Birth of the Prison*, trans. Alan Sherman (New York: Random House, 1995); Jacques Derrida, *Writing and Difference* (Chicago: University of Chicago Press, 1978).

4. Taylor, "The Moral Topography of the Self," in *Hermeneutics and Psychological Theory: Interpretive Perspectives on Personality, Psychotherapy and Psychopathology*, ed. Stanley B. Meser, Louis A. Sass, and Robert L. Woolfolk (New Brunswick: Rutgers University Press, 1988), 302.

5. Muriel Dimen, *Sexuality, Intimacy, Power* (Hillsdale, NJ: Analytic Press, 2003); Virginia Goldner, "Toward a Critical Relational Theory of Gender," *Psychoanalytic Dialogues* 1 (1991):

249–72; Adrienne Harris, *Gender as Soft Assembly* (New York: Routledge, 2008); Rachel Hare-Mustin and Jeanne Marecek, "Sex, Lies, and Headaches: The Problem Is Power," in *Women and Power: Perspectives for Therapy*, ed. Thelma Jean Goodrich (New York: Norton, 1991), 63–85.

6. Kimberlyn Leary, "Race, Self-Disclosure, and 'Forbidden Talk': Race and Ethnicity in Contemporary Psychoanalytic Practice," *Psychoanalytic Quarterly* 66 (1997): 163–89; Derald Wing Sue and David Sue, *Counseling the Culturally Different* (New York: Wiley, 1999).

7. Steve Botticelli, "Return of the Repressed: Class in Psychoanalytic Process," in *Relational Psychoanalysis: Volume 3 New Voices*, ed. Melanie Suchet, Adrienne Harris, and Lewis Aron (Mahwah, N.J.: Analytic Press, 2007), 121–34; Stephen Hartman, "Class Unconscious: From Dialectical Materialism to Relational Material," in *Relational Psychoanalysis*, 209–25.

8. Frank C. Richardson, Blaine J. Fowers, and Charles B. Guignon, *Re-Envisioning Psychology: Moral Dimensions of Theory and Practice* (San Francisco: Jossey-Bass, 1999), 199–276.

9. Foucault, *Discipline and Punish*; Jacque Derrida, *Of Grammatology*, trans. Gayatri Spivak (Baltimore: Johns Hopkins University Press, 1976); Nikolas Rose, *Governing the Soul: The Shaping of the Private Self* (New York: Routledge, 1990); Robert Fancher, *Cultures of Healing: Correcting the Image of American Mental Health* (New York: Freeman, 1995); Thomas Szasz, *The Myth of Mental Illness: Foundations of a Theory of Personal Conduct* (London: Secker & Warburg, 1961).

10. Robert N. Bellah, Robert Madsen, William M. Sullivan, Ann Swidler, and Stephen M. Tipton, *Habits of the Heart: Individualism and Commitment in American Life* (Berkeley: University of California Press, 1985); Anthony Giddens, *Modernity and Self-Identity: Self and Society in the Late Modern Age* (Stanford: Stanford University Press, 1991); Jerome Frank, *Psychotherapy and the Human Predicament* (New York: Schocken, 1978); Ian Hacking, *Rewriting the Soul: Multiple Personality and the Science of Memory*, (Princeton: Princeton University Press, 1995); Philip Rieff, *The Triumph of the Therapeutic: Uses of Faith after Freud* (New York: Harper, 1966); Louis A. Sass, "The Self and Its Vicissitudes: An Archaeological Study of the Psychoanalytic Avant-Garde," *Social Research* 55 (1988); Richardson, Fowers, and Guignon, *Re-envisioning Psychology*.

11. Donna Orange, "Toward the Art of Living Dialogue: Between Constructivism and Hermeneutics in Psychoanalytic Thinking," in *Beyond Postmodernism: New Dimensions in Clinical Theory and Practice*, ed. Roger Frie and Donna Orange (New York: Routledge, 2009); Donnel Stern, "Witnessing across Time: Accessing the Present from the Past and the Past from the Present," *Psychoanalytic Quarterly* 81 (2012): 53–81.

12. Emmanuel Levinas, *Totality and Infinity* (Pittsburg: Duquesne University Press, 1969).

13. Philip Cushman, *Constructing the Self, Constructing America: A Cultural History of Psychotherapy* (New York: Da Capo, 1995), 15–33.

14. For a detailed description of this approach see Cushman, *Constructing the Self*, 278–331; Philip Cushman, "Clinical Applications: A Response to Layton," *Contemporary Psychoanalysis* 41 (2005): 431–45.

15. A longer version of this incident is narrated in Cushman, *Constructing the Self*, 302–303.

16. Stephen A. Mitchell and Lewis Aron, eds., *Relational Psychoanalysis: The Emergence of a Tradition* (New York: Analytic Press, 1999).

17. It is not just mainstream theory that must be questioned and interpreted politically. It

does not matter how new, current, trendy, or seemingly antinomian new theories or practices appear to be; they must all be interrogated for their political functions. Just because a practice is new and unusual does not necessarily mean it is not politically useful to the status quo.

18. Mitchell and Aron, *Relational Psychoanalysis*; Neil Altman, *The Analyst and the Inner City: Race, Class, and Culture through a Psychoanalytic Lens* (Mahwah, NJ: Analytic Press, 1995); Cushman, *Constructing the Self*, 348–53.

19. For an excellent example of this approach, see Lane Gerber, "Integrating Political-Societal Concerns in Psychotherapy," *American Journal of Psychotherapy* 44 (1990): 473–83.

20. Philip Cushman, "Why the Self Is Empty," *American Psychologist* 45 (1990): 599–611; Edward E. Sampson, "Cognitive Psychology As Ideology," *American Psychologist* 36 (1981): 730–43; Roy Baumeister, "How the Self Became a Problem," *Journal of Personality and Social Psychology* 52 (1987): 163–76; Seymour B. Sarason, "An Asocial Psychology and a Misdirected Clinical Psychology," *American Psychologist* 36 (1981): 827–36.

AFTERWORD

1. Quoted in Christopher Lasch, *The Culture of Narcissism: American Life in an Age of Diminishing Expectations* (New York: Norton, 1978), 14.

2. Donald Meyer, *The Positive Thinkers: The American Search for Health, Wealth, and Personal Power from Mary Baker Eddy to Norman Vincent Peale* (New York: Doubleday, 1965), title of chapter 2.

3. Lasch, *Culture of Narcissism*, 15.

4. Adolph Reed, Jr., "Nothing Left: The Long, Slow Surrender of American Liberals," *Harper's Magazine,* March 2014, 35–36.

5. Daniel T. Rodgers, *Age of Fracture* (Cambridge, Mass., and London: Harvard University Press, 2011).

6. William James, "The Hidden Self," http://en.wikisource.org/wiki/The_Hidden_Self.

CONTRIBUTORS

Badia Sahar Ahad is Associate Professor of English at Loyola University Chicago. She is the author of *Freud Upside Down: African American Literature and Psychoanalytic Culture* (2010). Her current research and publications focus on race, nostalgia, and narrative medicine.

Timothy Aubry is Associate Professor of English at Baruch College, CUNY. He is the author of *Reading as Therapy: What Contemporary Fiction Does for Middle-Class Americans* (2011). He is currently working on a book focused on the unacknowledged aesthetic commitments that shape contemporary literary scholarship.

Courtney Bender is Professor of Religion at Columbia University. She is the author of *The New Metaphysicals: Spirituality and the American Religious Imagination* (2010) and *Heaven's Kitchen: Living Religion at God's Love We Deliver* (2003).

Suzanne Bost is Professor of English and Graduate Program Director in Women's Studies and Gender Studies at Loyola University Chicago. She is the author of two books, *Mulattas and Mestizas: Representing Mixed Identities in the Americas, 1850–2000* (2003) and *Encarnación: Illness and Body Politics in Chicana Feminist Literature* (2009), and coeditor, with Frances Aparicio, of *The Routledge Companion to Latino/a Literature* (2013). Her current work focuses on the Gloria Anzaldúa archive, New Materialisms, posthumanism, and yoga.

Philip Cushman, Ph.D., is a member of the teaching faculty in the Psy.D. program of Antioch University Seattle and practices individual, marriage, and family therapy on Vashon Island, Washington. He is the author of *Constructing the Self, Constructing America: A Cultural History of Psychotherapy* (1995) and various articles on the history, moral understandings, political functions, and cultural meanings of psychotherapy. In 2001 he was invited to give the Mary Whiton Calkins Address for historical scholarship on underrepresented groups in the history of psychology, and in 2014, Division 24 of the American Psychological Association named him recipient of the Distinguished Theoretical and Philosophical Contributions to Psychology Award for lifetime scholarly achievement.

Tanya Erzen is Associate Professor of Religion at the University of Puget Sound and a Soros Justice Media Fellow of the Open Society Foundation, currently writing a book about religious volunteers in American prisons and the conservative movement for prison reform. She is the author of *Straight to Jesus: Sexual and Christian Conversions in the Ex-Gay Movement* (2006), *Fanpire: The Twilight Saga and the Women Who Love It* (2012), and the coeditor of *Zero Tolerance: Quality of Life and the New Police Brutality in New York City* (2001).

Joseph M. Gabriel is Associate Professor in the Department of Behavioral Sciences and Social Medicine at the Florida State University College of Medicine. He is the author of *Medical Monopoly: Intellectual Property Rights and the Origins of the Modern Pharmaceutical Industry* (2014).

David Herzberg is Associate Professor of History at the University at Buffalo (SUNY) and is a cultural historian who specializes in the intersection between addiction, race, and twentieth-century pharmaceutical consumerism. Among other places, his work has appeared in *American Quarterly*, the *American Journal of Public Health*, the *Atlantic Monthly Online*, and in the book *Happy Pills in America: From Miltown to Prozac* (2010).

Jackson Lears is Board of Governors Distinguished Professor of History at Rutgers University and Editor in Chief of *Raritan: A Quarterly Review.* His books include *Fables of Abundance: A Cultural History of Advertising in America*, which won the *Los Angeles Times* Book Prize for History, and (most recently) *Rebirth of a Nation: The Making of Modern America, 1877–1920.*

Kathryn Lofton is Professor of Religious Studies, American Studies, History, and Divinity at Yale University. She is the author of *Oprah: The Gospel of an Icon* (2011) as well as many essays and article addressing the related histories of American religion and American culture.

Elizabeth Lunbeck is a historian of psychiatry and psychoanalysis and the author, most recently, of *The Americanization of Narcissism* (2014).

Gabriel N. Mendes is Assistant Professor in the Ethnic Studies and Urban Studies and Planning Departments at UC San Diego. His monograph, *A Deeper Science: Harlem's Lafargue Hygiene Clinic and the Promise of Antiracist Psychiatry, 1940–1960*, will be published in 2015 by Cornell University Press, in its History of Psychiatry series.

Rebecca Jo Plant is Associate Professor in the History Department at the University of California, San Diego. She has published work on the history of women and gender and the history of psychiatry and therapeutic culture in the twentieth-century United States. Her first book, *Mom: The Transformation of Motherhood in Modern America*, was published in 2010, and a coedited edited volume, *Maternalism Reconsidered: Motherhood, Welfare, and Social Policies in the Twentieth Century*, appeared in 2012.

Beryl Satter is Professor of History at Rutgers University-Newark. She is the author of *Each Mind a Kingdom: American Women, Sexual Purity, and the New Thought Movement, 1875–1920* (1999) and *Family Properties: Race, Real Estate, and the Exploitation of Black Urban America* (2009), which won the Organization of American Historians' Liberty Legacy Award for best book in civil rights history and the Jewish Book Council's National Jewish Book Award in History.

Elizabeth Spelman is Professor of Philosophy and Barbara Richmond 1940 Professor in the Humanities at Smith College. She is author of *Inessential Woman: Problems of Exclusion in Feminist Thought* (1988), *Fruits of Sorrow: Framing Our Attention to Suffering* (1997), and *Repair: The Impulse to Restore in a Fragile World* (2002). Her most recent book-length project, which is on the verge of publication with the title *Going to Waste*, explores our remarkably intimate ties with waste, trash, and other members of the detritus family.

Michael Sayeau is Lecturer of English at University College London. His monograph, *Against the Event: The Everyday and the Evolution of Modernist Narrative*, was published in 2013.

Michael E. Staub is Professor of English at Baruch College, City University of New York, where he teaches courses in American literature and culture. He is the author of *Madness Is Civilization: When the Diagnosis Was Social, 1948–1980* (2011), *Torn at the Roots: The Crisis of Jewish Liberalism in Postwar America* (2002), and *Voices of Persuasion: Politics of Representation in 1930s America* (1994). He is currently writing a book on the prehistory of the neuroscience revolution in postwar social psychology.

Trysh Travis is an Associate Professor in the Center for Women's Studies and Gender Research at the University of Florida. Her writing has appeared in venues ranging from *American Quarterly* and *PMLA* to *Inside Higher Ed* and *Bitch: Feminist Responses to Popular Culture.* Her book, *The Language of the Heart: A Cultural History of the Recovery Movement from Alcoholics Anonymous to Oprah Winfrey*, was published in 2009. She is the cofounder, with Joe Spillane, of *Points: The Blog of the Alcohol and Drugs History Society.*

Stevan Weine, M.D., is Professor of Psychiatry at the University of Illinois at Chicago College of Medicine, where he is also the Director of the International Center on Responses to Catastrophes and the Director of Global Health Research Training at the Center for Global Health. Weine is author of two books, *When History Is a Nightmare: Lives and Memories of Ethnic Cleansing in Bosnia-Herzegovina* (1999) and *Testimony and Catastrophe: Narrating the Traumas of Political Violence* (2006).

INDEX